Critical Consciousness

Critical Consciousness

A Study of Morality in Global, Historical Context

Elena Mustakova-Possardt

PRAEGER

Westport, Connecticut
London

Library of Congress Cataloging-in-Publication Data

Mustakova-Possardt, Elena, 1960–
   Critical consciousness : a study of morality in global, historical context / Elena Mustakova-Possardt.
      p. cm.
   Includes bibliographical references (p.) and index.
   ISBN 0–275–97911–3 (alk. paper)
   1. Psychology, Religious.   2. Consciousness.   3. Ethics.   I. Title.
   BL53.M98 2003
   126—dc21   2002029879

British Library Cataloguing in Publication Data is available.

Library of Congress Catalog Card Number: 2002029879
ISBN: 0–275–97911–3

First published in 2003

Praeger Publishers, 88 Post Road West, Westport, CT 06881
An imprint of Greenwood Publishing Group, Inc.
www.praeger.com

Printed in the United States of America

The paper used in this book complies with the
Permanent Paper Standard issued by the National
Information Standards Organization (Z39.48–1984).

10 9 8 7 6 5 4 3 2 1

To my parents, Roza and Michail Mustakov, whose inner dignity, love of truth, beauty and goodness, and unfailing generosity and caring have built me up and strengthened me through the years. To my husband, Earl Possardt, whose noble mind and heart and respect for life have been my guiding light through the latter part of this journey. To all the beautiful, courageous people who crossed my path and whose journeys spun webs in my heart. To my friends, those remarkable women who inspired me and whose inner light and endurance helped sustain me, to Vessela Markova, Terry Carlson, Nourieh Jalalzadeh, Janna Essig, Carol Rutstein, Beth Bowen, Eunice Possardt, and all the others. To my son Alipi, who tried me and forgave me again and again as we grew together. To my dear stepdaughter Jackie, and to my little daughter Rosie whose formidable spirit breathes the fragrance of a new world being born. To those who survived through oppression and injustice and were able to keep their faith, and to those who did not make it. To all of you, and to all of us.

O SON OF BEING!
Thy heart is My home; sanctify it for My descent. Thy spirit is My place of revelation; cleanse it for My manifestation.
The Hidden Words, Baha'u'llah

Contents

Illustrations

FIGURES

Acknowledgments

This work would not have been possible without the democratic commitment of the University of Massachusetts at Amherst, which enabled my transition out of totalitarian communist Bulgaria and offered me a dynamic and healing environment in which I could pursue my life's work. My deepest acknowledgment goes to Maurianne Adams for her significant help in the conceptualization stages of this project. This work was also inspired by the dialogue with a number of other remarkable colleagues, among them Gerald Weinstein, John Carey, Anne Colby.

I would like to acknowledge also the Henry A. Murray Research Center for the Study of Lives, whose Dissertation Award supported the cross-cultural part of this research. Without its funding of my project "Critical Consciousness and Social Responsibility among Bulgarian Midlifers," I could not have substantiated the generic, cross-cultural value of the construct of critical consciousness or begun to document the journey of optimal consciousness under communism. I am also deeply grateful to all those wonderful people who trusted me with their life stories. I have been profoundly touched by their journeys.

Finally, I would like to thank Sangeeta Dave for her dedicated technical assistance, and to Alex Agle and Jim Olle for the technical consultation they provided.

Introduction

The task I face feels overwhelming, and at the same time lucid and simple, a perfect example of the split between mind and heart with which most of us struggle: the heart knows, and the mind has to figure out. Each has its task and its powers, and in synergy they are an undefeated team. Yet, it is so easy to become frightened, and then the mind begins to spin its wheels, taking us further and further away from the inner vision of the heart.

We do not grow up knowing our capacity for this beautiful harmony inside. We are not taught to recognize the wisdom, the love-knowledge of the heart, or its capacity to work in concord with the understanding of the mind. We grow up acquiring knowledge that often pulls us further away from the intuitive wisdom of the heart. Sometimes, the voice of the heart becomes so muted that we no longer recognize it and we learn to ignore it. For those of us who never stop hearing this voice, it is in constant tension with much of our learning and habits of mind and with the choices we make.

Spiritual traditions call the heart "the seat of the revelation of the inner mysteries of God" (Baha'u'llah, [1931] 1983, p. 192). As the mind grows and develops its reasoning capacity, it constructs progressively more encompassing meaning out of these revealed mysteries. But the mind's capacity to reason and construct meaning can also be exercised in relative separation from the discernment of the heart. The harmonious working of mind and heart throughout the human lifespan is a precarious balance, which few people seem to achieve. The general condition of the world shows a pervasive split and imbalance between the two.

However, in every age, there have been people who never lose the truth of the heart, and in whom it gets only stronger with the development of their minds. After many years of observing and pondering this phenomenon, I came to call it the ontogenesis of critical consciousness, using the term coined by the radical Brazilian educator Paolo Freire, who became known through his work for the empowerment of ordinary people. Critical consciousness is a way of being that we recognize and admire, and every chapter of human history has had its individuals who have exhibited this empowered unity of rational mind and inner vision. The most outstanding among these people have become known as moral and spiritual leaders, whom the rest of humanity has viewed as people of a different quality. Their names and stories fill the world's treasury of the human heritage.

What is the nature of this way of being? People who exhibit it strike us as both independent and original thinkers and deeply connected to the rest of humanity, individuals with presence and integrity but not individualists. They identify with no one particular ideology, class, group, or philosophy—they draw on the best in all; yet their personal understanding is not eclectic but deeply integrated. These are people who recognize truth in whatever shape or form it appears, who respond to life with wisdom and enter into an ongoing dialogue with it, not in order to outsmart life with their personal theories but out of awe and reverence for life. These people always stand out, and others are attracted to them and threatened at the same time, because these people fit no easy mold and are not guided by personal interest. These people's lives are about truth and service, both outdated and discarded words; but they are not moralists. If anything, they are lovers, lovers of humanity, lovers of life. Their hearts embrace and respond deeply to the human condition. Their minds powerfully cut through the rubble of detail and the smoke of words and reach for inner meanings, harnessing knowledge into understanding, never just caught in the trimmings of knowledge. These are people who are loved and feared and hated but who, whether we like them or resent them, represent our best hope for ourselves, that hope which we don't even dare entertain. These are the people who recognized Christ in His day as clearly as they recognized the betrayal of His message in some of the later practices of Christianity; who tremble with the power and mystical beauty of the words of Mohammad and do not for a moment confuse them with the threat of fundamentalism; who inhale deeply the words of wisdom of the Buddha but do not pose to the trendy Western world as enlightened Buddhists; who are neither of the East nor of the West but have made the world their home even if they never had a chance to leave their native land. These are people who know deep in their hearts, beyond all intellectual debate, that Truth exists, even though they will never fully understand it; people whom the trends of the times leave untouched. About these people the prophet Baha'u'llah wrote:

This people have passed beyond the narrow straits of names, and pitched their tents upon the shores of renunciation. (Baha'u'llah, 1988, p. 74)

Yet, many of us get caught in names; our hearts become progressively overlaid with "the dust of acquired knowledge" and conditioning, and our minds begin to erect fearful walls. Life becomes an agony of separation with, at best, a compartmentalized and carefully maintained semblance of happiness and, at worst, a deep alienation from ourselves and from the world.

The deceivingly simple story of this book is about the journey of integration of heart and mind on an individual and on a collective level. As I have traveled to and lived in different corners of the globe, I have come to believe that this story of painful and compelling emergence, of gradual integration of mind and heart, characterizes not only each human journey but also the very global historical processes that provide the context for individual emergence. I have come to realize that collective human civilization itself, with all its history of dignity and betrayal, in fact manifests stages in the evolution of collective consciousness. Human civilization is now poised on the brink of this emergent integration at the turn of the twenty-first century, in the midst of profound collective angst and polarization. Therefore, understanding the individual potential for critical consciousness, for a powerful unity of mind and heart and the lifelong transformations in this capacity, is essential in creating the kinds of educational, social, and international institutions that can foster individual empowerment and peaceful global integration.

My thinking about the construct of critical consciousness began inductively, through trying to organize and name my personal experience and observations around questions of social responsibility and citizenship while living and working in several different societies and cultures: Bulgaria, where I was born and grew up, Libya, the United Arab Emirates, Zimbabwe, and the United States. In Bulgaria, I taught adults, in whom I observed a chasm between the majority, who seemed to feel that in order to survive they had to accept the norms of a deeply corrupt social and political system, and a minority, who seemed to rely on a different internal resource which made them resilient to forces of collusion. While many criticized social reality in private, few really chose to search in their hearts for an understanding of what made the prevailing absurdity of the communist system and its fifty years of existence possible. Most people simply compartmentalized the system's destructive requirements to the point where they became the unconscious norm, profoundly undermining the fabric of social life and collective moral standards. Those who resisted, primarily from the so-called intelligentsia, eagerly and earnestly sought ways to educate their minds and hearts, in order to overcome fear and powerlessness and to gain a sense of agency amid inimical social conditions.

At first it appeared to me that, in comparison with the freedom of the Western world, the spirit of the majority of East Europeans was simply crushed by the iron fist of totalitarianism. However, my thinking changed as I lived in Libya, traveled throughout Eastern and Western Europe, lived and worked in the United Arab Emirates, and taught at a teacher training college in newly liberated Zimbabwe. In these different contexts, I began to encounter disturbing similarities with the limited understanding of citizenship in my home environment. I saw various expressions of compartmentalized or limited social responsibility.

In Zimbabwe, where my work was the most socially involved, I witnessed the uncritical naiveté with which the atheistic communist ideas were embraced by intelligent people as a seeming panacea, regardless of the historical experience of the whole Eastern bloc. Here again people were divorcing social reality from historical experience and allowing themselves to be submerged into the present, in reaction to an equally compartmentalized white Rhodesian culture of the past, which was somehow trying to continue its existence into the new historic era of postcolonialism.

In 1990, I came to the United States, the place that East Europeans most frequently associate with the idea of freedom. I soon found out that freedom is a relative thing. American society also turned out to be embedded in mass myths and ideologies, only of a technologically more advanced kind. The homeland of democracy has largely turned into an alienated, compartmentalized, consumer society, which subtly entices people to remain locked in a limited reality and breeds mindlessness and disempowerment for many. Even amid the elite U.S. culture of advanced progressive thinkers, I have encountered a deep compartmentalization and disharmony between minds and hearts, a radical individualism which seems to lock people in its fearful, self-protective grip even when they believe they are transcending it; a deep-seated distrust of the other despite postures of "openness"; lots of politics on every level, an abundance of words and a failure of love.

The construct of CC (critical consciousness) began to take shape as I contemplated the gap between the sophisticated and unsophisticated people I met who showed a unity of will, reason, and love, and the majority of people. The inner power of those people seemed to come from a loyalty to a greater truth and an internal deeply held moral core. The question I started asking was: how did these people arrive at this place? In what way and under what influences was their way of being constructed so differently? What role did formal and other kinds of education play, and what kind of education, offered by whom? How did social forces, family, educational, institutional, political, and spiritual, interplay with their internal construction of reality in a way that generated the ultimately liberating capacity these people showed to engage in a wholesome, lived dialogue with reality from a place of faith in life and integrity? What fundamentally distinguished these people was a relative unity of mind and heart, which equipped them to deal with corrupt and confused societies with dignity and truthfulness.

The questions occupying me clearly were related to existing concepts such as integrity, critical thinking, discernment, moral reasoning, empathy, permeability, motivation, altruism and prosocial behavior, moral commitment, social responsibility, faith, and agency. Yet, none of these concepts by themselves could explain the phenomenon I was observing. Not even Freire's (1973) understanding of CC seemed to grasp the whole phenomenon I was pondering, but it pointed in the right direction.

Why critical consciousness, many have asked me. How is that different than moral development? Critical consciousness is a whole-person phenomenon, a way of being in the world. It includes, but is not limited to, what moral psychology currently calls moral development. It also includes what critical theory and praxis call historical agency and empowerment; what Maslow calls mental health and authenticity; what Fowler calls the development of faith and the quest for meaning; what ancient wisdom traditions and transpersonal psychology describe as an orientation to growth, unitive understanding, interconnected ways of being, and transcendence. Then why collapse all these things together, some colleagues ask. Because this wholesome way of being can only be understood in a holistic interdisciplinary way.

In contrast, the current scientific specialization into subfields and areas has begun to look like clubs, each of which speaks a somewhat different lingo and has different ontological and epistemological assumptions, which makes dialogue and integration hardly possible, or even desirable. An example of this tendency is the gap between moral psychology, and Freirian thought and critical theory. While both study the theory and practice of moral agency, one has developed inside the Ivory Tower, much of its research funded and claimed by highly exclusive upper-class institutions by far not exemplifying a commitment to justice and equity in the world. The other has emerged outside the affluent Western worldview, or in philosophical opposition to it, and has been taken up by radical thinkers, academic institutions, and activists. Both speak to critical consciousness in fundamental ways, as do social and transpersonal psychology, and a number of other relatively disconnected areas in the humanities and social sciences.

Against this background of scientific compartmentalization that lags behind the realities of human life on the planet, I began my work, not knowing in the least where it was leading me. It has turned out to be a profoundly spiritual journey, one I did not anticipate. When I began, I was a European-bred agnostic existentialist to the bones. Having experienced the questionable nature of social groupings and the hollowness of much organized Christianity, I saw religion or any form of group identity as a way of relegating the authority and responsibility of one's existential choices to external powers. In the past ten years of work on critical consciousness, my view of religion, spirituality, and social life has changed profoundly, as I discovered the Baha'i spiritual philosophy and through it the wisdom of other world spiritual traditions and, most of all, the wisdom of my own heart. I came to realize that critical consciousness is nothing else but the personal and social expression of an activated depth dimension of existence, of an awakened spiritual potential in a human being.

This realization has been summed up for me in one of the Hidden Words of Baha'u'llah, the founder of the Baha'i wisdom tradition:

O son of Spirit! The most beloved of all things in My sight is Justice; turn not away therefrom if thou desirest Me, and neglect it not that I may confide in thee. By its aid thou shalt see with thine own eyes and not through the eyes of others, and shalt know of thine own knowledge and not through the knowledge of thy neighbour. Ponder this in thy heart; how it behoveth thee to be. Verily justice is My gift to thee and the sign of My loving-kindness. Set it then before thine eyes. (Baha'u'llah, 1991, p. 10)

This quote makes a compelling claim: that we have the capacity to choose to discern justice in our hearts, and that if we were to love truth and justice enough, we would learn to see through the veils of reality. CC, then, is a matter of choice and love, as well as of critical discernment. The question for me became how we cultivate so powerful a love for truth and justice that allows people to fully come into their powers, and yet that is tempered by a deep awareness of the limitations in our understanding of truth, and our interdependence in the pursuit of justice. This is the fundamental question that moves me as an educator, and I will come back to it in later chapters.

I have adopted Freire's (1973) term critical consciousness because the phenomenon I study is the very quality of human consciousness, not just some of its dimensions. I use the term *critical* in the sense in which the Frankfurt school of critical theory used it in the early part of the twentieth century: as capable of understanding and de-reifying one's sociohistorical context and economic conditions, breaking through ideological veils, and standing in a responsible relationship with the historical tensions of the times, using thought to provide social alternatives from a perspective of the primacy of moral ends.

The first guiding premise of this book is that critical consciousness represents not just a particular stage or level in the development of consciousness, but an optimal path of human development, and has been the goal of much human thought. The best thinkers of each age, people as diverse as Rumi, Plato, Tolstoy, Dostoyevsky, and Baha'u'llah, to mention a few, have highlighted the full range of aspects of this phenomenon, which has to be studied in an interdisciplinary way. The path of critical consciousness is manifested in an infinite variety of ways and degrees, and people move through them in widely different timeframes, which have a lot to do with their life circumstances. Some may be negotiating advanced forms of CC in their mid-twenties; others may be struggling with earlier forms until late in life before they fully discover their agency. Regardless of where they are developmentally, these people always strike us as more authentic, independent minded, and resilient human beings.

The second guiding premise is that CC cannot be fully understood if viewed on a purely individual level, as has been the tendency of much Western philosophy and most of Western psychology. This, I believe, is the reason why the phenomenon of CC has not been described as an integrated whole yet. Collective consciousness is only just evolving the capacity to view itself in terms of its relationship to a global world. Until now, all such efforts have been partial, focusing on one dimension of that complex relationship at the expense of others.

For example, existentialism (Kierkegaard, Nietzsche, Jean-Paul Sartre, Martin Buber, Sidney Jourard, Abraham Maslow, Irvin Yalom, Victor Frankl, Rollo May) has explored in profound ways the capacity for authentic experiencing of meaning and choice by the individual and the psychopathology resulting from thwarting that capacity. However, existentialism focuses exclusively on the self and does not view individual awareness against the background of a comprehensive and equally humanistic understanding of collective human history, which acknowledges the painstaking evolution of the idea of social justice throughout human civilization. Instead, in existential philosophy, the individual striving toward authenticity is viewed as poised against basically inimical and static so-cial forces. Lacking is a broad enough historical perspective from which the striving of human civilization toward authenticity can be encompassed. Hence, while existentialism has elucidated many aspects of individual CC, it has not been able to capture the individual evolution toward CC as part of a collective evolution. Vygotsky is one of the few psychologists who strove to see individual development in its unfolding historical context, but Vygotsky's thinking did not have time to mature. At best, historical context is present in the perspective of critical theorists, but they too do not view historical context in its large-scale unfolding.

Revealed spiritual traditions, more than any other secular source, have spoken to the balanced and interdependent movement toward CC on an individual and collective level. However, much of that understanding has been buried under centuries of interpretation and ignorance and fear-bred distortions. Also, since most world religions have emerged at much earlier times in collective history and have responded to the needs of specific sociohistorical and cultural contexts and earlier levels of development of collective consciousness, their social teach-ings have not articulated explicitly a clear global vision. Nevertheless, a funda-mental vision of balance between the individual and the world is at the core of their moral and ethico-spiritual teachings.

The first religious tradition revealed since the onset of modernity, and there-fore explicitly and appropriately speaking to the individual and collective chal-lenges of modern consciousness, is the Baha'i Faith, which is widely unknown and as of yet unexplored in terms of its contributions to resolving the modern tension that is the focus of this book. My work on CC is firmly grounded in this tradition, although I discovered it late in my research.

Finally, the third guiding premise of this book is that, while CC has always existed as a minority way of being among people of every age and culture, in this age it is an attainable goal of adult development, due to the global trend toward universal education and lifespan development, information networks, and the growing appreciation for the untapped human potential.

I offer this book in the hope that it can contribute in some small way to our ability to set ourselves free, to rediscover the powerful unity of mind and heart which is our human endowment, and to have the collective wisdom to rise to the challenge of this painstaking global transition and establish the foundations of a peaceful world civilization for our children.

Chapter 1

The Current Tension in Our Collective Consciousness

> This is a new cycle of human power. All the horizons of the world are luminous. . . . You are loosed from ancient superstitions which have kept men ignorant, destroying the foundation of true humanity. The gift of God to this enlightened age is the knowledge of the oneness of mankind and of the fundamental oneness of religion. War will cease between the nations, and by the will of God the Most Great Peace shall come; the world will be seen as a new world.
>
> Abdu'l-Baha, 1982, pp. 19–20

We live at a time of transition. The twentieth century, which has been recognized as "the most turbulent in the history of the human race," has come to a close (Universal House of Justice, 2001, Preface). This past century has seen an old world dying and a new and not yet clearly understood world struggling to be born. At this threshold, we have witnessed the mind-boggling expansion of a material civilization that has brought into sharp contrast the limitations of our understanding, which has fallen far behind our knowledge of the material aspects of the universe.

We are members of a human race that possesses the knowledge required to feed itself and to provide education and a life of relative health, comfort, and cooperation for all in the context of a globally peaceful and ecologically sustainable planet. Yet, we are still polarized and compartmentalized, torn by racial, ethnic, and class hostilities, religious and sectarian antagonism, and competing special-interest groups and ideologies and steeped in politics as usual, lacking the collective will to extricate ourselves from this quagmire.

In the twentieth century, we have largely managed to shake off the powers of patriarchal oppression, colonialism, and dictatorship and to release on a large scale the human hunger to know from the grips of dogma. Yet, the development of our capacities to love and to exercise our free will responsibly has lagged far behind our power to know. This reality is illustrated starkly by the fact that every two seconds a child dies of starvation across this small planet, and every day 34,000 people die of starvation, while we continue to throw food away in order to maintain the high prices of the global markets (UNICEF, Feb. 2002). We are part of a global economy that concentrates all the world's resources into fewer and fewer hands.

Examples of the distance between knowledge and understanding abound. One of the highest causes of death in Africa is malaria, which can be prevented by a simple $2 mosquito net. Yet, the annual death toll from malaria rivals that from AIDS in the world—approximately two to three million people, of whom over a million are children. In the meantime, we in the West develop new and more sophisticated lifestyles to somehow fill our boredom and relieve the stress of the rat race known as career. While our medicine has advanced to the point where it can now routinely perform organ transplants, in the United States it has also become a corporate business, as a result of which over 30 percent of the children in the richest country in the world lack basic medical insurance.

As we continue to develop economically, we alienate ourselves from the very earth that sustains us. We poison it and ourselves while pursuing profits. We try to restrict the efforts of ecologists and wildlife biologists as they lobby on our collective behalf, on the grounds of the preeminence of individual rights.

This condition of an extreme materialistic civilization, which has reached its limits, has been vividly captured and was foreseen 150 years ago by the founder of the Baha'i spiritual philosophy, who reiterated in fresh and contemporary insights the eternal call of the ancient spiritual traditions:

So blind hath become the human heart that neither the disruption of the city, nor the reduction of the mountain to dust, nor even the cleaving of the earth, can shake off its torpor. (Baha'u'llah, [1952] 1976, p. 39)

These words are that much more poignant and disturbing in the wake of September 11, 2001, when the world experienced the literal reality of one of the greatest cosmopolitan centers of civilization being consumed by an explosion of hatred and desperation. For most of us, that scale of absurd atrocity came as a surprise. Many months after September 11, we are still mostly in denial of the obvious connection between the tragedy of September 11 and the rampant materialism of the twentieth century, and its staggering chasm between knowledge, love, understanding, and commitment to justice on a global level.

We continue to be caught in dualities: individual rights versus collective rights, profit versus compassion and responsibility, convenience versus truth, limited identities and nationalism versus a common humanity and global justice—these are some of the manifestations of the deep tension in the midst of which we all negotiate our lives.

Yet, across the globe, there is also a new will arising, an increasingly visible grassroots movement for change. A range of people from all cultural, religious, and social backgrounds are slowly coming together to develop a global understanding of our unity and interdependence on this small planet. United by an ethic of social responsibility and service to the common good, these groups and nongovernmental organizations in various ways point to the political paralysis of will in current adolescent forms of governance. Thus, the foundation is being laid for truly mature international institutions of global governance. As an example of this grassroots movement, the Beijing Women's Conference in 1995 brought together the largest oppressed majority in the world in a spirit of sisterhood and empowerment. The Beijing Conference made it clear that the mothers of the world stand for universal peace and international arbitration.

Are the people around the globe who are active participants in the emergence of a new and more humane global civilization free of the tensions of the age? It does not seem so. Yet, they seem to be negotiating these tensions differently.

THE PHENOMENON OF CRITICAL CONSCIOUSNESS

What are the psychological dimensions of this new consciousness which is struggling to emerge on a larger scale than ever before in human history? In its developmental emergence, it engages in an intuitive and progressively more conscious critical moral dialogue with the world, spurred by a quest for truth and justice. It moves the individual into moral agency, while the understanding of truth, justice, and agency is continuously developmentally reconstructed. In its fully developed form, it is characterized by moral maturity and empowerment. This consciousness exhibits a qualitatively different level of integration of its cognitive, volitional, and affective capacities. In other words, even in its early forms, it is marked by a greater consistency between what we know, what we love, and how we exercise our will.

Ironically, these three fundamental human faculties have so far been studied separately in psychology, with an exclusive emphasis on analytical ways of knowing, a rather tentative examination of the human capacity to love, and a limited examination of agency. Yet, as psychology has in recent decades begun to move past the fragmented materialistic and primarily behaviorist approach and toward a more holistic, Socratic (Burnett, 1916) view of the human psyche, we are beginning to understand more about how these faculties work together (Danesh, 1994; Diessner, 2002; Mills and Spittle, 2001).

We have come to see the human capacity to know as including all kinds of knowing—conscious, subconscious, unconscious, intuition, insight, inspiration—which develop through experience, cognitive and intellectual pursuits, self-reflection, meditation, and prayer. As Danesh (1994) points out,

Although these various forms of knowing have been accessible to humankind from the dawn of consciousness, our understanding of them has been vague, disjointed and uneven. However, we are now arriving at a new phase in our capacity for knowledge in general and self-knowledge in particular. Even though the remarkable growth of science during the last one hundred and fifty years has, for all practical purposes, dominated all other forms of human knowledge relegating them to either secondary status or irrelevancy, nevertheless there are now strong indications that this imbalance is beginning to be corrected. (p. 64)

People who exhibit critical consciousness manifest a much clearer balance of the full range of different ways of knowing. In contrast, other people seem to favor a particular way of knowing, be it heavily intellectual, predominantly unconscious, or some other type.

Love, perhaps the least studied of the three human faculties, has been recently described as "an active force of attraction to beauty, unity, and growth" (Danesh, 1994, p. 67). Love is a creative activity that varies in force of attraction. Even more importantly, as Danesh (1994) points out, its quality is closely related to the nature of the object of love, as can be seen when we examine humanity's continuing love affair with war. People exhibiting critical consciousness stand out as creative agents in their communities, forces of attraction that seem to draw out the best in others. The quality of their love is notably more all-embracing and is manifested in a deep compassion for the human condition.

The human will, understood as "our freedom to choose between good and evil, between action and inaction, and to determine the direction and quality of our lives" (Danesh, 1994, pp. 70–71), is a much broader phenomenon than agency. Danesh points out the tension in contemporary thought between, on the one hand, the tendency in psychology to reject the primacy of the role of will and to place much greater importance on forces beyond the reach of volition, such as childhood experiences or drives, and on the other hand, the philosophical tendency to absolutize free will. As is usually the case, the truth lies somewhere in the middle, and is suggested by Danesh's (1994) metaphor:

In many respects, life is like sailing. To sail we need a boat (the body) and a sailor (the soul with its power of will). The boat must be sea-worthy. The wind provides the motive power to the boat. The sailor determines the direction and destination of the journey. Notably, the presence or absence of wind is not decided by the sailor. . . . We can use our will in an intelligent and loving way, or live a life of ignorance, close-mindedness, and selfishness. . . . The human will can be either abused or creatively employed to improve the quality of life. (pp. 71–72)

In critically conscious people, we see a strong sense of personal choice. Regardless of what life has handed them, they tend to take responsibility for their own choices. They also live with a deeply felt responsibility to initiate work for positive change and to respond to the needs of the world.

The human powers to know, to love, and to exercise will are directed in life toward concerns with self, with relationships, and with the larger dimension of time (Danesh, 1994). With that in mind, the predominant current condition can be described in the following way. With regard to time, knowledge seems particularly focused on the here-and-now, with a limited understanding of history and mortality, not to mention immortality. With regard to relationships, knowledge seems to focus on the sameness and differences of people, or at best on their uniqueness. Only rarely is there a realization of the oneness of the human family. With regard to self, knowledge seems expressed primarily in self-experience and self-discovery, and relatively much less in true self-knowledge (Danesh, 1994).

Further, as part of the global disintegration of social structures supported by the old ethic and the resulting pervasive social breakdown syndrome (Lambo, 2000), people's actual experience of connectedness has become increasingly limited. However, it is the lived experience of connection that naturally strengthens our capacity to love and to exercise our will in a way that is consistent with what we love. As a result, there is a general feebleness in our capacity to love, which lags far behind our fragmented knowing and fails to engage the exercise of our will. The most common expressions of love seem to be self-preoccupation, struggles with the acceptance of limited others, and struggles with biological and secondary family. Only rarely do we see an expansion of love beyond that, to embrace increasingly larger circles of the human family. Correspondingly, the use of will seems mostly directed toward cultivating self-control and self-confidence, competition in relationships on every level, the meeting of desires, and the making of day-to-day decisions. Rarely does will seem expressed in an expanding sense of responsibility, an orientation to cooperation and equality in relationships, not to mention service to humanity (Danesh, 1994).

Altogether, as Danesh points out, most of people's difficulties are the result of the abuse of our capacities to know, to love, and to will, or of a discordance among them. In contrast, CC people can be distinguished by the way they use their powers to know, to love, and to will. Mature CC, or optimal consciousness, exhibits a general orientation toward genuine self-knowledge, growth, and responsibility, a deepening appreciation of the oneness of people, the need for unity, and a commitment to service, along with an awareness of mortality, history, and transcendence. CC people seem to operate with a relative unity of the three capacities of knowledge, love, and will, a unity which becomes more deeply integrated with development and which is the basis of the resilience, equanimity, and strength that distinguish these people.

In summary, in our age, which has been described as the golden age of information (Hart, 2000), the accessibility of knowledge that was unthinkable for previous generations, and its staggering pace of multiplication, has created an immense gap in human consciousness. As Hart points out, the transformation of information into knowledge requires direct experience and involves a selective process of valuing and co-construction. This process is mediated by individual and collective ethical and moral frames of reference. However, one of the central characteristics of this historical epoch is the profound questioning and changing of all existing ethical and moral frames of reference. In this context of fast-paced change and confusion, valuing has acquired an increasingly pragmatic quality, and there is a general fragmentation of knowledge, which, according to quantum physicist David Bohm, has "helped to lead not only to a dangerously irresponsible use of knowledge, especially scientific, but even more to a general loss of meaning in life as a whole" (Bohm, qtd. in Hart, 2000, p. 18).

Yet the introduction to this book describes people from different walks of life, different cultures, and different levels of education who manifest a common thread in the quality of their being: a relative unity of mind and heart, an ultimately liberating capacity to engage in a wholesome, lived dialogue with reality from a place of faith in life and integrity. What accounts for the significantly greater integration of human powers and human concerns in these people?

Critically conscious people live with what Marcuse (1989b) called an activated depth dimension of existence, manifested in a primarily moral understanding of life. CC is distinguished by a preeminently moral motivation that can be discerned even in childhood; moral motivation interacts with the structural development of mind, resulting in a graded sequence of progressively more complex and expansive moral ways of being.

What is moral motivation? The people studied for this book exhibited a yearning after truth so deep, and often expressed so early in life, that it began to dominate other, more expedient motives, centered around meeting other needs. Such a yearning leads a person to increasingly "know his own self and recognize that which leadeth unto loftiness or lowliness, glory or abasement, wealth or poverty" (Baha'u'llah, qtd. in Noguchi, Hanson, and Lample, 1992). This knowing expresses the spiritual nature of a person, that aspect of a human being which recognizes that, intrinsic as the material world is to our existence, there is something more fundamental to life. As Noguchi, Hanson, and Lample (1992) point out, a human being's "material nature is the product of physical evolution, and is shaped by the struggle for survival. . . . [I]f it is allowed to dominate consciousness the consequences are injustice, cruelty and egotism" (p. 6).

We all seem to come into the world with this innate undifferentiated knowing that there is something greater to life. We can see it in children in their spontaneous attraction to beauty, goodness, and knowledge, which manifests itself along with the other impulses of their material nature. To the extent that this spiritual knowledge and attraction are fostered, they increasingly manifest themselves in life as love, mercy, kindness, generosity, and justice; in other words, the individual's depth dimension of experience is activated, and this depth dimension becomes prominent in their way of being. That is *moral motivation*—an awakened spiritual nature, an attraction to beauty, truth, and goodness, which defines a person's choices.

In most of us, motivation represents an uneasy tension between moral and expediency concerns, but where a moral orientation predominates, people exhibit critical consciousness and can be identified as happier, more actualized and integrated, regardless of their developmental level. To the extent that motivation is governed by other, more expedient motives, regardless of the person's ideological or religious claims, she or he manifests the non-CC pathway. Such a person experiences greater tensions and contradictions between mind and heart and varying degrees of disempowerment. The relative weakness of moral motivation leaves structural development more vulnerable to circumstances, which results in a suboptimal pathway of the development of consciousness.

The different developmental pathways of CC and non-CC themselves represent a continuum, because a predominant expediency motivation can at any point in life be transformed into predominantly moral motivation (often as a result of peak experiences, such as losses, disease, near-death experiences, and education). This continuum is represented in Figure 1.1. In it, the structural-developmental axis is shared by both CC and non-CC pathways. The motivational axis is bisected by the two forms of consciousness, with CC characterized by predominantly moral motivation and non-CC characterized by predominantly expediency motivation.

Hence, any assessment of the current quality and level of consciousness in an individual is only a snapshot in time. While this author has not observed cases where adults switch from the optimal CC pathway, once they have already developed moral motivation and resiliency, this author did observe many cases where people seemed poised at the brink of a transition from a suboptimal non-CC life path to an awakening of their spiritual potential.

THE CHASM BETWEEN EAST AND WEST, NORTH AND SOUTH

The same tension between CC and non-CC, which characterizes individual consciousness, is also reflected in the condition of the world. The fragmented nature of contemporary consciousness was recently most painfully brought home to all of us through the tragedy of September 11. This massive culmination in the split among our capacities to know, to love, and to exercise our will responsibly has illuminated the chasm that divides the Global North from the Global South. It has also brought into sharp relief the particular nature of the twentieth century "betrayal of the life of the mind through surrender to ideologies as squalid as they have been empty" on both sides of this dividing line (Universal House of Justice, 2001, p. 1). In the wake of September 11, we have come to realize that our world will never be quite the same; that we face a need to examine our ways more pressing than ever before.

In this context, it is helpful to revisit the work of Freire and the critical theorists, who engaged poignantly the particular brand of mindlessness so characteristic of the twentieth century.

Freire's (1973) work sheds light on some obvious societal factors that inhibit the development of CC and challenge people in less developed countries in the South and in the East—poverty and illiteracy, religious fanaticism, oppressive regimes and cultures, economic dependence. However, a critically conscious dialogical relationship with one's environment does not seem any easier to develop in the relatively open and democratic Western societies, where universal

Figure 1.1
Diagram of the Full Range of the CC/Non-CC Continuum

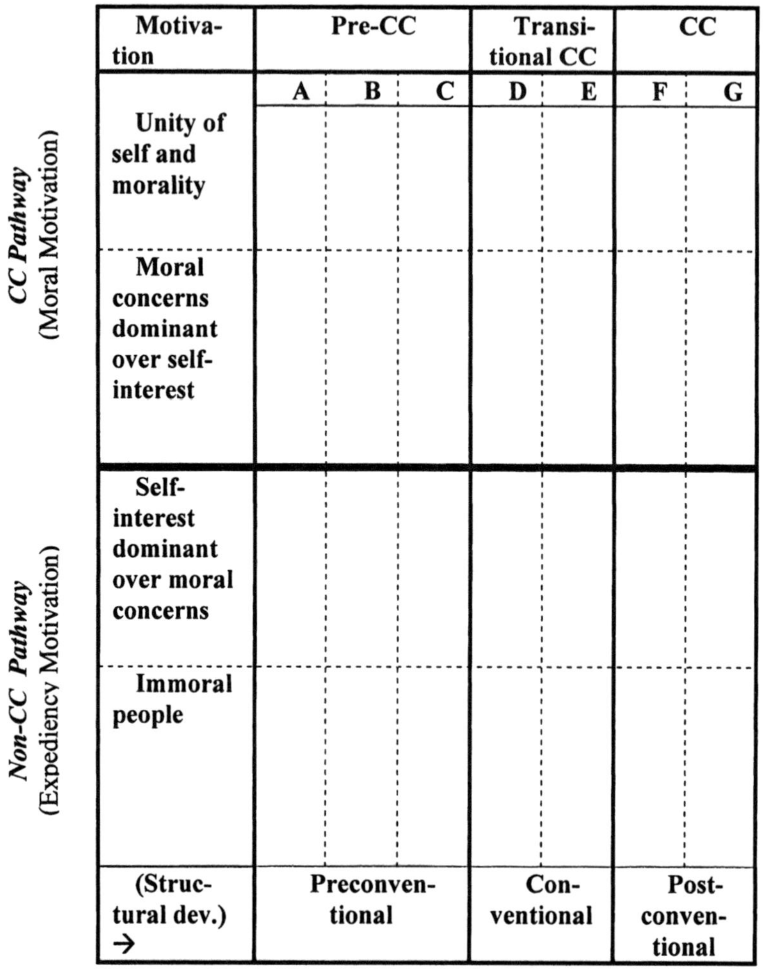

<table>
<tr><td rowspan="2">Motiva-tion</td><td colspan="3">Pre-CC</td><td colspan="2">Transi-tional CC</td><td colspan="2">CC</td></tr>
<tr><td>A</td><td>B</td><td>C</td><td>D</td><td>E</td><td>F</td><td>G</td></tr>
<tr><td>Unity of self and morality</td><td></td><td></td><td></td><td></td><td></td><td></td><td></td></tr>
<tr><td>Moral concerns dominant over self-interest</td><td></td><td></td><td></td><td></td><td></td><td></td><td></td></tr>
<tr><td>Self-interest dominant over moral concerns</td><td></td><td></td><td></td><td></td><td></td><td></td><td></td></tr>
<tr><td>Immoral people</td><td></td><td></td><td></td><td></td><td></td><td></td><td></td></tr>
<tr><td>(Structural dev.) →</td><td colspan="3">Preconventional</td><td colspan="2">Conventional</td><td colspan="2">Postconventional</td></tr>
</table>

CC Pathway (Moral Motivation) — applies to "Unity of self and morality" and "Moral concerns dominant over self-interest"

Non-CC Pathway (Expediency Motivation) — applies to "Self-interest dominant over moral concerns" and "Immoral people"

Key:

A: Moral interest
B: Moral authority
C: Personal responsibility
D: Expanded moral and social responsibility
E: Sociopolitical consciousness
F: Philosophical expansion
G: Historical and global vision

education and information are available to the majority of people. The forces
that inhibit the evolution of a liberated, critically conscious way of being are
subtler in the developed world but no less powerful.

Fromm's (1989) critical social analysis suggests that in the large information
societies of the West, mass media, advertising, ideologies, and politics on every
level have greatly shrunk the personal space where the individual's standing in
the world is negotiated. With almost every aspect of life subject to public scrutiny and the influence of powerful business and political interests, people are not
really free, but are disempowered. Although to all appearances the individual
has more rights, or can at least talk about them, ego-strength is undermined by
forces of massification and indoctrination. It takes a strong and grounded individual to negotiate successfully the worldwide information flow and the ever-
expanding radius of our social world.

How do we develop this groundedness, and groundedness in what? Many
people experience globalization as intimidating as they struggle to define their
place and their lives in relation to not just a single immediate community but to
complex, impersonal, and often perplexing national and international forces, to a
fast-changing global commons (Daloz et al., 1996).

The last few centuries, culminating in the twentieth century, have subjected to
a profound scrutiny all the established social and moral values in which individual consciousness has been grounded for many generations. This radical questioning in all areas of human life has brought to the surface the most undermining inconsistencies and has spurred a breakthrough in collective consciousness—nothing short of a qualitative shift in human civilization in the direction
of greater congruency and universal responsibility. It has so deeply shaken our
trust in the reliability of any ideals, however, that it has left the average person
with little ground to stand on. The result has been a paralysis of will and a deep
internal divorce of the human will from the capacity to know and to love.

In the West, knowing and loving have become much more superficial and
compartmentalized, while will, ungrounded in a deeper knowing and loving, has
amounted to a lot of frenetic activity and hollow busyness (Daloz et al., 1996).
As minds spin faster and faster, trying to compensate through quantity of activity for the tenuous quality of the connection between mind and heart, inner instability and alienation grow deeper. According to Bryson (1999), 500 million
people in the wealthy developed nations suffer neurotic, stress-related, and
somatoform illnesses, and 200 million more have mood disorders such as
chronic and manic depression. The crisis of meaning is evident not only in the
increasingly common mental disturbances but also in the quality of ordinary
social life. Social critics such as Bellah et al. (1985) point out that, in the U.S.
context, the idea of work as calling has become a more and more outdated phenomenon, replaced increasingly by work as career. Lifestyle enclaves have begun to replace interdependent and all-inclusive communities; lifelong commitments, transcending lifestyles and the sectoral organization of life, become
harder and harder to come by.

This combination of precarious relatedness and a utilitarian and morally relativistic approach, which dominates the Western world and is directly opposite to

critical consciousness, increasingly infiltrates the less developed countries as a mistaken symbol of progress and advanced thinking. Centuries-old bonds of interrelatedness are breaking, and new ones are difficult to formulate. In the meantime, the more we recognize the need for the cultivation of character, the less we know how to bridge our differences and create a shared context in which the cultivation of character can become possible. Our internal oppression has reached a new level: we are now contending not just with corrupt social forces, but even more with a deep spiritual vacuum which both reflects on a personal level the state of the world and perpetuates it.

In the East, where all world religions have originated and still have a strong hold on collective consciousness and where the ramifications of the Renaissance and the modern age have not been interpreted as undermining the very essence of the religious quest, the modern mind has developed more slowly than in the West, in a relatively greater balance with the heart. Modernization has been tempered by a historically more deeply rooted spirituality, on which the West, in its desperation, has increasingly begun to draw (as illustrated by the spread of Eastern spiritual forms of practice such as yoga, Taoism, Buddhism, and Sufism). However, even if more slowly and cautiously, people in the East have also begun to examine the double standard of many traditional practices and have experienced the destabilization of traditional values. This has brought about three different but related processes.

First, amid better educated people, there is a growing trend toward an ambivalent secularization and a more precarious Western balance of living. Second, less educated people have held on to their traditions, translating them into ritualized practices suited to specific local contexts and retaining a measure of stability while contributing to the fragmentation of centuries-old cohesive traditions into infinite local sects and cults. Third, the ruling religious elite has reacted to the first two processes with paranoia due to the loss of control and has initiated violent efforts to hold on to the past, breeding religious fanaticism and intolerance and attempting a crackdown on basic human rights and dignities.

The Global South, which has remained materially undeveloped and has been severely exploited by the Global North for almost the past five centuries, has also experienced its fair share of destabilization. Exploitative Western practices have disrupted the structures of tribal societies without replacing them with authentic education and development. The ruthlessness of "civilized" Western colonizers has reinforced tribal aggression while undermining the ethico-spiritual foundation of those societies, resulting in such horror stories as the genocide in Rwanda. Rapid changes throughout the Global South are wiping out old and traditional ways, offering no viable substitutes.

Altogether, as Deputy Director-General of the World Health Organization (WHO) Adeoye Lambo (2000) points out, the world is experiencing a social breakdown syndrome, reflected in "a rising incidence and prevalence of psychosomatic diseases, mental disorders, anxiety and neurosis, prostitution, crimes, political corruption, and a variety of sexual diseases, including AIDS." (p. 114) "The human race today, engaged in a mighty outward and inward struggle for a new and universally binding order of life, stands at a point where two worlds meet, amid an almost inconceivable devastation of traditional values" (Lambo, 2000, p. 122).

In this global climate, despite our enormous technological and intellectual advances, the ideal of human health as "a state of complete physical, mental and social well-being, and not merely the absence of disease or infirmity," as espoused by WHO, is as remote as it is urgently needed (Lambo, 2000, p. 116). A guiding principle in the work of WHO is that health is a fundamental condition for global peace. As Sir Wolstenholme (2000), president and founder of Action in International Medicine, points out, unequal development endangers all.

Despite this fact, and despite the efforts of people of conscience who participated in the North-South dialogue initiated by former German president Willy Brandt, in the words of Lester Brown, president of the Worldwatch Institute, "Our world today is two worlds, one rich, one poor; one literate, one largely illiterate; one overfed and overweight, one hungry and malnourished; one affluent and consumption-oriented, one poverty stricken and subsistence-oriented" (qtd. in Lanza, 2000, p. 122).

According to recent United Nations reports, poverty in the world is deepening, rather than becoming alleviated by technological advances.

More than two billion people in the world are forced to exist on less than thirteen percent of the global income. . . . [I]n 1950, the per capita Gross National Product of the poor countries was 7.9 per cent of the per capita GNP of the rich countries; in 1975 it was only 7.6 percent. To the extent that poverty generates ineffective or inappropriate resources usage, the resource cost of global poverty could be extraordinarily high. . . . [I]t is clear that the developing world commands a significant share of the world's resources. It is in everyone's interest to see them used as efficiently as possible. (Lambo, 2000, p. 122)

The conclusion is that "education must extend its influence from intellectual training, which is its center, to a refinement of sensibility—to the cultivation of understanding, imagination, sympathy and tolerance, and to the fostering of talent of the kind of individuality that operates harmlessly and beneficially within the framework of a free society" (Lambo, 2000, p. 114).

Such an education is education for critical consciousness, which brings into a balanced development minds and hearts and combines a systemic awareness and critical global perspective with ego strength and an activated depth dimension of human experience. Despite the growing awareness of that need, the collective condition in most parts of the world is still one of inner split between minds and hearts, reflected in the chasm between East and West (as very general categories).

The West, on the one hand, has achieved a great deal in the cultivation of minds and has created a standard of education, ethics, organization, and intellectual and scientific development that serves as a model for the rest of the world. However, the West has developed the mind largely in separation from the capacity of the heart for love and compassion and has therefore bred anomie and an increasingly alienated, positivistic, and frequently arrogant culture, which has generated its own psychological problems.

The East, on the other hand, has preserved its emphasis on the mysteries of the heart. It has continued to contribute to humanity peaks of mystical and poetic understanding and a generally much more spiritual and interconnected view of life. It has, however, greatly neglected the education of minds, and so the capacity for love has often wrapped itself around questionable objects, breeding religious fanaticism and destructive wars, as well as intellectually suffocating and socially rigid environments.

Generally speaking, neither East nor West has found a healthy balance between cultivating minds and cultivating hearts, and each part of the world seems locked in its own biases and problems, viewing the opposite camp with a good measure of contempt and distrust. September 11 brought that reality home.

The obvious solution seems to be the emancipated integration of East and West, a unity in diversity which can happen only between equals and which would allow each to learn from the strengths of the other without necessarily losing diverse identities. Such thinking is scary for most people, however, since unity is frequently misunderstood to mean unification, sameness, rather than an organic principle characteristic of all healthy living systems (Woodall, 1996).

Caught in this vacuum between opposing views, people tend to absolutize whatever most immediately seems to make sense, which can be seen in the modern world by people's embrace of fanatical religious beliefs, ideology, consumerism, sport, rock music, hero worship, political figures, health foods, working out, computers, addictions, and animal rights. This tension between mind and heart burdens people, and leaves many feeling voiceless and submissive or overwhelmed and defensive. The tendency is to delegate responsibility for the central issues in one's personal life to external sources of authority—state laws, political parties, intellectual ideologies, organizations, trends, public pressure, or simply fate. Under such conditions of internal oppression, it seems natural to isolate oneself in the domain of private life, where one can feel a measure of control, and to limit one's sense of relatedness to immediate others. The chasm between public and private life grows deeper.

In the face of this pervasive internal oppression, progressive integrative thinkers are beginning to suggest that we may have completely missed what constitutes the human psyche and that we may need to return to that foundational question before we can integrate into a helpful understanding and change of heart the vast accumulated scientific knowledge (Diessner, 2002; Mills and Spittle, 2001; Wilber, 1998). It is becoming clearer that the current thwarting of the most fundamental human yearning for a transcendent balance of the true, the good, and the beautiful has resulted in a polarized and paranoid world replete with human suffering.

Large-scale education for critical consciousness is a global enterprise which has to draw equally on the strengths of both East and West, North and South, integrating them into a new whole. We now face the task of understanding what the characteristics of that whole might be.

UNEASY GLOBALIZATION AND ITS HIDDEN SPIRITUAL DIMENSION

Our postmodern predicament has been well summarized in the First International Dialogue on the Transition to a Global Society, held at the Landegg Academy in Switzerland in 1990 under the auspices of UNESCO. That forum pointed to the variety of imbalances that many societies exhibit in the relations between the three main sectors of every society: economic order, sociopolitical order, and spiritual order (Malaska, 1993). Western societies in the main were viewed as obsessed with economic development, with rampant materialism overshadowing the sociopolitical and spiritual orders. Eastern European societies were regarded as representing the collapse of societies as a result of the dominance of the sociopolitical order over both spiritual and economic orders, and some countries in the Muslim world "serve to demonstrate societal dissonance . . . because of the marked dominance of the spiritual order" (Malaska, 1993, p. 47). "Certain African societies illustrate what happens when none of the sectors makes an adequate contribution to the societal whole" (Malaska, 1993, p. 47).

As we are moving steadily toward globalization of the planet, people face correspondingly greater complexities, ambiguities, and responsibilities and search in ways movingly described by social critics such as Wuthnow (1991) and Bellah et al. (1985). We are held back by old habits of thought (Mills and Spittle, 2001; Thich Nhat Hanh, 1991), while changes are happening fast. As Vaclav Havel, president of the Czech Republic, points out:

There are good reasons for suggesting that the modern age has ended. Many things indicate that we are going through a transitional period, when it seems that something is on the way out and something else is painfully being born. It is as if something were crumbling, decaying and exhausting itself, while something else, still indistinct, was arising from the rubble. (Havel, 1994)

There is a felt sense of this emergence, individually and collectively, that seems to be especially prominent in the Western world and is at the root of the mass speculation of disaster associated with the new millennium. It is not hard to see in the "Y2K" and other apocalyptic prognoses a deeper collective angst, the result of a lack of vision and understanding of the kind of individual and collective challenge we are facing. Chaos always precedes the emergence of a larger frame of reference; in the midst of this movement into unfamiliar ground we are frightened.

This all-pervasive fear and turmoil at the point where a collective materialistic civilization has reached its limits, and has to face the depths of its motivation, has been powerfully captured in the metaphorical language of the prophecies of world spiritual traditions.

Today, humanity is bowed down with trouble, sorrow and grief, no one escapes; the world is wet with tears. (Abdu'l-Baha, [1917] 1969, p. 110)

Its sickness is approaching the stage of utter hopelessness, inasmuch as the true Physician is debarred from administering the remedy, whilst unskilled practitioners are regarded with favor, and are accorded full freedom to act. . . . The dust of sedition hath clouded the hearts of men, and blinded their eyes. . . . Most of the people are bewildered in their drunkenness and wear on their faces the evidences of anger. . . . We see them rushing toward their idol. Say: None shall be secure this Day from the decree of God. This indeed is a grievous Day. We point out to them those that led them astray. They see them, and yet recognize them not. (Baha'u'llah, [1952] 1976, pp. 39–41)

In the evil age to come, living beings will decrease in good qualities and increase in utter arrogance, coveting gains and honors, developing their evil qualities, and being far removed from deliverance. (Lotus Sutra qtd. in Wilson, 1995, p. 775)

But understand this, that in the last days there will come times of stress. For men will be lovers of self, lovers of money, proud, arrogant, abusive, disobedient to their parents, ungrateful, unholy, inhuman, implacable . . . swollen with conceit, lovers of pleasure rather than lovers of God, holding the form of religion but denying the power of it. (2 Timothy 3.1–5 qtd. in Wilson, 1995, p. 775)

The time is near in which nothing will remain of Islam but its name, and of the Qur'an but its mere appearance, and the mosques of Muslims will be destitute of knowledge and worship; and the learned men will be the worst people under the heavens; and contention and strife will issue from them, and it will return upon themselves. (Hadith, qtd. in Wilson, 1995, p. 778)

Spiritual traditions have also prophesied that these times of painful spiritual awakening will mark the long-awaited and hoped-for spiritual maturity of a collective humanity.

The whole human race hath longed for this Day, that perchance it may fulfill that which well beseemeth its station, and is worthy of its destiny. (Baha'u'llah, [1952] 1976, p. 39)

It is our duty in this radiant century to investigate the essentials of divine religion, seek the realities underlying the oneness of the world of humanity, and discover the source of fellowship and agreement which will unite mankind in the heavenly bond of love. This unity is the radiance of eternity, the divine spirituality. (Abdu'l-Baha, 1982)

Many individual thinkers have already anticipated the gradual shift to a spiritualized civilization, able to muster its collective will to solve the economical and ecological problems facing the planet, on the basis of an understanding of the universal spiritual principles that govern life (Abdullah,1995; Aull, 1988; Chopra, 1993; Huddleston, 1999; Laszlo, 1989; Ruhe, 1994; Schaefer, 1994; White, 1989). Wilber (1998) conceptualizes this shift as a new level of integration of the now fully differentiated cultural value spheres of morals, science, and art, as the respective expressions of the good, the true, and the beautiful, the intersubjective, objective, and subjective "faces of Spirit as it shines in this world" (p. 201). He recognizes as the most important topic of the modern world the integration of science and religion, which preserves the "dignity of modernity."

In a recent interview (Novak, 1998), Norman Mailer said that he sees religion as the last frontier. Vaclav Havel asserted that today's crisis of moral responsibility in this "first atheistic civilization in the history of humankind" is the result of our loss of the feeling that "the Universe, nature, existence and our lives are the work of a creation guided by a definite intention" (qtd. in Novak, 1998). As *New York Times* journalist Michael Novak (1998) points out, through the "great intellectual struggles" of the twentieth century, we have come to realize that democracy and free enterprise are the way of the future, but they leave open the question of how we should live and bring forward, once again, moral and religious questions.

For some five centuries, a leading secular elite has held that moral questions can be resolved on the plane of reason alone. Some still believe that. But it has become even more apparent that such a belief is only a belief, a faith, a kind of religion of its own. For who, looking at the butcher's bench that was the 20th century, finds it self-evident that reason is adequate to its own defense? . . . All around us, post-modernists, nihilists and relativists have been assuring us that reason has no particular grip on reality. . . . This inadequacy is the more apparent when one thinks not of the rare individual but of the whole social order, in all its teeming varieties of passion, ignorance, ambition, and talent. . . .
Faith in reason alone had as its premise the belief that humans are not naturally religious. Therefore, to be religious was in some way to be alienated from oneself and to exhibit a form of weakness. The fearful might cling to a blanket or need a crutch, but not the free and the brave, not the mature. Today, however, the religious question arises most insistently among some of the most successful and the most powerful, and not at their moments of weakness but during their hours of greatest triumph. . . . Just when they have achieved everything they once thought would make them happy, they bump into their own finitude—and their infinite hunger.
Some of the leading spirits of our age have begun to sense that humans are naturally religious. They have found that to discover God, one does not have to be driven down on all fours. Today it is often the brightest and the most able and the most fortunate who are becoming aware of their true nature. This very nature sings to them of God. (Novak, 1998)

As people like Mailer and Havel emphasize the new importance of religion, and as Novak points out that the movement beyond an adversarial attitude between science and religion has already quietly begun in medicine and theoretical physics, it becomes clear that the best thinkers of our times are not advocating a return to antiquated religious dogmas. Many are now trying to conceive of a spiritualized, sustainable global civilization in the twenty-first century. Wilber (1998), who seriously explores the emerging integration of science and religion into a deeper understanding of life and human functioning, does so with a deep sense of responsibility to the "dignity of modernity" (p. 44).

In many ways, the governing principles of the hundred or so democratic nations in today's world are in fact the principles of modernity—that is, the values of the liberal Western Enlightenment. These include the values of equality, freedom and justice; representational and deliberative democracy; the equality of all citizens before the law, regardless of race, sex, or creed; political and civil rights (freedom of speech, religion, assembly, fair trial, etc.). . . . None of the pre-modern religions anywhere in the world delivered these dignities and rights on any sort of large scale. . . . Whatever it was that allowed modernity to bring forth these noble values will be a necessary ingredient in the integration of the best that both epochs have to offer. (Wilber, 1998, pp. 44–45)

To unite the premodern, modern, and post-modern epochs in a truly new level of understanding which can encompass a global world requires no less than critical consciousness, a consciousness that brings systemic thought and an engaged dialogical relationship to reality from a place of unity of mind and heart. In this context of a painfully emerging global society, which is being negotiated in every person's life, the role of individual critical consciousness becomes significant. It allows people to become moral and caring agents in a fast-changing, transforming global world.

As mentioned in the preface, this author's thinking about the individual and collective movement toward CC has been profoundly enriched by the Baha'i spiritual paradigm. Since it is widely unknown, it seems important here to clarify its principles that inform the study of the above-described tendencies.

BAHA'I SPIRITUAL PRINCIPLES THAT INFORM THE STUDY OF CC

This most recent wisdom tradition (150 years old) rearticulates, in ways consistent with our contemporary level of understanding and social development, fundamental psychospiritual and ethico-moral principles, which are present in all earlier wisdom traditions. It offers a profoundly hermeneutical model of the individual and collective evolution of consciousness and brings a distinctive perspective on the current process of globalization. Its psychology, which is still widely unknown, has much to offer to the study of CC.

Baha'i understanding helps demystify the notion of spiritual potential and links it in clearer terms with overall psychological functioning and moral motivation. In that understanding (and consistent with quantum physics), every living thing on the material plane reflects some of the qualities of infinite divine potentiality, and that represents its particular beauty, dignity, and purpose. Human beings are endowed with a unique potentiality, which it is the purpose of their lives to manifest more fully—the human spirit, or rational soul.

The rational soul, embraces all beings, and as far as the human ability permits discovers the realities of things. . . . The mind is the power of the human spirit. Spirit is the lamp; mind is the light which shines from the lamp. . . . Mind is the perfection of the spirit and is its essential quality. (Abdu'l-Baha, [1930] 1999, pp. 208–9)

The mind is seen as the link between body and soul. Hence, it is the purpose of life to develop the mind, and through the spirit of faith, to let it illumine the world with understanding.

Upon the inmost reality of each and every created thing He hath shed the light of one of His names. . . . Upon the reality of man, however, He hath focused the radiance of all of

His names and attributes, and made it a mirror of His own Self. (Baha'u'llah, [1952] 1976, p. 65)

All created things except man are captives of nature and the sense world, but in man there has been created an ideal power by which he may perceive intellectual or spiritual realities . . . through the attribute of reason, when fortified by the Holy Spirit, he may penetrate and discover ideal realities . . . of the world of significance. (Abdu'l-Baha, 1982, pp. 302–3)

With the purpose of human life being to attain "the Tree of Knowledge" (Baha'u'llah, [1952] 1976, p. 78), human beings do that only to the extent to which they are not captives of their own personal minds. When we forget that the human mind is the essential quality of spirit, when we deny spirit and confine ourselves to a physical, materialistic outlook, we become attached to the constructions of our personal minds and eventually locked in their prison. Then, even our greatest achievements and most honest efforts are tinged with bitterness, if not cynicism, as studies of some moral leaders show, and we are left estranged from our own powers (see Virginua Durr in Colby and Damon, 1992). The human soul, "unless assisted by the spirit of faith, does not become acquainted with the divine secrets. . . . It is like a mirror which, although clear, polished and brilliant, is still in need of light" (Abdu'l-Baha, [1930] 1999, pp. 208–9).

Baha'i psychology recognizes at the heart of human motivation the desire for transcendence, an attraction to and a desire to know truth, beauty, and goodness: "These endowments have enabled humanity to build civilizations and to prosper materially. But such accomplishments alone have never satisfied the human spirit, whose mysterious nature inclines it towards transcendence, a reaching towards an invisible realm, towards the ultimate reality, that unknowable essence of essences called God." (Universal House of Justice, 2001, p. 17)

It is that reaching out that is so unique in CC individuals, who seem relatively indifferent to their material circumstances and who bring vision to their lives. As Baha'i spiritual philosophy points out, this precisely is the uniquely human endowment. If we were meant to simply partake of our animal propensities to eat, drink, wander about, and sleep, then any animal is "nobler, more serene, poised and confident" in the satisfaction of these needs, while we are fraught with anxiety and unrest (Abdu'l-Baha, 1982, pp. 184–85). But we are meant to attain toward "moral sublimity and intellectual perfection" (Abdu'l-Baha, 1978, p. 288), and when we do that, we are fulfilled, as CC individuals show. We have a double nature that, in this life, we learn to integrate:

Man is in the highest degree of materiality, and at the beginning of spirituality . . . at the last degree of darkness and at the beginning of light. (Abdu'l-Baha, [1930] 1999, pp. 235–36)

Thou art even as a finely tempered sword concealed in the darkness of its sheath and its value hidden from the artificer's knowledge. Wherefore, come forth from the sheath of self and desire that thy worth may be made resplendent and manifest into all the world. (Baha'u'llah, 1991, p. 47)

In us are the potentialities for all the necessary qualities that ultimately allow us to attain knowledge and understanding through a unity of mind and heart. But these potentialities have to be developed in a balanced way, so that they can become virtues, or powers, rather than disintegrate into self-destructive characteristics. Evil, in Baha'i understanding, is not a separately existing power, but the outcome of ignorant and misguided imbalance.

In creation there is no evil; all is good. Certain qualities and natures innate in some men and apparently blameworthy are not so in reality. For example, from the beginning of his life you can see in a nursing child the signs of greed, of anger and of temper . . . greed, which is to ask for something more, is a praiseworthy quality provided it is used suitably. So if a man is greedy to acquire science and knowledge, or to become compassionate, generous and just, it is most praiseworthy. If he exercises his anger and wrath against the bloodthirsty tyrants . . . it is very praiseworthy . . . but when the natural qualities of man are used in an unlawful way, they are blameworthy. (Abdu'l-Baha, [1930] 1999, pp. 214–16)

The premise is that the universe is governed by spiritual laws, which religion continuously reveals to humanity in accordance with its readiness at each stage in its collective evolution. Hence, religious revelation is not absolute but progressive: its sociohistoric teachings change, accounting for much interreligious misunderstanding and conflict, while the ethico-moral teachings remain essentially the same.

Therefore, when a human being's natural proclivities are cultivated in a balanced alignment with spiritual laws, this person's powers unfold and ultimately manifest his or her true spiritual potential. When we look at the lives of moral leaders, it becomes evident that they do not live locked in their narrowly analytical personal self-definitions, but rather with a sense of greater nobility and power. Every time ordinary people access that understanding in themselves, they become extraordinary, as recent findings increasingly show (Banks, 1998, 2001; Mills and Spittle, 2001).

While children carry this spiritual potential, and it manifests itself in moments of flow as profound intuitions and glimpses into the mystery of life, their minds have not yet been developed to attain the strength of a fully manifested spiritual potential. There is a significant difference between the purity of heart of a child and the purity of heart each adult needs to strive for in order to fully actualize his or her spiritual potential.

The hearts of children are of the utmost purity. They are mirrors upon which no dust has fallen. But this purity is on account of weakness and innocence, not on account of any strength and testing . . . whereas the man becomes pure through his strength. Through the power of intelligence he becomes simple; through the great power of reason and understanding and not through the power of weakness he becomes sincere . . . his heart becomes purified, his spirit enlightened, his soul is sensitized and tender—all through his great strength. (Abdu'l-Baha, 1982, p. 53)

Baha'i philosophy recognizes the existence of transcendent awareness from the moment of conception, which characterizes the powers of the soul, and explores in depth the relationship of those powers to the growing powers of the individual mind after birth.

[T]he spirit is connected with the body, as this light is with this mirror . . . the rational soul is the substance through which the body exists. The personality of the rational soul is from its beginning; it is not due to the instrumentality of the body, but the state and the personality of the rational soul may be strengthened in this world. (Abdu'l-Baha, [1930] 1999, p. 240)

Recent studies that explore the place of prenatal consciousness in the lifespan evolution of consciousness (Wade, 1996) point to the same understanding, namely, that in the developmental life journey, to the extent that the powers of the mind are developed and become increasingly integrated with the soul knowledge of the heart, the resulting consciousness is of a new and much more expansive quality. Baha'i philosophy emphasizes the need to direct the mirror of consciousness from the beginning to the divine center of all life and to nurture and cultivate transcendent awareness in children. Such awareness can become a solid foundation on which developing brain-based consciousness can then erect the edifice of knowledge, and ultimately, knowledge and understanding can become one in the fully developed and fully awakened mind.

Although to acquire the sciences and arts is the greatest glory of mankind, this is so only on condition that man's river flow into the mighty sea, and draw from God's ancient source His inspiration. When this cometh to pass, then every teacher is as a shoreless ocean, every pupil a prodigal fountain of knowledge. If, then, the pursuit of knowledge lead to the beauty of Him Who is the Object of all Knowledge, how excellent that goal; but if not, a mere drop will perhaps shut a man off from flooding grace, for with learning cometh arrogance and pride, and it bringeth on error and indifference to God. (Abdu'l-Baha, 1978, p. 110)

This warning rings particularly familiar in the face of our advanced society's ultimate split between mind and heart, and the overall tension in the world between technological knowledge and severely lagging understanding, exemplified by the fact that 1.2 billion people live in utmost poverty and frequent starvation in our rich and advanced world.

The implications are clear: a consciousness that is not tuned to its transcendent source will become locked in an incorrect, imbalanced use of analytical thought, which will function in circular and ultimately blinding ways. On the other hand, continuously redirecting the mirror of consciousness toward transcendent truth, and our own transcendent essence, allows the human mind to function in balanced and wise ways and to truly illumine the world of material reality and penetrate it with the light of understanding.

Hence, a child needs to be reminded from the very beginning of its noble nature, because in that awareness is an energy that can illumine the human world. As illustrated in the life stories of moral leaders (Bembow, 1994; Colby and Damon, 1992; Gandhi, 1927), such encouragement of the noblest intuitions and yearnings of the heart fosters searching and questioning and brings about intensive structural development and expansion of the mind. Hence, the evolving of critical consciousness becomes an ongoing interaction of heart and mind, of moral motivation and structural development. This interaction has been poignantly illustrated in the case studies of contemporary individuals who have devoted their lives to a discerning and committed service to humanity (Daloz et al., 1996). Here is how the Baha'i paradigm distinguishes between these two kinds of consciousness:

The mass of people are occupied with self and worldly desire, are immersed in the ocean of the nether world and are captives of the world of nature, save those souls who have been freed from the chains and fetters of the material world and, like unto swift-flying birds, are soaring in this unbounded realm. They are awake and vigilant . . . their highest wish centereth on the eradication from among men of the struggle for existence, the shining forth of spirituality . . . the exercise of utmost kindness among people, the realization of an intimate and close connection between religions and the practice of the ideal of self-sacrifice. Then will the world of humanity be transformed. (Abdu'l-Baha, 1978, pp. 281–82)

Today the confirmations of the Kingdom of Abha are with those who renounce themselves, forget their own opinions, cast aside personalities and are thinking of the welfare of others. . . . Whosoever is occupied with himself is wandering in the desert of heedlessness and regret. The "Master Key" to self-mastery is self-forgetting. The road to the palace of life is through the path of renunciation. (Abdu'l-Baha, qtd. in Hornby, 1997)

According to the Baha'i macrodevelopmental philosophical perspective, human consciousness is now challenged more than ever to face and resolve this tension between mind and heart. In the past, human consciousness has gone through its stages of collective infancy and childhood, with their typical tensions and contradictions. In our modern age we are facing the historical process of humanity's emerging from its turbulent adolescence, and slowly and painstakingly entering its age of collective maturity. Hence, the primary task of this stage in human civilization is the widespread development of critical consciousness—in other words, such a level of individual and collective consciousness which will allow humanity to attain fully the kind of unity in diversity, and peaceful global civilization, for which we certainly have the knowledge but need to cultivate the understanding.

God has created in man the power of reason, whereby man is enabled to investigate reality. God has not intended man to imitate blindly his fathers and ancestors. He has endowed him with mind, or the faculty of reasoning, by the exercise of which he is to investigate and discover truth, and that which he finds real and true he must accept. . . . The greatest cause of bereavement and disheartening in the world of humanity is ignorance based upon blind imitation. It is due to this that wars and battles prevail; from this cause hatred and animosity arise continually among mankind. . . . Each human creature has individual endowment, power and responsibility in the creative plan of God. Therefore, depend upon your own reason and judgment and adhere to the outcome of your own investigation; otherwise, you will be utterly submerged in the sea of ignorance and deprived of all the bounties of God. (Abdu'l-Baha, 1982, pp. 291–93)

EMPIRICAL BASIS OF THE STUDY

The following chapters explore real-life vignettes of ordinary contemporary Americans and Bulgarians who exhibit different levels of CC and can help us grasp further the nature of this empowered moral consciousness and way of being. These vignettes are drawn from the cross-cultural study *The Ontogeny of Critical Consciousness* (Mustakova-Possardt, 1996), which involved twenty U.S. and eight Bulgarian interviews.

The U.S. interviews constituted a statistically selected subsample of Colby and Damon's (1994) study of midlife social responsibility, supported by the MacArthur Foundation Research Program on Successful Midlife Development (MIDMAC). The original Midlife Development in the United States (MIDUS) survey was based on a demographically representative sample of 6,000 Americans in midlife (aged thirty-five to sixty), selected by the MacArthur Foundation Research Program on Successful Midlife Development (MIDMAC). Colby and Damon's study on social responsibility was an in-depth follow-up study of a subsample of about one hundred, roughly half men and half women, residing in or around five urban areas throughout the country, namely Atlanta, Chicago, Boston, San Francisco, and Phoenix. The Boston area interviews provided the subsample of the Social Responsibility study used to explore CC.

The Bulgarian interviews, supported by the Dissertation Award of the Henry A. Murray Research Center for the Study of Lives, constitute an unrepresentative sample consisting of four men and four women, five of them living in the capital, and three living in a town in the heart of the country (Mustakova-Possardt, 1995b). In 1995, when these interviews were done, this author was shocked to discover the extent to which the connected, people-and-relationships-oriented Bulgarian life she had left behind had changed. With the turmoil of the transition out of communism and the efforts to articulate free and conscious public and private choices in the context of a steadily globalizing world, Bulgarian society had become deeply antagonized. Lifelong connections between family and friends had been torn, as each person's inner reality shined clearly in their choices. There was a deep sense of a dramatic historical shift, in the context of which motivations, previously veiled underneath lifelong connections, had become defining, and could no longer be hidden. A time of change, a time of pain, a time of distinct and autonomous choices now bore explicit global ramifications in a shrinking world. The construct of CC proved very helpful in the author's understanding of those choices.

The Appendix offers a table describing the occupation and specific characteristics, as well as the CC/non-CC ratings, of the twenty U.S. and eight Bulgarian interviewees.

This cross-cultural research has allowed the differentiation of the generic from the contextual characteristics of CC. There are some important overall contextual similarities and differences between U.S. and Bulgarian cultures. The United States and Eastern Europe share a similar westernized materialistic and individualistic context, colored by a generally recognized Christian framework. However, there are differences in the degrees of materialism and individualism and their particular expressions. In contrast to the fundamentally individualistic cultural tradition and collective discourse of the United States, as described by Bellah et al. (1985) and Wuthnow (1991), East European societies come out of more collective cultural, social, and religious traditions. Individualism developed there as a reaction to the oppressive totalitarian claim on consciousness, and is not so deeply rooted in the fabric of the society itself.

These social configurations create culture-specific images of the ideal self (Csikszentmihalyi, 1993; Sloan, 1992). In the United States, the preponderance of the economic order fosters predominantly sensate individualistic ideals. In contrast, in East European societies, the preponderance of the sociopolitical order fosters idealized collective ideological images, as well as idealistic individualistic counter-tendencies. As a result, Bulgarian society is much more dominated by ideas, and there is a deep rift among ideology, raw materialism, and idealism. However, in spite of the somewhat more idealistic images in East European culture, people in both societies struggle with CC.

Chapter 2

Critical Consciousness as an Individual Way of Being

The springs that sustain the life of these birds are not of this world.
Baha'u'llah, [1952] 1976, p. 341

You will know the truth, and the truth will make you free.
John 8.32, qtd. in Wilson, 1995

The fetters of the heart are broken, all doubts are resolved . . . when He is be held who is both high and low.
Mundaka Upanishad 2.2.8, qtd. in Wilson, 1995

JIM: AN AFRICAN AMERICAN ACTIVIST

A simple-looking, short and stout black man who works on the railroads and lives in one of the poorest and most crime-ridden slums of a big city, Jim is as remarkable an individual as his appearance is inconspicuous. He is a wonderful example of mature CC, or optimal consciousness, as described in chapter 1. He manifests a distinctive unity of the three capacities of knowledge, love, and will, which is the basis of his resilience, equanimity, and strength. The central themes of his life story are an abiding orientation toward genuine self-knowledge, growth, and responsibility; a deepening appreciation of the oneness of people and the need for unity; and a commitment to service to the human family, coupled with a growing awareness of his mortality and capacity for transcendence.

From a critical interpretive perspective, Jim illustrates what Sloan (1996) considers relatively liberated, "pure" consciousness. Sloan describes freedom in the following way: "Most analyses locate freedom in the deliberation phase. This takes us nowhere. It would be more accurate to hold that individuals are free to the extent that they interpret problems, deliberate, commit, and act with a deep awareness of the contexts that influence and determine their perspectives and inclinations" (Sloan, 1996, p. 142).

Jim is remarkably aware of his own context and the context in which each of his significant life decisions was made. Unlike most people, in whom, according to Sloan, this kind of awareness is only a glimpse of "pure" consciousness at turning points in their lives (Sloan, 1996, p. 142), Jim seems to live with an abiding sense of the forces at work in his life, a capacity to consciously align himself with these forces by tapping into his inner resources, seeing things fresh, accessing good feelings, and acting with commitment and whole-heartedness, out of wisdom and understanding. This capacity has been recently described in research on wisdom (Mills and Spittle, 2001).

Jim's freshness of perspective reveals a relative freedom from ideology, which Sloan (1992) defines as "a complex structure of affect, cognition, and action that functions so as to maintain social relations of domination and to reproduce the social order founded on those oppressive relations" (p. 75). This freedom from the oppression of ideology, and his ability to access and respond to life fresh in each moment, bringing to bear a relative harmony of knowledge, love, and will, constitutes critical consciousness. How did Jim come into this way of being?

A first look into Jim's life reveals a world richly populated with meaningful human connections and relationships with an expansive circle of others. His home and heart are always open to people, and in the community he is "kind of like a resource type person": "I'm always the one to get called upon, round the clock." He provides financial and physical help, counsels people, gets men into detox programs, helps them find jobs, connects them to support programs or to the right people, and provides other kinds of assistance. His habitual morality (Colby and Damon, 1992) makes responding the most natural thing. Jim is a creative agent, and a force of attraction in his community, continuously drawing out the best in others.

Jim has done many things in his life. An excellent college student on a full scholarship in the sixties, he left school and became active in the civil rights movement. His early thinking reveals idealism as a central component of his identity and a strong and clear inner standard, which became articulated in the encounter with racism:

I wasn't willing to compromise my ideas for a mark or a grade. I just knew it wasn't for me. I went down South. I had worked heavily on the desegregation process. I was involved with a group of people from North Carolina that went and struggled for educational and human freedom in their town.

He later joined the Air Force, and faced "truly combative, racist attitudes that were around me every day." His army experience of daily humiliations as a black minority in the Air Force was a significant experience of cognitive dissonance, or "catching culture in a lie"—a common theme in the lives of moral leaders (Bembow, 1994, p. 153). His time of greatest despair coincided with the assassination of Martin Luther King.

Even in the worst moments of discrimination and injustice, Jim did not compromise his principles. Under misplaced allegations in the Army, he refused to give out the names of others in order to exonerate himself. Although many of his friends "turned their backs on" him when he was reduced to "a pariah," he kept his faith in people: "I met some wonderful people there, and we're still friends today." He showed both spirit in the face of hopelessness and little bitterness when he spoke about it. His ability to forgive and his ultimate faith in human nature are reminiscent of those of prominent moral leaders (Colby and Damon, 1992). In the long run, his competence and intelligence prevailed in the Air Force. Jim eventually became "Airman of the Month" twice.

Jim's encounters with racism continued through his later experiences as a nontraditional student at Tufts University. He stood by his convictions and bore himself with the utmost dignity and character in the face of injustice. Here is an example:

The professor in the embryology class would go right to the end. My chemistry class was way over on the other side of campus. So I would get there, there would never be a seat. So I would sit alongside of the wall. Then finally the instructor breaks his chalk on the board, and he walks right up to me. I'm the only black in this 200-person class, and he walks right up to me, and he says, what the hell are you doing sitting on the floor? So I said, I can't see the board from the back, so I have to sit up here. He says, well you wear glasses. Maybe you should get some new ones. So now I said, excuse me sir, but you might not have noticed that I'm not a child. I said, maybe you're used to teaching children. I don't know. But, I'm not a child. I have a name. I said, if you wanted to talk to me about this, you could simply say, please see me after class. I think that's the proper way.

When he took this to the dean, Jim met more insensitivity and injustice. Facing the wall of systemic racism, he had enough perspective to see the pettiness of all these encounters, and not to allow himself to become consumed with them. He withdrew from school and pursued an alternative path. Nothing in the way he tells his story suggests the slightest sense of victimization; he remains a moral agent in his life, and takes responsibility to find opportunities to work for positive social change.

He started working for the railroads and found in that a wonderful opportunity to combat racism and help other black men build lives for themselves. He speaks with understanding about the systemic predicament of black men like his father, while retaining a strong sense of personal moral responsibility and agency.

My father was a very productive person up until his mid-twenties, and then he began to drink alcohol. And he was an alcoholic for a long time. And it's kind of interesting to know because most of his friends kind of went through the same kind of process, and they're a group of bitter black men. They probably never reached their potential, and a lot of that had to do with opportunity, basic education. . . . I think that my father was—I can't call him a victim of this system; I think he's a product of it, 'cause I believe you have some control in your destiny, and he proved that in his last 20 years of his life. He cleaned up his act.

We hear in these words a central theme for CC people—the theme of choice, of free will despite circumstances. As in the case of most moral leaders (Colby and Damon, 1992), Jim's will to pursue the right choices snowballed. He stuck with his job for the railroads for seventeen years, grew in it, and discovered ways to make changes happen. He had his pitfalls, "dabbled" with gambling, marijuana, and drinking; fought anger and negativity; put his family at risk. But through it all, he "learned to accept and count my blessings." His struggles deepened his compassion and understanding for others but never crushed him. The spiritual nature of his path is expressed as one of the participants in Bembow's (1994) study of committed people describes it—as "one of an increasing ability to empathize with people and ideas" (p. 140).

He says he continued to face other "waterloos," as he calls them, but he sums it all up in the following way: I have had a very rich, long life. I've packed a lot into it, and I'm thankful for it. I'm able to take care of my family. I'm able to help friends along the way, and I have relatively decent health. I make it to work every day. That's the good life.

Jim lives with a deep faith in the wisdom and meaning of life and an ongoing quest to align himself with life's meaning as best understood. His vision of social change comes from an understanding of the conditions of ordinary people and an appreciation of the role of social networks and interconnectedness. He exhibits unity of self and morality, which Colby and Damon (1992) describe as "little separation between moral, personal, and professional life," and no compartmentalization of concerns (p. 16). His life is a perfect example of what he believes.

Jim's history of volunteer work is so closely knit into his life that it is hard to separate the two. In fact, his life seems characterized by continuously expanding circles of empathy. In the military, he volunteered to work with dependents and help them with their homework, because he felt for their "nomadic" life and lack of opportunity to become rooted in place and friends. Then he worked with youths in the prison system. At Tufts, he helped young people from out of town, "trying to give them a sense of community." In all these different places, he set up structures to help involve youths and give them supporting frames of reference.

He gained humility from raising his own daughters and dealing with their struggles and translated that into a better understanding of how to help other young people. He raised the daughter of a friend who died from cancer. In his community, he did "a lot of volunteering around housing issues," as well as crime watch. At work, he does a lot to keep others employed and help them deal with racism. In every sphere, he is a leader, an organizer, and a visionary, a moral agent with a high standard of personal moral responsibility.

I look at life like this: If in fact you're not responsible for yourself, who the hell are you responsible for? So when people approach you in negative ways, if you play into that negative way, then in fact you become part of the same game. If you refuse to play the game, then in fact you've insulated yourself against that. And no matter what, no matter how unfair that might be, that you have to play your life that way, that's a reality of your existence. There's many times that negative racist things have tried to impact me, where

I've refused to play the game. And I've accepted the fact that I don't have the same deal that some other people have in this world. I wasn't born rich. I wasn't born famous. I'm a black man in an essentially white world. All these things I've accepted. But I've also accepted the fact that doesn't limit me, how I have to lead my life.

Jim sees the source of his moral knowing in "maintaining a spiritual base in your life, a belief in God." He recognizes his own moral contradictions and grapples with them with honesty and humility. He brings a spiritual life philosophy to his differentiated understanding of social patterns, and takes on the responsibility to break the cycle of hostility by transcending it. And for others who do not seem strong enough to do the same, he builds networks of support, seeking the cooperation of similarly minded souls both on the job and in the community. His high personal standards and lack of self-pity are tempered by humility and compassion for others struggling.

We see Jim moving toward a progressively more principled understanding of social justice, transcending the limited point of view of the grievances and interests of his racial group.

It's not just black people. We've addressed the issue of women, which has been handled, actually, a lot better than the issue of black males. We've addressed also the issue that there are other people involved, whether they be Asian people or whatever. . . . So the issue goes beyond just black people. We can't afford to fight for just black people anymore. We all have to open up the workplace. It has to be a policy, an institutional thing, and they can't hide behind all these little other sub-issues.

In struggling to evolve a fully systemic understanding, Jim grapples with historical processes, as well as with the increasing recognition of the relativity of his own point of view. Throughout this negotiation, he tries to remain open and permeable to reconstructing.

America is changing. It's changing too fast for me in some instances, and too fast perhaps for other people, but that's America. It's changing. . . . We always think that our politics is the only real politics, and I guess I'm becoming kind of like a centrist, that I'm willing to accept other points of view and hopefully shape them more to be mine. I'm willing to accept more into my life than before.

He applies his critical discernment to global politics, as well as local and national issues, and shows an astute assessment of international problems, such as Bosnia (the interview took place in 1995, when the war in Bosnia was still raging). He ponders questions of no lesser magnitude than global peace.

The policies that I perceive that are taking place—benign neglect, letting something grow until it's almost out of control. . . . It just seems to me that somebody is pushing a button for war. I mean, I know it's big business. I know everybody makes money. But it just seems like that's always the solution to get the world going again.

This quote continues the theme of the tension Jim experiences between his own creative leadership and a fluctuating, not yet fully formed sense of agency, limited by his early systemic understanding. In the face of political corruption, he chooses to maintain intelligent political involvement on the local level and focus predominantly on grassroots social activism in the neighborhood and the community. Jim has some understanding of class issues but tries not to become consumed with them, guided by a spiritual vision of transcending differences and alienation and uniting around social justice. He wages his "own personal battle against becoming cynical." To the degree that he struggles to "stay the course" (Bembow, 1994, p. 142) and not lose his sense of agency, he is reminiscent of other, more prominent moral exemplars and their unfailing positivity and faith (Colby and Damon, 1992). Here are his closing words:

I love the human race. I think that we're destined to better ourselves at some point. . . . If you read the Bible carefully and listen to what people are saying, the whole human experience can't be for what we're experiencing now. It just doesn't make sense. . . . There has to be a kind of coming together.

What accounts for Jim's ability not to become caught in the bitterness of black counter-racism and separatism (Rutstein, 1997), but to be conscious of it as an ideology equally problematic as the one it opposes? What accounts for his capacity to see with compassion and understanding both the sociohistorical predicament of blacks and the way they choose to exercise their free will, without feeling the need to absolutize one and deny the other? Why is he not caught in the cross-fire of the clashing ideologies of his world? What allows him to both understand the forces that shape his own thinking and yet in a subtle way transcend them, despite the fact that his cognitive development has not yet fully evolved to metasystematic reasoning (Commons et al., 1990)? Finally, what allows this prominent congruency in Jim between what he knows and understands, what he loves and feels compassion for, and the choices he makes in his life?

This capacity to embrace life in a fresh and responsive way, unmediated by ideology, is fueled by a deeper motivation. Herbert Marcuse (1989b) describes this critical faculty as a consciousness capable of "breaking through the material and ideological veil" (p. 281). He sees such liberation as "predicated upon the opening and the activation of a depth dimension of human existence." (Marcuse, 1989b, p. 280) This depth dimension is the innate transcendent yearning after the true, the good, and the beautiful in a Socratic (Burnett, 1916), Platonic (Plato, 1937), and Aristotelian (Aristotle, 1991; Moravcsik, 1974) sense.

If we understand the psyche as soul, the nonphysical essence of a human being (Diessner, 2002), the seat of the potentiality for knowledge, love, and goodness and of the desire to actualize this potentiality through development in life, then we can detect this yearning in the childhood of all moral leaders and critically conscious people. In them, this yearning, characteristic of all people to some degree, has been particularly nourished through the presence of ideals in their early environments, poignantly embodied in significant models of moral authority. Often, these ideals were drawn from an overtly religious orientation, present in their early environments, to the divine essence of life; but in many cases, they came from subtler spiritual attitudes of moral rectitude. Regardless, the presence of these embodied ideals seems to have strengthened the innate yearning of the soul, in contrast to it becoming overlaid by other considerations in the lives of the majority of people. In the course of life, this yearning then developed into a dominant moral motivation and an overarching spiritual depth dimension to their lives, more central than any ideological influences.

Jim, for example, grew up in a traditional black close-knit extended family and community, held together by significant figures of authentic moral authority. The central pillars around which the large extended family revolved were two remarkable African American women, Jim's mother and his grandmother on his father's side.

When Jim's parents divorced, the extended family put pressure on Jim's mother to give up the children. However, Jim's mother showed resilience and character: she "refused, and she did a fine job raising us" without relying on welfare. Her mother-in-law, Jim's grandmother, whom he describes as "a peacemaker" and "a tough woman," supported his mother, helped her, and kept the extended family together in spite of the disagreement. Jim says about his grandmother: "She was a union leader in the garment industry, and . . . she didn't mince a lot of words. If there was something to fight for, she'd be there. She would stand up, and I think that's one of the things that my mother respected."

Jim's life seems guided by the example of "these good women," and he exhibits many of the values and virtues of character that he describes in them. He was most impacted by his mother. In talking about her, a theme pervasive throughout his life story came up, the theme of personal growth shared with others. He says his mother was seventeen when she got married, and they all (he and his siblings and his mother) practically grew up together. His mother "had such an impact on" his life that he calls her "the rock of the family." Jim describes her as a woman of remarkable courage, spirit, and understanding. In spite of serious heart problems, from which she died at a young age, she was "involved in many organizations":

She was always there for a lot of people. She started at least three organizations that revolved around the issues of women, and the issues of workers, and the issues of professionalizing workers. Even today I get called from people that sometimes forget that she is not with us. And it's just amazing, the things that she accomplished in ten years . . . she reached her potential. I think that she took her innate native skills of communication, organization, and ability to be brutally honest with people without tearing them down. She had a way of looking into people, very spiritual. My mother was extremely spiritual, and she could tell people what they already knew, and she could tell them in such a way that they would be able to come in peace with that. . . . And a lot of times she'd gather groups of people together that would want to work on an issue, and she had the ability to keep that group together for long periods of time until that process was completed. She was voted Greyhound woman of the year. She got another award for a community organization as the community activist of the year. . . . She was a woman of the '90s way back in the '70s.

Jim believes that his success and that of all his siblings ("of five siblings three have Masters degrees") was due largely to "her strength and ability to show the way."

Both his mother and his grandmother were deeply spiritual women and seem to have awakened a depth dimension of experience in Jim's life. The whole conversation with Jim was suffused with self-reflection. At forty-eight, he says he feels his mortality because his mother died at forty-nine, having accomplished an impressive amount of things. He is in a continuous dialogue with himself concerning the purpose in his life.

Jim seems to have received what appears to be an ideal foundation for CC: strong family rootedness, good education, spiritual awareness, and openness to the world. His early environment was dynamic, solid, connected, and open. It fostered the formation of an inner place that progressively included not just the immediate community but the wider world. This is an important theme in the lives of many activists and moral leaders (Bembow, 1994; Daloz et al., 1996): the early exposure and receptiveness to the dynamic presence of other significant figures who synchronistically crossed his path.

I was exposed to a lot of people that are today kind of movers and shakers in the world, at a very young age, and they were young at the time, and I think we all grew together. Bishop Burgess for one, and Ed Ridnor for another. All these people today are movers and shakers, not only in the church, but also in the community. Reverend Father Avery, and Reverend, you know, Hastings. . . . All these people. And I think that along with my educational base, they gave me a thirst for wanting to learn, to try and understand not what's being said, but what's behind what's being said.

Like other activists (Bembow, 1994), he talks about being on a path of life-long growth, the role of his family values in staying on that path, and taking the responsibility to learn and to investigate reality. Jim shows respect for life and spiritual understanding of its purpose and meaning: "this thing called life is not a guarantee. So if you don't treat it like it's important, you miss the whole thing. And it's tragic: too many people miss it."

Jim's ordinary and yet extraordinary life reveals the potential for this wholesome consciousness in ordinary adult development—a basic premise of this book. The way of being of people like Jim was beautifully captured in a recent interview with poet laureate Stanley Kunitz, in which the ninety-five-year-old poet said:

Sometimes, of course, one fears the future. One fears the loss of the search for the sacred, for the beautiful, for the true. But I think that we will always have individuals who will carry on the great tradition of the prophets and the poets. I have such a fierce conviction about the value of existence that I know there must be many, many others who feel the same way and who will always be here on earth. That gives me hope (Matousek, 2001, p. 29).

Kunitz is right—people like Jim are everywhere; others recognize them, even if they often don't know what to do with them. These people are lovers of life.

They do not defend against growth; they embrace it, with all the pain that it comes with. And they become life forces to be reckoned with in their environments, perhaps not of the magnitude of Kunitz, but impactful in their own right.

When a friend of Kunitz came to him after her brother had just died of AIDS, describing her pain as something that had her in its mouth and was chewing her up, he said, "It is, and you must wait to see who you are when this thing is done with you." This is just how Jim lives his life, open to each new trial, with faith in the ultimate integrity of life, active commitment to social justice, and boundless resiliency.

THE CONSTRUCT OF CRITICAL CONSCIOUSNESS

The Brazilian educator Paolo Freire (1973), the father of the construct, believed that "one can only know to the extent that one 'problematizes' the natural, cultural and historical reality in which s/he is immersed." (p. ix) He called this capacity critical consciousness, and emphasized its difference from the technocrat's "problem-solving" stance (p. ix).

This important distinction is further developed by critical theorists. Marcuse (1989a) identifies the "neutrality" and "instrumentality" (p. 124) introduced by the new scientific method as forces of domination, causing a split in human consciousness, and taking the place of natural immediacy, wholesomeness, and personal involvement. In contrast to much contemporary science, Freire (1973) saw the process of knowing the world as related to the extent to which a human being engages in relationships with the world.

To be human is to engage in relationships with others and with the world. . . . Animals, submerged within reality, cannot relate to it; they are creatures of mere contact. But man's separateness from and openness to the world distinguishes him as a being of relationships. (p. 3)

Jim is a wonderful example of a human being engaged in relationships on every level. He stands in contrast to many non-CC people, for whom interactions with others are mostly fleeting contacts and who seem to share, in varying degrees, the implicit assumption that the world and other people's experience stand apart from their own and are not particularly knowable.

All human beings are in some "relation to reality" which "results in knowledge," regardless of "whether or not they are literate," and even if this "knowledge is mere opinion" (Freire, 1973, p. 43). Knowledge becomes critical to the degree to which causality is apprehended. This statement may seem obvious common sense in view of the emphasis Western societies place on a rational-analytical approach to life. However, it is important to remember the Buddha's observation 2,500 years ago that much of what we call rationality is, in fact, rationalizations of our desires; or, as brain research shows, the tendency of the lower limbic brain to bend cortical capacities to its needs and emotional reactions (Wade, 1996). Hence, the scientific approach does not automatically protect against rationalizations and apprehend true causality. As Kuhn (1970) has shown, it often reproduces its own world view.

Spiritual traditions have long insisted that for true causality to be apprehended, people need to cultivate the spiritual condition of detachment, emptying from self, which is a lifelong process. Moreover, knowledge, the true apprehension of causality, includes more than the rational analytic process. It also involves the understanding of the heart, referred to in Eastern spiritual traditions as the love-knowledge of the heart. To the extent to which science has separated its approach to causality from the processes of the heart, it cannot fully apprehend causality. Such separations lead to simply creating communities or enclaves of like-minded people with whom we share the same blind spots, a prominent tendency in U.S. society, as Bellah et al. (1985) showed.

In Jim, we see a knowledge continuously brought vis-à-vis his intuitive spiritual discernment and turned inward as much as outward. He takes none of his own opinions or inclinations for granted, but reflects on them continuously. His ongoing soul-searching keeps him open and developmentally alive.

Freire (1973) understood CC in broad developmental terms, as a cognitive disembedding from reality passing through three or four stages. He described early social consciousness as "semi-intransitive," characterized by a sphere of perceptions limited to biological necessities and lacking "a sense of life on a more historical plane" (p. 17). Since perceptions are "impermeable" to other than biological challenges, there is "a near disengagement between men and their existence"; "discernment is difficult," and people "fall prey to magical explanations because they cannot apprehend true causality" (p. 17). "Magic consciousness . . . simply apprehends facts and attributes to them a superior power by which it is controlled and to which it must therefore submit. Magic consciousness is characterized by fatalism" (p. 44).

This consciousness, in which the erratic attractions of the heart lead the way, relatively untempered by the reasoning faculty, is more common among poor, illiterate, and oppressed people in developing countries. Gradually, horizons expand but responses still have a magical quality, which marks the "naive transitive consciousness." Freire describes naive transitive consciousness as characterized by "an over-simplification of problems; by a nostalgia for the past; by underestimation of the common man; by a strong tendency to gregariousness; . . . by fragility of argument; by a strongly emotional style; by the practice of polemics rather than dialogue" (p. 18). "Naive consciousness sees causality as a static, established fact, and thus is deceived in its perception" (p. 44).

This kind of public consciousness, in which reasoning is still relatively separate from the heart's attractions and is used mostly to rationalize inclinations, is currently very common in former Eastern Europe, and it accounts for much of the social gridlock experienced there. A typical example is the conspiracy theory (Nicolov, 1988), popular in Bulgaria, according to which dreary historical processes are set into motion by a ruling moneyed global elite. Such thinking, though perhaps not entirely ungrounded, grossly oversimplifies world history and current realities and renders people prone to much polemic speculation and a general sense of helplessness.

The further development of consciousness depends on two conflicting tendencies: the tendency (1) to adapt to social reality and (2) to inquire into its contradictions and integrate them. To the degree that the tendency to adapt predominates, a massified, gregarious, mythical perception of social reality develops, characterized by a deeper split between reason and emotional attraction, by accepting ready myths and mass ways of thinking about the social world. Freire calls this "fanaticized consciousness." Obvious examples here are Islamic and Christian fundamentalism and nationalist movements around the world, as well as the massified consciousness cultivated by Western consumer societies.

If the second tendency predominates, there is a movement toward critical consciousness. A key concept in Freire's definition of CC is transitivity:

As men amplify their power to perceive and respond to suggestions and questions arising in their context, and increase their capacity to enter into dialogue not only with other men but with their world, they become "transitive. . . ." Transitivity of consciousness makes man "permeable." It leads him to replace his disengagement from existence with almost total engagement. (1973, p. 17)

Transitivity, or permeability, as a central characteristic of critical consciousness is, as we saw, prominent in Jim's life. The question Freire does not address is, what is the source of this transitivity, at what point does it emerge in people, and what fosters it? This is the central question that has guided this author's research on the ontogenesis of critical consciousness.

When we look at young children in relatively healthy environments, it is easy to notice how curious and responsive they are to every fluctuation. Not only are they alert and perceptive, but they also exhibit an innate empathic response, which, with optimal parenting practices of moral induction and with cognitive growth, develops into levels of empathy (Hoffman, 1983, 1989, 1991). It makes sense to view these faculties in children as the early expression of the psyche's potential spiritual capacities to know, to love, and to exercise will accordingly. This permeability in children can become amplified, or it can become overridden. When this spiritual potential, which is striving to become manifest, is amplified, it is progressively expressed in an evolving moral motivation to engage deeply with life and to discipline other inclinations in the self.

Recent research on children's spirituality (Dillon, 2000; Robinson, 1977) amply confirms the presence of this spiritual awareness and force of attraction long before it can be cognitively made sense of. In its fully developed form, permeability, as a central characteristic of CC, points to an ultimate way of being which thinkers from explicitly spiritual frames of reference have called "interbeing" (Daloz et al., 1996; Thich Nhat Hanh, 1991).

Another important component of Freire's definition of CC is the capacity to disembed from the lock of the present moment, to gain perspective on one's situation and its historical context, and to take responsibility for one's choices and actions. This broadly developmental understanding suggests a structural cognitive evolution toward disembedding from social context and engaging in a critical moral dialogue with one's personal and social reality. An important question here is, what are the cognitive dimensions of such a development, and their developmental threshold?

Four central structural dimensions of consciousness need to develop (a) the ability for logical and causal reasoning; (b) the social-cognitive ability to know oneself in social situations; (c) the evolving sense of self and other; and (d) the evolving ways of knowing. Mature CC involves the capacity for systematic reasoning (Commons et al., 1990), or the capacity to link individual phenomena and patterns systemically, to see them critically as part of a system. It also requires pattern self-knowledge (Weinstein and Alschuler, 1985), an ability to identify patterns in one's relationships with the social world, to reflect critically on one's stable internal responses to classes of situations, and to recognize the choices one makes, rather than experience oneself as a recipient of circumstances. Mature CC also involves a postinstitutional, at least 4/5 ego-system (Cook-Greuter, 1990; Kegan, 1982, 1994; Lahey et al., 1988; Walker, 1995), able to open itself to an interdependent inter-individual process. Finally, it involves contextual relativism and commitment in relativity (Kitchener and King, 1990; Perry, 1968), or an understanding that while we cannot know absolute truth and our constructions are always context-specific, certain constructions are still more worth getting behind than others. Another way to refer to that epistemology is what Belenky et al. (1986) call constructivist knowing.

These are four different aspects of the capacity for critical reflection. As Brookfield (1998) points out, the development of critical reflection has been conceptualized by moral psychology in a variety of ways: dialectical thinking (Basseches, 1984, 1986; Irwin, 1991), epistemic cognition (Lohman and Scheurman, 1992), double loop learning (Argyris and Schon, 1978), cultural literacy (Bowers, 1974, 1984), critical literacy (Kretovics, 1985; Lankshear and Maclaren, 1993), conjunctive faith (Fowler, 1981), embedded logic (Labouvie-Vief, 1980), informed commitment (Perry, 1970), constructivist thinking (Belenky et al., 1986), practical intelligence (Sternberg and Wagner, 1986; Wagner, 1994), everyday cognition (Rogoff and Lave, 1984), relativistic operations (Lee, 1994), and postformal thinking (Cavanaugh, 1991), transformative learning (Daloz et al., 1996; Mezirow, 1991; Cranton, 1994), learning to learn (Smith, 1990; Tuijnman and Van Der Kamp, 1992), educative learning (Stanage, 1987), emancipatory learning (Shor and Freire, 1987; Hart, 1985), experiential learning (Cell, 1984: Boud et al., 1993), and reflective learning (Boyd and Fales, 1983; Boud et al., 1985).

Embedded in all these concepts is an interpretation of the process by which adults become critically reflective regarding the moral assumptions, beliefs and values which they have assimilated during childhood and adolescence . . . assessing the accuracy and validity of these moral norms for the context of adult life. (Brookfield, 1998, p. 291)

With this cognitive development, people become what Freire (1973) describes as subjects.

Men relate to their world in a critical way. . . . And in the act of critical perception, men discover their own temporality. . . . As men emerge from time, discover temporality and free themselves from "today," their relationships with the world become impregnated with consequence. . . . As men create, re-create, and decide, historical epochs begin to take shape. . . . Whether or not men can perceive the epochal themes and above all, how they act upon the reality within which these themes are generated will largely determine their humanization or dehumanization, their affirmation as Subjects or their reduction as objects. . . . If men are unable to perceive critically the themes of their time, and thus to intervene actively in reality, they are carried along in the wake of change. (pp. 3–7)

This powerful understanding is even more poignant in the wake of September 11, 2001, as millions of people are facing the overwhelming question of what it means to act responsibly in the face of such violation of humanity.

Freire's praxis of liberatory education relies on engaging people who have capitulated to reality into a dialogue about reality. While the idea of dialogue has many similarities with ethical reflection as developed by Kohlbergian moral education (Higgins, 1995), it has an important distinction: its clear articulation of the dimension of historical agency, which is generally absent from moral psychology. Most developmental psychology associates such historical understanding primarily with advanced development. Yet, critical theorists see the general absence of historical understanding as a function of what they call the postliberal society (Bronner and Kellner, 1989). Marcuse (1989a) points to the ahistorical quality of industrial society, the "atrophy of historical transcendence" (p. 119), and its embeddedness in the here-and-now of economic efficiency and profit. This limited and selective understanding of, or interest in, world history is particularly prominent in U.S. society.

In summary, several components stand out in Freire's formulation of CC, which clearly reaches far beyond the specific context of the closed Brazilian society in which the concept was born and is directly applicable to various social, cultural, and educational environments. First, it involves the ability and inclination to pose questions, which in much contemporary Western education is known as critical thinking. Second, it involves a critical analysis of causality in our relationships with specific aspects of reality, as different from opinion. Third, it is characterized by transitivity, that is, the power to perceive and respond to critical needs through engagement with others and with reality. Fourth, it involves the responsibility of the human subject to grasp the historical themes of the time, disembed from the present, and discover temporality. Fifth, it involves conscious, responsible, and creative relationships with reality in reconstructing it and joining the historical process. Sixth, it is a way of knowing which Freire considers the only true way of knowing.

While the best examples of education in critical thinking contain the first two dimensions (weaker examples seem to draw on mere opinions), moral psychology works in varying degrees with five out of the six components. The component of historical understanding is seriously underestimated, and with the exception of the postmodern discourse, generally absent from the conversation. Despite the contributions of postmodernists in introducing an awareness of the historical nature of the way we construct our contexts and they construct us, the overall relativism of the postmodern view leaves it utterly lacking in any understanding of historical agency comparable to Freire's and that of the critical theorists. Altogether, an integrated approach to empowered human consciousness is yet to emerge. This reality is amply illustrated by the way our public culture tends to confuse polemics with the practice of genuine dialogue, and emphasize the first at the expense of the second. Table 2.1 summarizes the important contrasts that Freire draws between CC and alternative, less developed forms of social consciousness.

Table 2.1
Freire's Contrasts between CC and Less Developed Forms of Social Consciousness

CC	Alternative, Less Developed Forms of Social Consciousness
Knowing to the extent that one "problematizes" the natural, cultural and historical reality in which she or he is immersed	Technocrat's "problem-solving" stance
Consciousness: intentionality towards the world; that is, separateness from and openness to the world, engages in relationships	Creatures of mere contact
Relation to reality results in knowledge: critical understanding to the degree to which causality is apprehended	Opinion, magical, or naive understanding: apprehends facts and attributes to them a superior power, or sees causality as static
Sense of life on a more historical plane; discovery of temporality; relationships with the world impregnated with consequence; total creative engagement with reality	Perceptions impermeable to other than biological challenges; disengagement between people and their existence; discernment difficult; narrow horizons (semi-intransitive consciousness)
Tendency to inquire into contradictions in social reality and integrate them; Transitivity (permeability): power to perceive and respond to suggestions and questions arising in their context; enter into dialogue	Tendency to adapt to social reality, accept ready myths and mass ways of thinking; over-simplifications of problems, gregariousness, fragility of argument, polemics, impermeability (naive consciousness and fanaticized consciousness)
Human subjects	Reduction to objects

Critical theorists have enriched Freire's multidimensional description of critical consciousness with a profound multidisciplinary analysis of the contextual forces that trap modern consciousness, stunt its capacity for historical under-standing, and prevent it from developing toward its critical potential (Bronner and Kellner, 1989).

Marcuse (1989b, 1989c) shows how economic conditions in an advanced in-dustrial society are responsible for the social frameworks in which reality is or-ganized. Ironically, it was Karl Marx who professed the primacy of economic means in his philosophy of dialectical materialism. Even though the West devel-oped in opposition to many of his premises, which were adopted by communist societies, the West shared with communism the basic worldview of economic materialism. As Marcuse points out, the dialectics of profit integrate and absorb all forces of opposition, producing a "one-dimensional society" and a "one-dimensional man" (Bronner and Kellner, 1989 p. 9). This classic analysis is an-other way of referring to an alienated, self-absorbed, consumer society.[1]

Marcuse (1989c) argues that the direct socialization of individuals into cur-rently pervasive cultural institutions such as mass media, schools, sports, and peer groups, unmediated by the ego-building tensions of a strong family unit, tends to eliminate the conflict between individual and society, producing mas-sive social conformity and weak egos.[2] Here is how Marcuse (1989c) describes the impact of conditions in postliberal societies on the lives of individuals:

transition from free to organized competition, concentration of power in the hands of an omnipresent technical, cultural, and political administration, self-propelling mass produc-tion and consumption, subjection of previously private, asocial dimensions of existence to methodical indoctrination, manipulation, control . . . reduce the "living space" and the autonomy of the ego and prepare the ground for the formation of masses. (p. 235)

He further describes the formation of consciousness under these circum-stances:

weakening of the critical mental faculties: consciousness and conscience. . . . Conscience and personal responsibility decline "objectively" under conditions of total bureaucratiza-tion. . . . The more the autonomous ego becomes superfluous . . . in the functioning of the administered, technified world, the more does the development of the ego depend on its "power of negation," that is to say, on its ability to build and protect a personal, private realm with its own individual needs and faculties. (p. 238)

This "power of negation," or the critical faculty of the consciousness, is easy to misunderstand. Both liberal activists and conservative isolationists often un-derstand it as a negative, polemical, and oppositional stance to contemporary global processes, an effort to return to a less centralized past and a less global-ized culture. This author understands this critical faculty differently, as a con-sciousness capable of "breaking through the material and ideological veil of the affluent society" (Marcuse, 1989b, p. 281), where affluent society is seen as "growing on the condition of accelerating waste, planned obsolescence, and destruction, while the substratum of the population continues to live in poverty and misery" (p. 280).

Liberation, Marcuse writes, "is *predicated upon the opening and the activation of a depth dimension of human existence*" [emphasis added] (1989b, p. 281). This depth dimension is the internal spiritual awakening already detectable across the globe; the same amplified spiritual potentiality that we saw manifest in Jim's critical consciousness. Coupled with knowledge, such a personal development allows one to move into the future without fear and to support the progressive aspects of globalization while becoming an agent in transforming its more negative, exploitative aspects. The critical faculty, understood as an awakened spiritual dimension of life, fosters both a realization of the interdependence of the global human family and the power to contemplate and participate by choice in large-scale historical processes.

Marcuse (1989a) points out how the Western scientific method, narrowly understood, has illegitimized the spiritual dimension of life and has "destroyed the idea that the universe was ordered in relation to a goal, to a teleological structure" (p. 120), substituting for it the almost "metaphysical" universal applicability of technology in the place of ontology. This captures the deeply paralyzing contexts we are all negotiating and from which we need to emancipate ourselves.

In the past, illiteracy and ignorance prevented the majority of people from cultivating the love of truth and justice. This is still the case in large parts of the developing world. However, in the Western world, it is not the lack of education but the lost force of moral and critical ends, the debunking of the very idea of truth, and the prevailing anomie that stunt people's ability to love and pursue truth with passion.

Such an understanding has allowed critical theorists to draw a generative distinction between direct versus mediated socialization, and to describe the formation of contradictory personality tendencies as a result of mass culture. Some of these common contradictory tendencies are pride in being an individualist and constant fear of not being like the others and jealous guarding of one's independence coupled with an inclination to submit blindly to power and authority (Adorno, 1989; Fromm, 1989). These phenomena continue to be pertinent in the contemporary Westernized context, which includes Eastern European societies. Table 2.2 summarizes the important contrasts that critical theorists elaborated between CC and mass consciousness in relation to context.

In summary, as a result of the massification of society (Fromm, 1989), modern individual consciousness faces some significant tensions:

1. Fear of the challenges of a wider and more complex world versus a sense of empowerment and courageous acceptance of those challenges;
2. A sense of being lost versus a sense of freedom and fulfillment;
3. Frantic one-sided reactions to a confusing world, with one aspect of the self living at the expense of another, that is, compartmentalization versus inner wholeness and union of emotional, sensory, and rational faculties and aspects of life;
4. Lack of inner models and organizers of experience versus their strengthening presence (e.g., unselfish love, creativity, explicit moral and spiritual frames of reference); and

5. Alienation and limited loyalties versus openness to the world and recognition of the continuity among a human being, their world, and nature. (Maslow, 1959b, pp. 86–92)

The second side of these tensions constitutes the benchmark characteristics of the presence of CC, as we saw illustrated in Jim's life.

Table 2.2
Critical Theorists' Contrasts between CC and Mass Consciousness in Relation to Context

Context Conditions	Mass Consciousness	CC
Market economy reliance on fear and competition	Atomized and alienated	Integrated and interconnected
Technology and scientific rationality	Thought serves to make prevailing system more efficient and raise technical means over normative ends; moral and critical ends lose their force; centrality of technological questions	Thought functions to provide alternatives to existing society; moral and critical ends central; centrality of ontological questions
Industrial society embedded in here-and-now of economic efficiency and profit	Ahistoricity; neutrality; instrumentality; split between private and public	Natural immediacy; wholesomeness; personal involvement, coupled with a sense of history
Advanced economic conditions absorb forces of opposition	Consumer consciousness; alienated; self-absorbed	Service to others and the world; transcendence of economic conditions
Direct socialization into pervasive cultural institutions (mass media, sport, peer groups); weak family unit; bureaucratization	Massive social conformity; weakened critical mental faculties; decline of conscience and personal responsibility	Power of resistance built in strong family units; knowledge and moral judgment capable of breaking through veil of duplicated reality
Mass culture duplicating reality; material and ideological veil of affluent society	Contradictory personality tendencies: pride in being an individualist and fear of not being like the others	Opening and activation of a depth dimension of human existence; personality integration

CC people are remarkably open to growth in their quest for truth and meaning in life. Yet, as literature, philosophy, psychology, and religion have forever known, such an orientation is not very common among people.

Growth involves movement into the unknown and often requires surrendering familiar ways of being. Consequently, we tend to fear growth. The tragic result is that . . . we actually deny and defend against our greatness and potential. These meta-defenses, as we might call them, have been described in many ways. The humanistic psychiatrist Erich Fromm viewed them as mechanisms of escape, while Maslow called their net effect "the Jonah complex," after the biblical prophet Jonah, who tried to escape his divine mission. The existential philosopher Kirkegaard described how we seek "tranquilization by the trivial," while others speak of "the repression of the sublime". . . . Defenses against transpersonal development also operate in society. Cultures . . . mirror and magnify our individual ambivalence toward transcendence. (Walsh and Vaughan, 1993, p. 110)

As Maslow (1999) points out, the desire for transcendence is an essential part of human nature, and failure to recognize and fulfill it results in psychological distress. Hence, what we consider normal human development seems to exhibit a measure of psychopathology to the extent that it thwarts the desire for transcendence and cultivates a wide range of compensatory tendencies. In that sense, critically conscious people, in whose lives this desire remains defining and does not become overlaid by defenses or overwhelmed by circumstances, as it appears to be in the majority of people, are remarkably healthy people. Hence, CC people exhibit optimal human consciousness, and have a great deal to teach us about optimal development.

A growing number of researchers have recently begun to appreciate the wealth of new and more positive psychological understanding that can be drawn from the study of these lives. In addition, the historical process of globalization that we are facing has spurred a renewed interest in how moral leaders across cultures embrace our fast-changing world, and define and sustain lifelong commitments to humanity under conditions of swiftly growing ambiguity (Shapiro and Shapiro, 1992). It is impossible to encompass the full range of such studies; however, the outstanding commonality among these people from different cultures, historical periods, and ages is the centrality of moral motivation.

People who exhibit some level of CC consistently relate memories, even from early childhood, of being different, of hungrily seeking to become better people, to transcend their personal limitations and those of their environments, to bring about more justice, more kindness, to find deeper truth and meaning in life (Bembow, 1994; Colby and Damon, 1992; Daloz et al., 1996). These people actively negotiate their social relations from the point of view of preeminently moral frames of reference, and they resist both the forces of collusion with unjust or morally questionable status quos and the social effect on development described as "coercion to the biosocial mean" (Walsh and Vaughan, 1993, p. 110). The next section describes the nature of moral motivation.

MORAL MOTIVATION AT THE HEART OF CC

The understanding of moral motivation in this book both builds on Kohlberg's (1984) view of morality as the developing ability to "accurately take the perspective of others, their needs and rights, and to see one's own claims and obligations with similar balance, detachment and accuracy" (Fowler, 1980, p. 131), and goes beyond that. It shares Kohlberg's commitment to "a Platonic understanding of justice as the central and unitary moral virtue" (Fowler, 1980, p. 130) yet departs from his purely formalistic approach.

Moral development is more than the cognitive achievement of mature rationality, in which the individual is motivated by cognitive dissonance, and the pursuit of "an ideal equilibrium . . . born of the actions and reactions of individuals upon each other" (Piaget, [1932] 1965, p. 318). As Taylor (1982) points out, the moral is a much broader and more complex category than its "epistemologically-motivated reduction and homogenization" by utilitarian ethics to maximizing happiness (p. 132). It needs to include "the qualitative languages of admiration and contempt—integrity, healing, liberation, conviction, dishonesty, and self-indulgence" (Christians, 2000, p. 138). In fact, the vignettes in the coming chapters will show the complexity of morality and the impossibility to reduce it to only values, or character, or moral reasoning, or even commitment. This author's approach to moral motivation integrates disparate views on morality into an understanding of basic human yearnings.

As Kohlberg himself recognized, "to ultimately live up to moral principles requires faith" (Kohlberg, 1974, p. 14). Fowler (1980) points out that the question "Why be moral?" cannot be answered adequately within the terms of any of Kohlberg's stages without reference to a person's commitments to a wider frame of meaning and value (p. 139).

Fowler (1980) answers the question of moral motivation in terms of "a self's valued membership in groups or communities joined by commitments to meaning frames centering in shared values and images of power" (p. 141). The research conducted for this book confirms Fowler's findings that "because of ties of dependence and affection, and because of the pre-operational child's imitative interest in adult behaviors and values, there is already forming by stage 1 . . . a rudimentary loyalty to the *child's construction* of her or his family's 'ethos of goodness' " (Fowler, 1980, p. 140).

However, this author's approach to moral motivation is distinct from most of the work reviewed above in how it locates the source of moral motivation. Most current work on moral development is still based on the neo-Piagetian claim that "morality, as we know it, is initially 'external', at least with respect to the individual's natural impulses." (Blasi, 1995, p. 230) While it has been very helpful in understanding the development of reasoning and the construction of personal beliefs, the formation of personal continuities and the developmental transformation of goals in the direction of progressive unity of self and morality, it has failed to recognize the human spiritual impulse. This failure to recognize the human spiritual impulse, along with other, better recognized biological impulses fundamental to human nature (Wilson, 1975), stems from a materialistic ontology, teleology, and cosmology (Diessner, 2002).

This author adopts a spiritual perspective on moral motivation, where spiritual is understood in terms of Diessner's (2002) definition as:

1. Different than matter, where "matter and spirit are interactive, dialectical poles of a unified cosmos." (p. 11)
2. "Spirit is fundamental to matter; matter is an emanation or appearance of spirit. . . . Spirit is generative or creative." (p. 11)
3. "Spirit is abstract and transcends time and place." (p. 11)
4. "Spirit is an emanation from God, and God is all Goodness" (p. 11), understood in both Eastern and Western terms as harmony, balance, alignment (Chopra, 1993). Therefore, "spiritual becomes a normative or prescriptive modifier." (Diessner, 2002, p. 11)

A spiritual perspective on the primary source of moral motivation allows us to account for the fact that moral leaders consistently recollect a sense of core moral values or instincts having been with them from a very early age (Bembow, 1994). In many cases, this moral impulse led them to decisions which put them in conflict even with their early family environments, with which they otherwise largely identified. While these children appear to have been affiliated to their families' "ethos of goodness," as Fowler claims, they also show a consistent tendency to be primarily attracted to figures of authentic moral authority within those families, as well as to intuitively transcend that ethos in defining moments, at an age at which it is not reasonable to assume postconventional principled reasoning (see Bembow, 1994; Gandhi, 1927).

What allows a young child to discern and be attracted to particularly authentic embodiments of goodness, truth, and beauty in the midst of generally benevolent environments, and to carry those imprints in their hearts with an earnestness that spurs them to continuously redefine goodness, truth, and beauty beyond any affiliative standards?

It seems reasonable to assume that children carry an inherent spiritual potential for goodness, truth, and beauty, along with other inclinations, and that this potential is amplified and manifested in environments that themselves recognize and attempt to foster that potential. This potential is the "generative . . . motivational source" Bembow (1994) identified in her study of activists (p. 164), which interacts with various environments and progressively manifests itself in moral motivation, a defining attraction to living and acting in accordance with what one perceives as right.

Hence, we can define moral motivation as a progressively clearer developmental expression of inherent spiritual potential along four dimensions of developmental constructions: (1) identity; (2) relationships with external moral authority, and the emerging sense of internal moral authority, responsibility, and agency; (3) empathic concerns with others, with justice and caring; and (4) concerns with the meaning of life. These four dimensions of motivational development may or may not be predominantly morally colored, which appears to have much to do with formative environments. In that sense, each dimension represents a continuum between predominantly or exclusively moral and predominantly or exclusively expedient concerns. When morally colored, these dimensions can be statically described as follows:

1. Moral identity, anchored in universal moral values, and moral character predominate over and mediate the sense of identity derived from various social configurations such as class, race, gender, ethnic, or other group membership. Identity rooted in moral models and concepts, however simply understood, is the source of a moral imperative, that is, an inner need to do the morally right thing, which is stronger than self-interest, and strengthens and expands in the course of life.
2. External moral authority in significant others is first intuitively and then increasingly rationally scrutinized, as the individual constructs her understanding of authentic moral authority. With the growing critical discernment of and receptiveness to authentic moral authority, it is progressively internalized as personal moral responsibility. This process is accompanied by the emerging sense of internal moral authority and the tendency to reconstruct continuously internalized personal moral responsibility. A sense of moral agency develops, which prevails over the tendency to experience oneself as the victim of circumstances.
3. A central concern with relationships, where the person experiences herself in relationships, rather than just in contact with others. The person is empathically concerned with others, with good and bad, with being loyal and not hurting, and gradually expands that concern beyond interpersonal relationships, into larger social concerns with justice and equity.
4. A tendency to ask and value questions regarding the meaning of life. The lifelong search for authentic meaning is amplified by explicitly or implicitly spiritual environments, characterized by faith in the wisdom of life and acceptance of the responsibility it imposes. The search for truth provides a larger frame of reference from which to reflect on self and experience and spurs intense self-reflection and critical examination of reality, expanding toward principled, philosophical, historical, and global vision.

Table 2.3 presents the motivational template of the four dimensions of continuum between moral and expediency motivation. Moral motivation, understood this way, involves what Bishop Desmond Tutu refers to as "the opportunity to fulfill" one's "human and spiritual potential" (Colby and Damon, 1992, p. xii).

In summary, research (Mustakova-Possardt, 1996) has shown that behind the converging developmental paths and processes, characters, behaviors, and life choices of both moral leaders and ordinary people is a common phenomenon of critical consciousness, expressed in a lifelong synergistic interaction between evolving moral motivation and cognitive-structural development. This synergistic interaction at every developmental level accounts for the wholesome relationship among what critically conscious people know, what they are attracted to, and the choices that they make.

Knowing and being, mind and heart, center round a caring, increasingly interconnected, justice-and-equity-oriented view of life. With the structural developmental movement toward greater differentiation and complexity, people engage increasingly in a critical dialogue with themselves and their sociocultural world, have empathy toward fellow human beings in the larger social world, and integrate their social experience. This constitutes a developmental movement toward greater openness to and engagement with the world.

Table 2.3
Template of the Dimensions of Continuum between Moral and Expediency Motivation

Dimensions	Expediency Motivation	Moral Motivation
1. Identity	Identity predominantly rooted in social conventions (social identity) and lack of moral imperative	Identity predominantly rooted in moral values (moral identity) and moral imperative
2. Authority, responsibility, and agency	Limited personal authority and responsibility; lack of agency (fear, helplessness, skepticism in the face of external authority)	Personal moral authority and critical discernment of external authority; expanding sense of moral responsibility; moral agency
3.Relationships	Lack of empathy, alienation, impermeability, lack of concerns with justice and not hurting	Empathy, relatedness, permeability, concerns with justice and not hurting
4. Meaning of life	Self-referential frames of reference and limited goals	Larger frames of reference as vantage point for critical discernment and self-reflection; life purpose greater than self

NOTES

1. A brief anecdote may not be out of place here. When this author first came to the United States, she was shocked to discover that people publicly referred to themselves as consumers, for example in the mass media. She took that to indicate a remarkably self-critical spirit, since in her less developed and much more idealistic native Bulgaria, to describe somebody as a consumer was a singularly negative way to point to their lack of higher defining characteristics. She was even more shocked to discover later that consumer in the United States was not only not a pejorative term, but one people prided themselves in and with which they had named their whole society.

2. One of the most favored methods of obscuring social conflict that communists used was to artificially develop a culture, paid and supported by their establishment, in the arts, including literature, and in sports. They particularly emphasized sports, especially

soccer, and mandatory youth organizations, and deeply feared churches. The reader can contrast that with the favorite pastimes in the United States — football and shopping.

Chapter 3

Two Ordinary Lives:
The Tenuous Boundary between Mature CC
and Its Suboptimal Counterpart

The time is at hand when whatsoever lieth hid in the souls and hearts of men
will be disclosed. . . . Verily, God will bring everything to light, though it were
but the weight of a grain of mustard-seed.

Baha'u'llah, 1941/1988, p.107

Man should discover his own reality and not thwart himself. For he has the self
as his only friend or as his only enemy. A person has the self as his friend when
he has conquered himself. But if he rejects his own reality, the self will war
against him.

Bhagavad Gita 6.5–6, in Wilson, 1995

Critical consciousness is a precarious balance between mind and heart, where
each serves as a corrective to the other, as a result of which the faculties of love,
knowledge, and will function in relative unity. The heart has a deep capacity to
discern, be attracted to, and be moved by beauty, truth, and goodness. But that
capacity is feeble until strengthened by the relentless critical examination of an
ever stronger rational mind. The mind, on the other hand, can easily become
locked in circular self-referential reasoning without the corrective of a heart
aware of, attracted to, and moved by its spiritual source.

This precarious human condition has been poignantly epitomized in the
history of each new religious revelation, fraught with a painful mix of heroism
and betrayal:

One must understand the old story of Cain and Abel, the story of family jealousies which,
like a somber thread in the fabric of history, runs through all its epochs and can be traced

in all its events. . . . The weakness of the human heart, which so often attaches itself to an unworthy object, the weakness of the human mind, prone to conceit and self-assurance in personal opinions, involves people in a welter of emotions that blind their judgment and lead them far astray. (Rabbani, 1969, pp. 121–23)

Ever since the Enlightenment, the solution humanity sought to centuries of such betrayals has been to separate the attachments of the heart from all pursuits after truth and train the mind to be more rigorous. Freed from the superstitions of the past, we now have to reclaim the heart's deeper knowing and capacity for love and will, because, as chapter one described, we face a collective gridlock as a result of this unsustainable split. The mind, in isolation from the greater spiritual yearnings of the heart, has proven not much more reliable a tool than the heart divorced from the scrutiny of a disciplined mind.

In this and the next chapter, we will study more in depth the possibility for a dynamic balance between a strengthening heart and a strengthening mind. We will focus on vignettes of ordinary people from two cultures and sociohistoric contexts, in most of whom this dynamic balance is being currently negotiated. In other words, these are not people in whom CC has been firmly established and who exhibit the unity of self and morality that Colby and Damon (1992) found in their moral exemplars. Rather, these are people who gravitate toward the center of the CC/non-CC continuum and are relatively close to each other on each side of that spectrum.

In this way, we can appreciate more fully the tenuous boundary between a CC and a non-CC way of being and the infinite possibility for every human being in each next moment. The moral motivational dimensions along which we will contrast pairs in comparable developmental places will serve not to categorize people but to bring into focus the human potential. We will see how the inherent human spiritual impulse (Helminiak, 1996), when amplified into an activated depth dimension of existence, progressively manifests itself in people's lives as a growing moral motivation, which gives rise to many variations of optimal consciousness. At what level this consciousness will manifest itself has much to do with the individual's stage of social-cognitive development.

We can differentiate three levels of CC. Pre–critical consciousness (pre-CC) ideally begins in early childhood and reaches into young adulthood, when the structural conditions for CC can be achieved. Those conditions are at least early formal operational ability for a consistent analysis of causality (see Commons and Rodriguez, 1990), conventional social system and conscience orientation toward duty and responsibility to a larger human group than one's immediate circle (Kohlberg, 1984), early pattern self-knowledge and its accompanying ability for some self-reflection (see Weinstein and Alschuler, 1985), and an institutional internal organization of the self, able to differentiate personal goals and to articulate a coherent philosophy (Kegan, 1982; Lahey et al., 1988). At that point the adult individual manifests transitional CC, which still exhibits a significant tension between mind and heart, a limited capacity for critical reflection, and internal contradictions. With the advent of systematic reasoning (see Commons and Rodriguez, 1990) and the movement beyond the institutional self (Kegan, 1982; Lahey et al., 1988), the individual opens up to a more thorough and consistent examination of both self and world from principled moral reasoning (Kohlberg, 1984) and an understanding of the constructed nature of knowledge and social reality (Foucault, 1980). That is mature CC.

However, the social-cognitive development necessary for the formation of transitional CC in adulthood may not occur fully in childhood. If the structural-developmental conditions do not fully occur but the moral motivation develops, the individual is likely to continue to operate with pre-CC into biological adulthood. We will see an example of that in the next chapter. If predominantly moral motivation does not develop along all four dimensions, the individual will embark on a non-CC pathway of adult development. In that case, there is always the possibility later in life for circumstances to jolt the individual into a morally oriented reworking of those motivational dimensions that had remained predominantly expedient. This can result in a relative integration across motivational dimensions and a fuller activation of the depth dimension of existence as the individual embarks on a CC pathway.

In this chapter, we will examine the life stories of two Bulgarians, Danton and Ramina, who illustrate respectively the qualitative differences between mature CC and its suboptimal developmental counterpart. In the next chapter, we will examine the differences between pre-CC and transitional CC, and their suboptimal developmental counterparts.

Danton and Ramina form an interesting pair. Cognitively, they are peers. Both exhibit a metasystematic (see Commons and Rodriguez, 1990) capacity to compare, contrast, and synthesize individual perspectives and think across systems. Both are in transition out of their institutional (Kegan, 1982) self-systems, which in both of them are colored by existential individualism. However, there is a small but significant difference in how each of them negotiates the precarious balance between the love of truth and justice and the perennial human tendency toward self-focus and self-aggrandizement. While Danton's overall motivation is predominantly moral, Ramina's is predominantly expedient. This motivational difference seems to amplify their slight developmental differences and accounts for a much more uneven developmental profile in Ramina.

Ramina is not as consistent in her metasystematic reasoning, because her thinking does not benefit from the consistent corrective of feedback loops, but tends to be more of a closed system. While both Danton and Ramina tend to live in the busy world of their own thought, in Danton this tendency is somewhat counterbalanced by his empathic inclination to be summoned by another and to access his deeper understanding and wisdom as he responds. Ramina is much less able to be summoned by the world outside her thoughts. Danton's and Ramina's self-systems exhibit a small but significant difference. In Ramina, a relatively closed and defended institutional internal organization prevails, although there are persistent glimpses beyond that (4(5) along Lahey et al., 1988). Danton operates out of a transitional space between two full self-systems, the institutional and the interindividual, with a predominance of the second (5/4 along Lahey et al., 1988).

Overall, Danton and Ramina occupy developmentally comparable and relatively close places on both sides of the motivational dividing line between CC and non-CC (see Figure 5.1).

While both Danton and Ramina are cognitively more advanced than Jim, there is a poignant difference between Ramina, on the one hand, and Jim and Danton, on the other. Jim's and Danton's self-systems are both predominantly interindividual (Kegan, 1982), open ended and oriented toward a process of growing interdependence with others. Though in different ways, their lives are grounded in a greater moral purpose and meaning, and therefore fulfilled. Ramina, however, struggles within the prison of self, unable to really trust humanity and embrace life beyond cautious and defensive contact.

Danton and Ramina share common cultural, philosophical, and social backgrounds. They are both intellectuals in the East European sense, widely read, existentially inclined, continuously reflecting on the meaning of life. They both identify their roots in strong patriarchal families, with prominent morally colored authority figures from whom they clearly derived ego strength. Their sense of identity is grounded in basic moral values, and they both perceive themselves as people who stand in opposition to prescribed social identities and dominant configurations.

At first glance, Danton and Ramina appear to share a predominantly moral orientation along three out of four motivational dimensions—(1) identity, (2) authority, responsibility, and agency, and (4) meaning of life. On closer examination, however, it becomes clear that Ramina's lack of a clear orientation toward empathy, relatedness, and permeability and her relative alienation from her world have held back the fully moral development along dimensions (2) and (4). Although acutely discerning of authentic moral authority, she is unable to live consistently by her internal sense of moral responsibility and experiences a paralysis of moral agency. Although deeply drawn to reflections on the meaning of life, she is unable to articulate a larger frame of reference than the self, and she remains trapped in a self-referential world and limited goals. Her motivational profile offers a clear example of how the four motivational dimensions are interrelated, and if one is particularly rudimentary, the others cannot develop fully. Therefore, in Ramina we see a poignant conflict between what she is attracted to and the choices by which she lives; between her mind's reasoning and the love-knowledge of her heart.

Danton's life story reveals that he shared Ramina's motivational condition well into adulthood. However, his professional orientation toward psychology eventually allowed him to fully elaborate his orientation toward empathy and concerns with justice (dimension 3) and to begin to integrate his motivational dimensions, leading to a moral shift into critical consciousness. Psychology, for Danton, became a spiritual experience.

This fact illustrates the contextual and highly relative nature of all identifiable causes. No particular realm of human activity can be viewed in and of itself as a guaranteed stimulation of the depth dimension of experience—neither psychology, nor religion, nor education. Within each, we have abundant examples of a self-serving orientation and resulting distortions. What ultimately makes a difference is the configuration of personal motivational choices, or what spiritual traditions call the exercise of our free will.

On both sides of the motivational continuum, there are decent, good people. But those on the predominantly expedient end are much more conflicted between mind and heart, less resilient, and with limited powers. As Baha'i scriptures say, "As ye have faith so shall your powers and blessings be. This is the balance—this is the balance—this is the balance" (Abdu'l-Baha, [1917] 1969, p. 40).

Let us now examine where Danton has chosen to put his faith and where Ramina has been unable to put hers. In the process, we will differentiate a host of motivational subthemes, each of which represents a continuum between moral and expediency motivation and with which a more detailed understanding of motivation will emerge.

DANTON: AN EXISTENTIAL HUMANIST

Danton is an average height, out-of-shape, slow and somewhat disheveled-looking man in his forties, with intelligent and alert eyes and a sensuous smile coming out of a puffy face. He is regarded as an outstanding psychotherapist within the Bulgarian context where the profession is relatively new; he is well read and uses three foreign languages. As he sits in his bare office with two armchairs, a small table and a bed, and many books around, he impresses one as a typical East European intellectual, narcissistic, reflective, and introverted. Yet, he turns out to be both that and its opposite, a deeply empathic and permeable man; an existential humanist.

In 1995, Danton was already a creative innovator in many areas of public life, working in teams with others, caring and practicing active love and service with dedication. He had done some radical work as a psychotherapist in a society that had, and still has, no appreciation for the liberating power of psychological understanding. He had participated in massive acts of civil opposition during the transition from communism to democracy. As a psychiatrist during the years of communism, he had established the first organized group therapy for alcoholics in the country, completely against the medicating and mind-numbing approach of the psychiatric communist establishment. Out of his years of efforts, the first Alcoholics Anonymous in Bulgaria eventually developed. He lives with an awakened sense of history, and despite his modest life, views himself as a citizen of the world.

Danton's way of being is rooted in extended family, place, and ethnic identity, all of which have been for him sources of moral authority. His story begins with the memory of the extended family and clan and a big house in which they all lived or gathered until one of his grandfathers and great uncles with their families left for Israel.

This clan took great pride in having lived in Sofia (the capital) for generations, ever since the fifteenth century. They remember how the city grew and developed, and they share a sense of permanence, loyalty, and pride. They are Jews, and it seems fundamental to their sense of identity to be observing of the laws, respectful, loyal, and reliable contributing citizens, so that in their own thinking, as Danton reveals it, they can earn the right to live in a particular country and be accepted. So it was very important to be well educated, well mannered, and honest and to excel both in the professions and in the arts.

This solid patriarchal cultural tradition with its interconnectedness and strong moral values seems to provide the very backbone of Danton's way of being. It is also the source of many contradictions and not immediately obvious forms of prejudice. There is a clear class identification and a certain distrust for the newcomers into the city, especially for the influx of people from the countryside during the years of communism. Altogether, Danton seemed to have fit well into the patriarchal Bulgarian society and male culture. Unlike Jim, he did not have to be an ultimate rebel and pathbreaker, because he was not on the fringes of society. He could afford a more gradual redefining of his culture and context, which is what his life story reveals. This may account for the nature of his CC, which appears to be a more intellectual phenomenon, without the deep spiritual integration we see in Jim and with a clearer tension between self and morality.

Danton remembers growing up in an old Sofia apartment building, where all the families belonged to the same social class and knew each other and the children played together under the protective supervision of the parents in that micro-community. It was a secure and happy childhood, with many relationships with both peers and adults, all colored by issues of loyalty and moral authority.

His grandfather on his father's side was a prominent lawyer and representative of the Jewish community. He was a member of Parliament before the communist revolution, and a social democrat. Danton makes a special point of the fact that his grandfather was not a member of the Grand National Assembly convened after the communist revolution, which sentenced most of the members of the anti-communist opposition to either death or labor camps. Later, Danton's father took his father's social democratic ideals further and became a convinced communist idealist. So the extended family had one foot inside and one foot outside the social system and was never truly persecuted or ostracized, although there must have been some anti-Semitic tension that accounted for many of his clan's moving to Israel.

The extended family gathered regularly around the grandfather in his house, and political discussions were common. Danton grew up with the larger world included in his inner space and a strong awareness of how world events reverberate in ordinary people's lives—a family pattern that Daloz et al. (1996) call "a home with open doors" (p. 28) and recognize as important in the lives of moral leaders. That, in combination with his sense of history and heritage, seems to have a lot to do with his openness to the world and moral agency.

Moral induction (Hoffman, 1991) family practices emphasized a strong sense of moral responsibility to the family and to the larger community to do one's best. Values discourse was an ongoing organizer of experience. Among those values, high standards of accomplishment, knowledge, and learning were central. Danton's story reveals a typical male socialization within a patriarchal society. The boys' earnest friendships were strongly encouraged, as was their competition to excel within acceptable limits; they played chess and developed their minds and acquainted themselves with philosophy and the social sciences. They resisted organized communist school life, read and wrote poetry, listened to serious music, and gathered to discuss social issues. Danton built a moral identity around earnest intellectual resistance to the prevailing political system, and his community of friends gave him a sense of balance between individual accomplishment and commonality of purpose shared by a community of thinkers. Again, this kind of moral earnestness, which Danton shares with many other moral leaders, appears in men from a relatively protected social niche (Gandhi, 1927). In contrast, people like Jim and Emily, whom we will meet in a later chapter, who are outsiders, develop a more feminist approach to morality.

Danton's first encounter with social discrimination came about during mandatory army service, where members of the intelligentsia from Sofia were targeted. Later, during the six-day war in Israel in 1967, he says he painfully realized that he was a Jew, and he could not embrace the official party line against Israel. In both cases, the realization that he did not quite fit in was accompanied by fear and anxiety, an important theme throughout his life and one that sets him apart from Jim, who never had such hopes in the first place and never knew the fear of losing them.

In this first direct encounter with social injustice, Danton didn't overtly adopt a cause; rather, he waited out circumstances, reflecting on his somewhat ambivalent position. This approach characterizes the nature of Danton's moral agency, which reveals a distinct tension between self-interest and morality, perhaps associated with the contradictions of his male patriarchal culture.

Danton went through medical school with academic success, belonged to a circle of friends who listened to The Beatles and sang about freedom, and felt intensely emotionally involved in the events of the Czech Spring in 1968. When the democracy movement was crushed, he withdrew into his studies and married life and later into his professional specialization.

With the same inner passivity and caution, he picked psychiatry because he had some connections there, and later he got his first job with the help of his father's connections. For the next ten years, he tried to adapt to the sociopolitical requirements, wrote what he considered useless pseudoscientific articles, and feigned scientific activity, even taking up a doctoral dissertation. In retrospect, he evaluates this as a wasted period of his life but takes little responsibility for it, rationalizing it as his efforts to survive. While negotiating his at the time institutional (Kegan, 1982) loyalties to the system, Danton even became a member of the Communist Party under pressure from his superiors. That cost him the loss of some friendships and initiated a lifelong struggle with his own conscience.

Danton's movement toward mature CC seems to have occurred through his encounter with psychotherapy in the face of a prominent Western specialist who visited Bulgaria. Here is how Danton speaks of this turning point in his life:

I was thoroughly shaken by his approach to freedom, to the profession, to people. I lived through a shock. . . . I saw my future in that psychotherapy and realized that I had to specialize in it and develop myself. The first thing that struck me is the accent that psychotherapy puts on human freedom, on the need for a person to be free, to fight for his or her freedom. . . . I was interested in existential literature; those were current issues at the time: freedom, Solzhenitsin. . . . And I probably went for it because I saw some personal issues that I would have to resolve. I saw the meaning of my life in working with people in real ways, as well as working with myself. I detested what was being done in the psychiatric clinic, where the system was impenetrable—the clinic is responsible for the person, there is no personal responsibility, and there is nothing you can do but despair.

For the next ten years he specialized in psychotherapy, "went through some severe catharses, despaired, decided to quit many times, and kept going back" to that psychiatrist's clinic in Greece for more training. In his own words, that was a time of intense personal growth and self-discovery. Since then, his work as a psychotherapist has become his calling and his greatest commitment, and, therefore, central to Danton's CC way of being. He sees it as an opportunity "to enter into a dialogue" with the worlds of his patients and build relationships; a constant challenge "to seek meaning" and change himself in order to understand others better.

Danton is permeable, and values "partnering, the dance of interaction." He is a moral agent through the work he does with people, frequently charging nominal fees for those who he knows cannot afford to pay, or even giving free services if necessary. He understands that, in the current sociohistoric context of Bulgaria, and perhaps even the world, the positive growth and personal responsibility orientation of the psychotherapeutic paradigm is ahead of its time.

The times are not the best suited for psychotherapy. People are not interested in rethinking their behavior. They just do things to meet their basic needs, to exist. . . . Now people are after quick fixes, and psychotherapy takes time. It is hard to redefine things in such a context.

In reflecting on his own challenges, Danton shows the same, not a lesser, degree of critical discernment:

My training is far from perfect. . . . And sometimes I have a hard time being spontaneous and relaxed. . . . I am a little vain; I want to be liked. I am ambitious; I have a hard time with criticism. . . . I would like to be more efficient; to understand more, not to investigate, but to understand people and myself more.

Danton is honest and open about the ongoing struggle with himself, and recognizes the tension between his capacity to reason and his deeper ability to understand. Although his moral motivation clearly predominates, this tension among self-interest, humanism, and moral imperative is negotiated differently in the different domains of his life. He seems a lot more engaged in his work than in his family life and parenting. He is somewhat aloof from his two sons, leaving the main responsibility for their raising to his wife and his parents—a traditional division of roles. He explains this with his wife's "more intelligent approach to practical issues," which suits him well. In his parenting, what he remembers most are the challenges, not so much any rewards. He remembers times in his life when he was so consumed with himself that he hardly noticed his children; in retrospect, he feels "a little guilty."

The same stereotypical gender roles are evident in what he sees as the most influential people in his life. Among them, his mother and his wife are seen as sobering models of how to be practical, grounded, and even skeptical at times. They are in contrast with people such as his father and his teachers, who taught him ideas. He also admires Jewish existentialist and proponent of civil opposition Martin Buber, who remained in the Jewish community in Germany until the last possible moment during the rise of Nazism and who later on in Israel resisted the predominant chauvinism. What Danton finds most valuable in Buber is that "he always sought the dialogue between people, and as early as 1948, started probing public opinion for the creation of a new culture, political and overall." Danton makes a point of not liking the figure of Christ, because he does "not like suffering" and is "connected with life in more grounded ways."

Danton's moral agency, the source of which is his humanism, seems to be somewhat weakened by his existential skepticism. On the one hand, his humanism is the source of his respect for people and life and his orientation toward an ongoing dialogue with history and the world. On the other hand, the secular existential part of it leaves him somewhat disoriented, trying to define intellectually the potential for harmony in the world and falling a little short every time when he attempts to conceptualize something beyond the moment of open interaction. His personal philosophy remains trapped in individualism, and he finds it hard to talk about universal moral values, remaining ambivalent and vague.

Danton's secular existential humanism is, in a paradoxical way, both his special strength and his greatest limitation. There is a particularly interesting aspect of it, which seems to have stamped his unique form of moral agency. Here is how he speaks about it:

I like losing causes. I find them more appealing. Perhaps, I do not see myself as somebody who is likely to succeed. But I also like myself that way. I think that losing gives me more than winning. It gives me a perspective on things, some wisdom. I see the bigger picture in life. . . . Progress happens gradually, and things develop, but good never wins. It's a paradox, but in the battle between good and evil, evil always wins. And yet things change. . . . So the point in human experience is experiencing it—even pain, war, everything. It all increases our sensitivity and understanding.

Danton shares with other moral leaders the philosophy of learning to accept life as it comes (Colby and Damon, 1992), but, unlike them, he cannot quite define the theme of self-transcendence. Hence, he does not have the same source of faith, positivity, and endurance. In spite of that, much like some of Bembow's activists (1994), he describes a notably courageous dance with history. Danton's complex distinction between individual battles between "good and evil" and historical progress is the key to understanding his specific form of moral agency. He sees himself as losing the battles but contributing to the historical process.

For example, while still working at the psychiatric clinic for alcoholics, for years he organized group therapy for alcoholics with the help of a couple of colleagues. Since there was no appreciation within the medical establishment of such services, he did it probono for nine years in his free time. The particular groups he organized always fell apart eventually, but out of his years of efforts, the first Alcoholics Anonymous in Bulgaria eventually developed. He gained nothing materially, yet he says that the work with alcoholism has given him as much as he has given to it. This is an excellent example of his professional and social vision.

Another example of his agency is his participation in the "City of Truth," a massive act of civil opposition organized in Sofia after the fall of the communist regime in November 1989 and during the preparation for the country's first free elections in fifty years. During those months, the former communists campaigned on people's fears and confusion around the transition to democracy. In response, the democratic opposition created this commune in the center of the city, right in front of the Communist Party House, which functioned as a mini-city camp within the city and governed itself democratically. The City of Truth lasted for over three months. The people who committed to it lived and slept there and collectively built democratic microinstitutions, while the rest of the city supported them by bringing food. Here is how Danton describes his participation, meaning making, and political vision around that heroic historic act:

I participated in the City of Truth because I understood it as civic service. I went and offered my counseling services for dealing with crisis situations of which there were all kinds. A couple of us therapists stayed there and offered therapy to individuals in crisis. It lasted throughout the summer. We were among the last to leave. I believe this was an attempt to create a truly civic, self-regulating society in Bulgaria. People went there, put up their tents, and took on different functions and responsibilities. They elected a mayor, a city counsel; there was a church, etc. It was an excellent example of the path that our society needs to take.

Danton approaches every issue on a complex systemic level. A contextual thinker, over the years he tried to work with "the isomorphic models with which people's minds operate in a particular context, the collective symbols." He examines how his own behavior and choice in the sixties, as well as those of his friends, parallel psychologically the behaviors and choices of young people in the nineties.

While exercising complex contextual systemic understanding of human experience, he does not lose touch with the immediacy of life. He describes his inspirational experiences with simple people of all walks of life during the first democratic elections, when he volunteered to take phone calls from various parts of the country to receive the final counts. His awe at those people's genuine engagement and sincerity of motive shows the same wholesome immediate relationship with reality that Freire considered the mark of a CC person.

Danton's cognitive and affective decentering and sense of belonging to a larger humanity come through in the way he talks about the war in Bosnia, with both lucid systemic understanding and passionate moral imperative.

For me Bosnia represents a moral dilemma, a missed opportunity since 1991. Three different ethnic communities used to live there in balance and even harmony. I think that the conflict was artificially ignited and escalated. Everyone could have done something at the beginning. Everyone means us (Eastern Europe, including Bulgaria), the West; but no one moved a finger. The Persian Gulf and Kuwait were more important at the time. And Serbia is a fascist state, right next to Bulgaria. But we seem to be blind. And the nonsense that is being said about neutrality and what not. . . . Such a violation—they burned a whole city, Zheppa, in the heart of Europe! And what's happening? Everybody is buying time, looking around, listening, talking about some hypothetical things. . . . And in the meantime, these are the countries in which there is a chance to develop the future socio-political structure of Europe. Because these are Moslems, but they are Serbs. Sarajevo is the only city in the world that saved its Jews during the Second World War. Moslems, Serbs, they all came together and saved the Jews. The only other places in Europe where something like that happened are Denmark and Bulgaria. But as a city, Sarajevo is the only one. So that's a wonderful example of tolerance . . . and what happened? How do things like that happen? It's clear that there is a dirty political game underneath. And Clinton is too soft. Violation and aggression have to be stopped with determination; then it is time for contracts. And what upsets me most is the horrible silence in Bulgaria. No real information, complete disinformation. Intelligentsia, intellectuals, all big words, and in fact they do not even comment on the Serbian actions—and that's a totalitarian fascist state! In the meantime, some Westerners come and start asking questions as though they are looking to us for information. Some Western psychiatrist stands in front of an audience here and asks: How did it come to that? It is his responsibility to inform himself.

Danton has been contemplating the idea of getting together a team of colleagues to go to the refugee camps in Bosnia and start crisis intervention counseling. This illustrates his personal standard and political and humanistic vision. The world is actively included in the inner private place from which he negotiates his choices. He says that neither his grandfather nor his father were zionists, because they did not believe that the future belongs to countries, and people should live where they live. We see here glimpses of his emerging global vision.

At the end of the interview, Danton confessed that the interview had actually been a wonderful opportunity to reflect on his life path. He takes deep responsibility for understanding his own meaning making, which is the closest he gets to an activated depth dimension of existence.

Danton's variation of mature CC shows a more sophisticated intellectual development and a less activated depth dimension, which illustrates the fact that CC is not the direct outcome of either structural development or moral motivation, but rather a synergistic product of the interaction between the two. His spiritual understanding is somewhat hesitant and ambivalent, developed enough to make him very permeable, but not enough to give him the courage and fortitude that his best intentions require. He is clearly a moral agent for positive social change, but, in comparison to Jim, not as empowered. He tries to conceptualize intellectually the possibility for harmony in the world, and even though he has existential faith in the historical process and in the power of the human spirit to overcome and find meaning, he tends to dwell more on the individual cases where "evil" prevails over "good," as he puts it.

RAMINA: AN INTELLECTUAL CAUGHT IN THE PRISON OF SELF

Like Danton, Ramina is in her mid-forties. She is a smart, strong, dynamic, and attractive woman with a mind of her own. An organic chemist by profession, when we meet her, she has survived communism with integrity despite the persecution of her family, has had a successful career as a researcher in the chemical-technological processing of metals in a government research institute in the communist years, and has switched to business in the years of transition out of communism. Her opening words are:

My life till now has been just an introduction. I have not begun to live yet; I am still in a state of expectation, as though I am yet to unfold. I feel that many things in my past life were not sufficiently consciously understood. I was good in my profession, then had to be good in steering my way in a society in chaos; but I still don't know what's good and what's evil. . . . The one thing that stands out is a beautiful childhood, in a beautiful home, around beautiful people, and a father who was a staunch anti-communist. . . . So my life growing up was home, school, home; trying to avoid communist public life as much as possible, and staying in the circle of those I loved.

This theme of a closed circle of others and of a deep split between her public and private life runs throughout the whole interview. If Danton tends to dwell on the individual cases where "evil" prevails over "good" despite his philosophical commitment to the power of the human spirit to transcend, Ramina has chosen to put her faith in herself only. She has actively chosen not to trust humanity, although her life, as do most human lives, shows a good mix of positive and negative experiences with people. Although she tries to live out her individualism with moral integrity, it often disintegrates into a negative view of the world.

Ramina is a complex character, not your ordinary expediency-oriented one-track mind. She struggles with a conservative, fear-based morality understood as inhibitions rather than as a positive vision of life and people. She is attracted to ideals, but those are still the ideals of an individualist, which fall short of activating the depth dimension of her existence. She is so locked up in the world of her own thinking that she sees others only momentarily. Around every issue, she shows an unresolved tension between her efforts to live with integrity and her expediency bent, a tension continuously rationalized through a personal philosophy of radical individualism.

Ramina considers her most generative period her fifteen years as a researcher, in the course of which she was motivated to be the best in her profession and was able to develop a number of innovations in the area of the vacuum processing of metals. She does not speak of herself as part of a team, but as a creative individual, coming the closest of the eight Bulgarian interviewees in this study to what is the U.S. ideal of freedom. In this way, Ramina's profile inadvertently captures the most salient limitations of this ideal and the ways in which it falls short of CC.

This was the most open period of my life, the purest. I had freedom of thought; I could create. I was alone on that front, and that worked well for me. I was creative, and for each person, the strongest time is when one is creative.

Even though in the years of communism personal recognition was usually not given without the right political status, her sense of fulfillment came from having participated in the development of a whole area of industry in the country and having left behind processes that are still in use today. With the fall of communism in 1989, she saw a swing into extreme pragmatism and chose to leave the research institute and get into business.

She took the selling out of the research institute in the years of transition as a confirmation of the mercenary and untrustworthy nature of humanity, and she decided it was not worth fighting for her professional ideas. Instead, she left for a bigger salary in sales and justified her choice with the needs of her family. She describes this period in her life as a time of dissociation from who she is, and she places the responsibility for that choice with the system. This sense of dissociation comes through even in the way she uses pronouns: when she refers to something she did that she considers good, she speaks in the first person; when she refers to her hard choices, she uses an overgeneralized "you."

I am happy that I realized before it was too late that what had been no longer was. . . . You become a pragmatist. You learn elementary things, such as how to import and export; how to avoid taxes. You lose your individuality. . . . You are forced to focus on the easiest form of the accumulation of capital, trade, the fastest circulation of means, which is not that easy at all. Production requires machines, equipment; it takes a long process to turn it into money. . . . I am forced to work with people who have been successful in a material sense. And I see how elemental their psychology is; but perhaps that's how you have to be today to be successful. You have to be brutal, arrogant . . . if you have complexes, and any intelligent person has at least some, or is maybe more self-critical, you cannot take the step that will take you to a higher material level. Now I've taken this step, but with the sense that it is not me. Because my child has to have a computer, a good start in life; to be able to travel abroad and see a larger world.

What kind of moral understanding is behind Ramina's choices? She says, "I tried hard to protect the morality which was given to me by the people I loved in my childhood, by my parents. To remain independent—a loving individualist, not an egotistical one. To remain faithful to my love for those people in my childhood." What were these standards of moral authority in childhood that still beckon to her so strongly in her forties?

A father, an architect, who graduated abroad; a super-intellectual and an extraordinary man. A mother full of heart and humanity, who cared for me, and for my older stepsisters; who was equal in both love and punishment; who found it in herself to love my wild nephews. . . . My older sister. . . . She was a very conservative and wise person, very ambitious toward herself, not with respect to worldly things, but with respect to developing herself. She taught me how to develop myself, how to be a thinking person. . . . She did not like trampolines; she preferred the slow unfolding of an idea, the gradual perspectival encompassing of the whole. . . . My middle sister—a warm-hearted person who taught me how to love, and how to manage the barbarism of totalitarianism and still be practical in providing opportunities for your family. . . . The smile of these people, their love—that was the most beautiful thing in my life.

Ramina identifies with intellectuals, whom she describes as people who work on themselves, have a realistic sense of who they are, are good in their profession, and have a broader and more generous worldview. In some ways, she embodies that ideal, but with a strange discrepancy between heart and mind, between what she loves and is attracted to, and what she chooses to enact in the world.

She grew up in what she experienced as a fortress of purity, beyond which was a corrupt and ugly world with which she wanted nothing in common. Her father narrowly escaped labor camp; her older sister married a vicious communist who harassed her mother after her father's passing when she was a teenager. Both of these facts embodied for Ramina what the larger world stood for and what she fought to keep at bay. This perception of a hostile world seems to have stifled her empathy and sense of relatedness to others.

She says she loves people but stays away from them because she sees their limitations. She seems to have identified most with her father and older sister, each of whom stood alone and in resistance and did not see themselves as part of any larger human whole even though they were admired for their integrity and loved by many others in the town. Each of them lived in a world of their own creation. Ramina's loyalties are with that world of the past, much like Faulkner's heroes. She is so caught up in her memories, and in the insecurity-driven escape in the world of thought that was modeled for her, that she does not really see the potentialities of the present.

Ramina's sense of agency parallels the limited agency of her authority figures. In a classic conservative fashion, the public world became the world to fight for survival and success, and the private world became the ideal to cherish. In the process, she describes herself as becoming somewhat wild, reactive, angry, socially awkward, ambitious, resentful, closed.

I hate the collective. Each one in the group tries to be a little better than you. But people are all the same. Each is great in themselves. There is no collective—that's a chimera, a communist idea. You cannot form a collective with a welder, with a custodian.

Asked if there are any other people she admires, she responds with a deep distrust and skepticism for the wider circle of humanity:

I admire only people I've known. I cannot admire people who have done this or that, but I do not know them. That's too relative. . . . To admire someone, I have to see them in a situation.

Ramina's motivational profile is as complex a mix of moral and expediency concerns as possible, but the overall configuration falls, even though very unevenly, on the side of expediency. Her identity formation, although grounded in moral values of integrity, is still predominantly influenced by social class; hence, rooted in social convention. Although she exhibits a strong character, grounded in some virtues, she is primarily self-absorbed and instrumental in her attitude to the larger world. Although she has internalized from her role models a strong sense of internal moral authority, she is self-righteous and with a limited sense of moral responsibility, preferring to view herself as a victim of circumstances.

When asked what she understands as moral courage, Ramina describes it as one's ability to overcome an inhibition in one's convictions and to act in the name of one's personal freedom; for example, to have an extramarital relationship if one's marriage is unsatisfying; to pursue success with drive. She considers herself morally more responsible than her abusive husband because she hid her relationships in the small town where they could otherwise become a humiliation for him, while he didn't bother to do that. She considers her greatest moral failure having married a primitive, brutal, violent, and abusive man and "having brought him to her mother, in that house with so much spirit in it." Her greatest pride is her son.

Ramina likes to help others if she can, but without making herself vulnerable. She describes her impatience with listening to others: "I hate for somebody to stand there and explain to me. I prefer that we act together, and in that moment of action we may even be at one."

She is distinctly on the run from herself, and action in the business world is her hiding place. She says she finds it impossible to apologize. She'll just try to make it up to the individual she thinks she has hurt but cannot bring herself to speak of her trespass. She does not trust other people's wisdom. "I've thought many times: man's both hands are sinful. Man is weak."

Ramina reads a lot. She grew up with a passion for serious literature. Her contact with the world classics was her medium for reflection on the meaning of life. But that reflection remained divorced from life. With an inner place not inclusive of others and no social consciousness or basis for enduring commitments beyond the self, she remains disengaged and alienated from her world. Her strong critical faculty developed into a negativistic, skeptical view of life. She dissociates herself from her democratic convictions, which suffer many disappointments with political reality in the transition period, and gives up on any public interest. "In international plan, nothing interests me either. Sometimes the beginnings of a world event may move me, but then I come to realize again that everything is a manipulated game of interest."

Asked what her spiritual philosophy is, Ramina answers that it is ethical, not spiritual. But her ethical convictions regarding treating others with integrity break down as soon as she starts speaking about goodness: "Naturally, goodness has its boundaries—cannot be infinite; because I start feeling stupid at the thought of infinite goodness which is infinitely exploited. People need to know their places."

Her negative and ultimately materialistic view of humanity becomes even clearer as she explains how she proceeds with others:

When people get in my way, I am firm in opposition, and do not stop till I reach my goal. My friends tell me I am undiplomatic. Or intolerant. Sometimes I step on people's toes. . . . I don't try to understand, because what does it mean to understand people? It means to understand specific individuals whom you have allowed close to you. What should I understand about people in general—about the ones talking to me on TV, or about my neighbor who throws his trash in my back yard? I don't understand them. And I don't want to understand that type of people. . . . Why should I try to understand humanity? I have no desire for that. I do not have that scope in me, that broad angle. I love my dog more than some people. Some people just disgust me with their attitude to others, with their malice, with their vengefulness, with their unscrupulousness.

Asked if she believes in God, Ramina explains:

I wouldn't call it God, but a unitary principle of justice, which rules over all of us, and leads us, something to which we are all subject. Whenever you think everything is as dark and hopeless as can be, an opening appears, and then there is light again, and you see that not everything is as bad as it seemed. That's why I believe in something greater than me. I believe there is a greater justice.

Later, she describes her intuitive sense of there being something more to life: "I am constantly preparing for something real, something big. I feel it in me, and have lived with this feeling in the last 20 years."

Unable to understand her own spiritual yearning, she quickly disqualifies it— "Perhaps it's my maximalism"—and then reduces it to flat conventional wisdom—"perhaps I need more experience in order to make that qualitative shift toward self-actualization." This is how we leave Ramina: poised on the verge of an awakening, but unable to make that step and place her faith with what she believes in. She is not very developmentally alive. In her own words,

My convictions have formed in me in my earliest years. My worldview was formed by 17–18. Later it was subject to some changes, but remained essentially the same. It is difficult for a person to change after 17—whether they increase the scope of their information, or of their connections with others, whatever they do, they are already formed by 17. There's a basic genetic factor.

Ramina professes what is a common secular materialistic assumption, fed by materialistic social science. She has no concept of her own spiritual potential or that of others. She is a typical product of the world we live in, and of prevalent education and psychological understanding.

SUMMARY OF MOTIVATIONAL DIFFERENCES: EXPANDED TEMPLATE

Danton and Ramina represent two opposites of postconventional consciousness and capture the characteristic challenges of many educated people in the West. Both of them have to face life's challenges without an explicit spiritual understanding of their own lives and of life's greater wisdom. Both have to negotiate in varying degrees the characteristic twentieth-century loss of faith and its concurrent split between mind and heart. The paralysis of such a condition becomes clear in view of Colby and Damon's (1992) finding:

A true integration of reflection and action rests on a unifying belief that must be represented in all the cognitive and behavior systems that direct a person's life choice. . . . The belief must be so compelling that it both preserves the stable commitments and guides the dynamic transformations of each system. . . . Many of our exemplars drew upon religious faith for such a unifying belief . . . a far larger proportion of our exemplars than we originally expected. But even those who had no formal religion often looked to a transcendent ideal of a personal sort: a faith in the forces of good, a sustaining hope in a power greater than oneself, a larger meaning for one's life than personal achievement or gain. . . . Although the substance of the faith and its ideals was too varied and too elusive to be captured in a final generalization, it can perhaps best be described as an intimation of transcendence: a faith in something above and beyond the self. The final paradox of our study is that the exemplars' unity of self was realized through their faith in a meaning greater than the self. (Colby and Damon, 1992, p. 311)

To the extent that Danton could transcend his self-referential intellectual inclination and locate a sustaining faith in the power of psychoanalysis to restore the freedom of the human spirit and faith in the ultimate prevalence of goodness, he was able to draw courage and purpose from his faith, to find a generative balance, and to become an agent of positive change in the world. Even though his heady intellectual orientation, unbalanced by spiritual practice, did not encourage in him moments of purposeful suspension of personal analytical thinking, which allow for direct insights into the wisdom of life (Mills and Spittle, 2001), his empathic capacity opened the door to occasional experiences of humility and awe in the presence of his clients. Although those glimpses into the human spirit were not sufficient to infuse him with the kind of power we see in Jim, they pulled him out of his personal world enough to make him capable of life on a larger scale. Ultimately, his faith, though not strong, was self-transcending enough to create the possibility for bringing reflection and action, mind and heart into a growing integration.

In contrast, in Ramina, who also held a philosophical conviction in the unitary forces of good, this conviction was not sufficiently supported by direct experiences of insight, humility, and awe to pull her forward. Her materialistic assumptions about a dog-eat-dog world kept her spinning inside her personal analytical world of thought, generating what she saw as further confirmations of her beliefs and digging for herself a deeper hole of isolation and inner dividedness.

Ramina's story illustrates the many aspects involved in amplifying the human spiritual potential into a consistent moral orientation, which can become the motivating force for the evolution of critical consciousness. Her immediate family environment certainly fostered her spiritual yearning to know and to love. It cultivated in her a sense of belonging and courage and offered her some models of critical moral discourse as organizers of experience. What it was not able to do for her was to cultivate openness and expanding engagement with the world. The beliefs that she infused from her environment about people and the larger world did not reflect an understanding of the collective spiritual potential of humanity.

Such understanding is profoundly lacking in most secular scientific circles, which, despite their commitment to work for the common good, are guided by basic materialistic assumptions about the nature of a human being and the nature of life (Danesh, 1994). As long as we are seen as governed by our biology and life is seen primarily in terms of survival, we have no vision of potentiality to offer in education and the social sciences, and public discourse is dominated by arguments over current and past forms. This breeds a climate of negativity, cynicism, and pessimism, which we see reflected in the mass media and in the general psychological state of the majority of people in the Western world.

Even those schools of humanistic thought that have tried to uphold a more positive view of human potential have failed to see that potential in the context of the larger historical process of the psychospiritual evolution of collective human consciousness (Saiedi, 2000). Humanistic psychology, which emerged as a positive corrective to excessively materialistic psychology, ended up magnifying the dangerous split between individual and collective consciousness and counterposing the fulfillment of individual potential to collective development. Ramina's life is a sad testimony of the high price of such a misconception. As Noguchi, Hanson, and Lample (1992) point out,

One cannot develop virtues and talents in isolation, but only through effort and activity for the benefit of others. Idle worship and prolonged withdrawal from society, advocated by some philosophies in the past, can neither promote individual development nor aid humanity's progress. To focus one's sense of purpose only on the development of one's own potential is to lose objectivity and perspective. With no outside interactions and social goals, one has no standard by which to judge personal progress and no concrete results by which to measure one's development. A person forgetful of the social dimension of moral purpose is prone to subtle forms of ego—combinations of guilt, self-righteousness and self-satisfaction. (p. 4)

These subtle forms of ego are themes that run through the whole interview with Ramina.

An understanding of collective spiritual potential is often lacking in current religious practices as well. As a result, many tend to breed a pervasive mentality of tribalism, hostility, and fear (Daloz et al., 1996), as is the case with the ambitious competition and intolerance between different Christian denominations, between Christianity and Islam, and between Christianity and Judaism. There is yet no understanding of how Christianity, Judaism, and Islam, as well as Eastern traditions, reflect a single unitary process of the evolution of collective human consciousness (Baha'u'llah, [1931] 1983). Hence, many people in the world have to negotiate the split we saw in Ramina.

Ramina's assumptions about humanity left her too fearful to be willing to loosen the bounds of her own thinking or to credit in any real way the spiritual frames of reference she came in touch with. Unlike Danton, whose profession as a psychologist was his saving grace, she was not challenged by her profession to embrace a bigger world. So her spiritual potential remains very unevenly manifested—mostly on the side of knowing, somewhat on the side of loving, with a painful paralysis of the will to act in accordance.

Using Danesh's (1994) model for the development of human spiritual powers with regard to the central human concerns, Ramina's knowing is focused on self-discovery, the uniqueness of others, and contemplation of mortality. She does not yet exhibit real self-knowledge, appreciation of the oneness of people, or understanding of immortality. Ramina's spiritual faculty of love is mainly manifested in self-development, acceptance of others, and negotiating separations. She shows little empathy with others or attraction to unity, and no attraction to building secondary unions beyond primary family. The exercise of Ramina's faculty of will is limited to issues of self-confidence, competition with others, and oscillations between dealing with her desires and the need for decisions. She shows no real self-responsibility, orientation to cooperation and equality, far less service, and no integrated action.

In contrast, Danton, who overlaps with Ramina in many areas, shows developed self-knowledge and self-responsibility, empathy with others and orientation to cooperation and equality, attraction to building secondary unions, and a capacity for integrated action. In Table 3.1, which represents Danesh's (1994) summary of the development of human powers and concerns, an asterisk on the left marks Ramina's developmental positions in the various areas at the time of the interview, and two asterisks on the right mark Danton's positions. That allows a greater appreciation of the existential individualistic overlaps between Danton and Ramina and the significant differences that still put them on different sides of the motivational continuum.

Table 3.1
Danton's and Ramina's Powers and Concerns

Primary Human Concerns	Main Human Powers		
	Knowledge	Love	Will
Self	Self-experience *Self-discovery Self-knowledge**	Self-preoccupation Self-acceptance *Self-development**	Self-control *Self-confidence Self-responsibility**
Relationships	Sameness of people *Uniqueness of people** Oneness of people	*Acceptance of others Empathy with others** Unity	*Competition Cooperation and equality** Service
Time	Present (here and now) *Mortality** Immortality	Primary union *Separation Secondary union**	Desire *Decision Action**

As is typical of contemporary intellectuals, Ramina and Danton are most developed in their concerns with self, with a significant difference between them as to what they take responsibility for. They share the typical postmodern focus on the uniqueness of people, as well as the secular existential inability to move beyond the contemplation of mortality. As is also characteristic of intellectuals, their capacity to love falls significantly behind their capacity to know and understand. In the exercise of will with regard to others, neither Danton nor Ramina has yet understood the spiritual significance of service. In that sense, even Danton's powers are limited in comparison with Jim's, not to mention with those of the moral leaders studied by Colby and Damon (1992) and Bembow (1994), all of whom are fueled by a remarkable unity of self and morality and reveal lives of undaunted service to humanity. Such a contrast brings into sharp relief the power of spiritual frames of reference to amplify human potential.

A closer look at the wealth of subthemes Danton and Ramina's lives exhibit along the four motivational dimensions and at the qualitative difference in the resulting consciousness allows further insights into the continuum between moral and expediency motivation. Table 3.2 presents an expanded motivational template, which can be used for the diagnostic assessment of profiles, as well as of a wide range of educational and other social interventions. In Table 3.2, one asterisk on the left marks Ramina's position along each subdimension, and two asterisks on the right mark Danton's position. In this way, it is easier to appreciate both the overlaps in their motivational characteristics and the significant departures.

However, since the template captures only two extremes, and not the many degrees in between, an assessment on one end or the other is only a matter of prevalence, not necessarily of absolute value. For example, in subdimension 2(e), Ramina's position should not be taken to indicate that she exhibits no inner conversation regarding issues of personal moral authority and responsibility, but simply that this conversation is not central or defining. In the interviews for this study, a few people exhibited the expediency extreme in most dimensions as absolute values, but those are exceptions rather than the rule. In the case of the relative positions of Danton and Ramina on each continuum, they are both close to the center, on either side of it.

Understood in terms of their relative dominance in people's ways of being, the motivational dimensions of difference between CC and non-CC allow construing CC not as another way to categorize people, but rather as a way to view the human continuum and its potential for development.

In the next chapter, we will trace the different motivational configurations in preconventional and conventional development in order to appreciate further the tenuous boundary between our current collective standard and setting a human being on the path of optimal consciousness. To understand more fully the challenges of our current collective standard, it is helpful to look at how cultural variations in social conventions play in the formation of optimal or suboptimal consciousness. For that purpose, in the next chapter, we will contrast Americans and Bulgarians, who, as pointed out at the end of chapter 1, represent variations of a similar Westernized materialistic context, colored by a generally recognized Christian framework. In the case of Americans, this context is also characterized by unfettered individualism. In the case of Bulgarians, we will see an uneasy tension between extreme suffocating collectivism and reactive individualism. This contrast will illumine further the need, discussed by Noguchi, Hanson, and Lample (1992), for moral education to transcend the limitations of both extremes and to orient itself to "a complementary and balanced approach to personal and collective transformation" (p. 5).

Table 3.2
Expanded Motivational Template

Dimen-sion	Expediency Motivation	Moral Motivation
1. Identity	Social identity a. *Rooted in social conventions**, unmediated by values, *precarious b. Lack of moral character grounded in virtues c. *Centrality of self-image and appearance concerns d. *Self-absorbed, instrumental consumer concerns e. Absence of habitual morality f. *No moral imperative	Moral identity a. Rooted in universal moral values, solid**, mediated socialization** b. *Strong character grounded in virtues** c. Peripheral self-image concerns** d. Normative ends** e. *Habitual morality** f. Moral imperative**
2. Agency and Responsibility	Lack of agency and limited responsibility a. Absence (or scarcity) of figures of authentic moral authority; no models b. Lack of opportunities to compare and discern authentic authority; *lack of respect for it c. Either no moral self-attribution and sense of personal moral authority or its opposite: *self-igteousness d. *Limited sense of moral responsibility, mostly derived from social and cultural stereotypes e. *No internal conversation around issues of moral authority and responsibility f. *No examples of true agency translate into skepti-cism, helplessness, fear of external authority	Moral agency and expanding moral responsibility a. *figures of authentic moral authority**; *models internalized** b. *Intuitive moral sense develops into critical discernment** of and respect for authentic authority** c. Moral self-attribution and sense of internal moral authority** d. Expanding personal moral responsibility continuously reconstructed** e. Centrality of internal conversation around moral authority and responsibility** f. Examples of moral agency translate into personal moral agency**

Table 3.2 (continued)

3. Relationships	Lack of empathy, alienation, impermeability, no concerns with justice and not hurting a. *Hostile environment stifles empathy and relatedness b. *Lack of/limited empathy c. *Isolated, individualistic way of being, in compe-tition with others d. *Lack of/mostly casual rela-tionships; just contacts; defi-ciency of attachments e. Centrality of receiving f. *Inner place not inclusive of others g. *No common purpose with others; no sense of commu-nity** h. Cognitive and affective pro-vincialism; *limited member-ship in immediate interest groups; no sense of belonging to a larger humanity** i. *Limited communication and sharing j. *Impermeability to meaning-ful social relationships k. *Compartmentalization and prejudice l. *Split between public and private life and alienation from public life m. *No concerns with justice and equity and not hurting n. *No social consciousness o. *No basis for enduring commitments beyond self, or work for the betterment of society	Empathy, relatedness, perme-ability, concerns with justice and not hurting a. Benevolent, empathic envi-ronment fosters empathy and relatedness** b. Levels of empathy** c. Rootedness in relatedness** d. Engaged in relationships on every level** e. *Centrality of giving** f. Inner place inclusive of oth-ers and larger world** g. Fulfillment derived from common purpose with others and sense of community h. *Cognitive and affective decentering**; sense of belong-ing to a larger humanity i. Value placed on open com-munication and permeability to others** j. Permeability to meaningful social relationships** k. Lack of compartmentaliza-tion and prejudice** l. Integration of private and public life** m. Concerns with justice and equity and not hurting** n. Social consciousness** o. Enduring commitments be-yond self and work for the betterment of society**

Table 3.2 (continued)

4. Mean-ing of life	Self-referential frames of refer-ence and limited goals	Larger frames of reference and life purpose as vantage point for critical discernment and self-reflection
	a. Sense of meaninglessness of life; no search or questions about meaning b. *No larger purpose than individual self	a. *Faith in meaning and wis-dom of life; search for it and ongoing questions** b. Life purpose seen in aligning oneself with life's meaning as best understood**
	c. *Peripheral concerns with right/wrong, good/bad, true/false; no vantage point outside self-interest	c. Continuous elaboration of connections between right and wrong, good and bad, true and false as vantage point** d. Critical discernment** e. *Self-reflection**
	d. *Negative criticism e. Reliance on habit and ritual f. No interest in establishing consistency in one's under-standing of life; no grappling with contradictions g. Embeddedness in sociocul-tural reality; status quo taken for absolute; tendency to be satisfied with opinions, stereo-types, polemics and fragile arguments h. *Impermeability to sugges-tions and questions arising from context i. *Surface functioning j. *Disengaged and alienated from one's world	f. *Efforts to integrate under-standing of reality and grap-pling with contradictions** g. *Problematizing of sociocul-tural reality from point of view of larger moral framework** h. Permeability to suggestions and questions arising from context** i. Depth dimension of existence activated** j. Engaged in wholesome and immediate relationships with reality**

Following are some general observations on the ways in which U.S. and Bul-garian cultural contexts each tend to be more conducive of different aspects of moral motivation and structural development.

CROSS-CULTURAL DIFFERENCES IN CONTEXTUAL SUPPORTS FOR CC

Although Bulgarian society is fairly Westernized, it still bears many of the characteristics of the East, and in that sense, the cultural contrasts between the two societies capture to some extent the respective strengths and limitations of East and West.

The East has, throughout the history of human civilization, been the dawning place of religion, spirituality, and mystic contemplation. Its attitude to life has been fairly passive, giving prominence to the richness of feeling and contemplation over the joys of action. To the extent that Bulgarian society is part of that tendency, it tends to favor the moral contemplation of broader philosophical concerns with life and meaning beyond immediate realities. It has fostered a wealth of emotional life, expressed in its thirteen-centuries-old culture and literature and strong communal traditions.

In contrast, the West has always been strong in its practical, down-to-earth understanding of the realities of life, its emphasis on creative action, and its focus on the creative powers of the individual mind. U.S. culture represents a pinnacle in this Western trend, and is, of Western societies, perhaps the least concerned with philosophical issues, and the most obsessed with action. Taken to the extreme, the tendencies of the East have resulted in fatalism, fanaticism, and totalitarianism, while the tendencies of the West have lead to arid individualism, materialism, and pragmatic expediency.

Aside from these most generic East/West differences in the two cultural contexts, the two societies also exhibit more specific contextual differences. The relatively young, multicultural U.S. society, with its long-standing tradition of public life and democratic commitment, seems most conducive to the development of permeability to different cultural and other ways and broader empathic concerns with social justice. With its traditions in citizenship and its emphasis on individual rights and freedom of self-definition, U.S. society also seems to encourage the formation of social consciousness and to foster the developmental aspects of the sense of agency.

Where the U.S. context seems to fall relatively short in comparison with Bulgaria is in its ability and willingness to draw on its diverse cultural and spiritual heritage, in order to provide enduring, convincing, and cross-culturally significant models of moral identity in which to ground national identity. In its youthful orientation toward change and growth and its quest to examine critically and to rethink every aspect of social life, this society has debunked as ethnocentric and hypocritical many of the models of the past and has not been able to evolve new and universally acceptable ones.

The very dynamic nature of U.S. society seems to account, as Erikson (1980) has aptly observed, for the rapid disintegration of social and communal networks which otherwise provide grounding and support for families and individuals. There is a resulting tendency toward a certain fragility of the sense of identity, and a tendency to extend the self-centered adolescent quest for self throughout the adult lifespan. Extreme individualism, as the shadow side of the respect for individual rights and freedom of self-definition, makes U.S. society less conducive to the development of an enduring moral sense of identity, personal moral authority and responsibility, and larger frames of reference than the individual self.

In contrast, the patriarchal Bulgarian society, with its relative historical absence of civic democratic traditions and its centuries of subjugation of the individual, fails to foster social consciousness and individual sense of agency. A relatively homogenous society, it also does not encourage permeability to different cultural ways. However, its strong philosophical, literary, artistic, family, and communal traditions foster a stronger sense of individual moral identity, authority and responsibility and broader philosophical concerns with life and meaning.

The following section examines these differences in contextual supports for CC in terms of the specific dimensions of moral motivation, and structural development.

Moral Motivational Dimensions

Moral Identity. The U.S. sample consistently exhibited a certain fragility in the sense of identity, related to the mobility and lack of rootedness and continuity in American society, as well as to the highly competitive organization of life. Since family connections appeared to have progressively lost their strength, a strikingly high occurrence of either dysfunctional or weak family contexts was evident, which did not seem able to mediate socialization. Hence, relatively few people exhibited a sense of identity primarily rooted in moral values. On the whole, social configurations such as class, role, interest group, and lifestyle enclave dominate as primary sources of identity.

The cultural moving away from explicit moral induction and moral discourse as organizers of experience, and relegating them to hypocritical and moralistic pseudo-religious or political practices, seems to create a vacuum for the individual. In this vacuum, individuals resort to either one of two extremes: becoming very prone to religious or political ideologies, from which people derive their sense of identity, or choosing to build character and identity in isolation, relying on occasional models and collective values which emphasize courage, liberty, self-reliance, righteousness, self-respect, honesty, and kindness. Overall, there seems to be a general lack of holding environments, which may account for the vulnerability of identity we will see in both Finnigan and William in the next chapter.

In contrast, the main cultural advantage of Bulgarian society is its solid rootedness in family and neighborhood, place and profession, as we will see in both Elliot and Ada, and a prominent moral values dimension in all these forms of identity. Traditional patriarchal values emphasize honesty, trustworthiness, high personal standard of education, work accomplishment, and work ethic, courtesy, generosity, forbearance, respect, hospitality, righteousness, and sacrifice. Child-rearing practices employ a lot of moral induction and moral discourse as organizers of daily experience. They build character and stimulate the development of habitual morality and moral imperative. The overall contextual configuration seems to foster a more morally mediated socialization.

External Moral Authority, Personal Moral Responsibility, and Agency. The U.S. sample exhibited a relative absence or scarcity of moral authority figures in the immediate or extended families and a general distrust for authority. Even in families that appeared more traditional in terms of gender and other roles, there seemed to be a shying away from explicit moral induction and a preference for more casual, peer relations. All of these seemed to speak to the significant difficulty of the interviewees in developing moral self-attribution and establishing a broader sense of moral responsibility. However, the general context of self-reliance fosters the development of agency, which is predominantly colored by either self-interest or moral motivation. Individuals with a predominantly moral sense of identity, moral imperative, and responsibility exhibit expansive moral agency, for which there seem to be unlimited possibilities.

The Bulgarian culture of permanence and hierarchical patriarchal relationships abounds in figures of moral authority in the immediate and extended family. The emphasis on classical education also introduces a host of other models of authentic moral authority into a child's life. The overall populatedness with models of varying degrees of moral authority gives young people a diverse exposure to examples that they internalize and the opportunity to compare and develop critical discernment. Also, the ongoing negotiation of these contrasts appears to make prominent internal conversations about issues of moral authority and responsibility. Hence, this traditional patriarchal culture seems to foster normative concerns and a pervasive sense of moral responsibility.

However, the agency modeled by most of these figures of moral authority is limited to interpersonal moral responsibility in an immediate circle and to gender and social roles. The patriarchal tendency toward authoritarian methods also limits agency, particularly in women and minorities. Conversations about larger civic responsibility abound, and the greater world seems consistently present in the understanding of family affairs, but the legacy of five centuries of Turkish subjugation followed by the totalitarian communist past and the current socio-economic havoc of transition has left people feeling rather powerless and distrustful of any opportunity to convert these conversations into reality.

Meaningful Relationship, Concerns with Justice and Not Hurting, and Social Consciousness. The U.S. sample demonstrated a significant disintegration in relatedness in the lives of the majority of U.S. individuals interviewed, which, coupled with the relative scarcity of significant figures, appears related to the predominantly casual, circumstance-driven, temporary nature of relationships. People seemed to have a hard time engaging fully and wholesomely in relationships and appeared somewhat precarious in their commitments beyond the self.

Despite that, this dimension was the strongest in the U.S. sample, since education promotes inclusive concerns with social justice and the democratic public culture emphasizes action, citizen participation, public process, permeability to differences and meaningful social influences, and overall social consciousness. Hence, even people who clearly tended to compartmentalize their empathic concerns related volunteering and other socially aware practices, which sets the U.S. scene in sharp contrast with Bulgaria, where volunteering is not a common concept.

This was the weakest dimension of the Bulgarian sample, despite the abundance of meaningful, wholesome relationships, and patriarchal interconnectedness, which foster an inner place from which choices and moral decisions are made inclusive of others. Patriarchal traditions are fairly impermeable to different ways and different cultures, territorial and self-protective, full of prejudices and stereotypes, and distrustful of differences. Patriarchal culture is strongly conformist (Wade, 1996), and its concerns with justice and not hurting are compartmentalized, so that they rarely extend beyond interpersonal relationships and group membership. Hence, social consciousness is limited. Fifty years of a totalitarian regime did not contribute to this cultural characteristic, but in fact deepened the protectiveness and distrust for different social groups and for collective social life.

Meaning of Life. In the United States, there is a general pragmatic cultural definition of life around personal success and material well-being, also described by Bellah et al. (1985). This cultural slant does not stimulate ontological concerns with the meaning of life. Hence, critical discernment and self-reflection appear somewhat secondary to problem solving for the purpose of immediate outcomes and more successful social adjustment.

In Bulgaria, ontological questions are as prominent in people's lives as instrumental questions. There is an overall tension between cultural traditions as sources of meaning, and individualistic, self-referential frameworks, the outcome of a general disillusionment with both religion and ideology. Critical discernment appeared frequently based on reactive self-definitions in opposition, or what Erikson (1980) called negative identity. The strong sense of history and a common past provide a larger meaning for people; however, there is no sense of future, other than the individual choice of profession as calling.

Overall, the Bulgarian sample showed a comparable tendency to compartmentalize public and private selves and allegiances and difficulty with critical self-reflection, permeability and empathy beyond familiar others as their American counterparts. Although living in a more communal and interconnected culture, the Bulgarians interviewed for this study were also struggling with individualism and difficulty building allegiances. Most of them were trying to negotiate the legacy of disillusionment with a debunk ideology and its destructive impact on the fabric of social life. That left them rejecting any collective frames of reference, developing a strong orientation toward educational achievement, relying heavily on their intelligence and critical discernment to the point of chronic skepticism and negativity. Hence, morally aware individuals expressed a sense of isolation, alienation, and lack of agency, which made their commitments beyond the self equally difficult.

Structural Development

Bulgarian society is still fairly interpersonal, and the collective norm seems to call for a mix of third and fourth order of consciousness (Kegan, 1994), depending primarily on gender roles. It fosters self-differentiation less than the U.S. context, and, depending on gender and social role, may even discourage it.

As a more developed society, the United States challenges individuals in the direction of greater differentiation and a higher order social-cognitive development; that is, what Kegan (1994) calls a fourth order of consciousness. There is a greater awareness of boundaries and of responsibility taken for self-definitions. The institutional (Kegan, 1994) fabric of social life seems to place before the individual an abundance of opportunities to exercise civic responsibility in different domains. Both individual freedom and the opportunity to exercise agency and individual responsibility seem greater.

The cultural disadvantage seems to be what Kegan (1994) identifies as inadequate social support systems, which foster the movement toward higher orders of consciousness. The public culture of work, family, and social life does not promote a sense of interdependence and does not invite individuals to reconstruct their boundaries in the direction of more interindividual (Kegan, 1982) structures of self. There is also a significant gap between the social support systems available for people from higher and lower classes. Some of the interviewees, who were among the poor class, received minimal education and exhibited the characteristic dysfunctionality and spiritual impoverishment of the U.S. culture of poverty.

Kegan's (1994) analysis points to an important difference between U.S. and more traditional cultures:

The great religions of traditional cultures, a paradigmatic example of one kind of effective culture-as-school, make use of all the regularly frequented arenas of ordinary human conduct to induct and inspire their members in the faith. How we eat, do business, make love, honor our mother and our father—supposedly private domains—are not handed over to independent, idiosyncratic, variably meaningful rules. The contexts for education are not shrunk down to the narrow confines of periodically attended church or school. On the contrary, the regularly frequented arenas of human conduct provide the most important opportunities for teaching. (p. 44)

Bulgarian society, although not particularly religious, shows clear evidence of these pervasive and strengthening traditions that are religious in origin. In the current fabric of U.S. society, there are no comparable, all-embracing frameworks to hold descendants of the culture of poverty. Hence, the U.S. sample contained a significant developmental gap between those who managed to make it within the social system, and those who found themselves on its outskirts early on.

Summary of the Cross-Cultural Contextual Supports for CC

The cross-cultural study of CC yielded some interesting insight into the nature of the historical time we live in. In the stories of the Bulgarian interviewees, one hears the account of a world in transition. A character-building past of rich and contradictory history had given most of them a sense of rootedness and personal moral authority and some of them critical discernment. Yet, few seemed equipped with the permeability and larger frames of reference needed to meet an indefinite future. The interviewees displayed a general apprehensiveness and sense of helplessness. CC is more of a goal than a reality.

The stories of the U.S. interviewees contained the same account of a world in transition, only differently expressed. The very nature of U.S. society, established fairly recently and out of a concoction of cultural traditions, seems to require from the individual different types of coping strategies. Because of the relative lack of rootedness in history and past, people are forced to rely more on their individual courage and self-sufficiency. CC seems to be a goal rather than a reality in the United States, as it is in Bulgaria.

The lack of agency and the sense of helplessness in the face of an indefinite future seem to bring about similar reactions in both samples. These reactions appear more polarized in the U.S. interviewees. On the one end seem to be people who close down into utmost alienation and compartmentalization; on the other end are people who plunge into reckless activity and activism; and in the middle ground are people engaged in existential resistance.

Hence, these two cultural contexts offered a glimpse of slightly different coping strategies in the face of a general lack of CC in a world of global transition. The Bulgarians tended to hold on to the strengths of their rich patriarchal tradition. The Americans sought solutions in the extremes of political conservatism or liberalism. Not many people seemed to know how to negotiate a balanced, permeable approach to the future guided by moral agency. The two cultural contexts manifested in different variations the same difficulty with frames of moral and spiritual meaning larger than the self. This appeared to be the fundamental challenge to most of the intelligent and caring people interviewed for this study in both parts of the world. Altogether, neither culture seems more conducive to the development of CC than the other. Rather, the value of the cross-cultural comparison is in its potential to show the strengths of each culture, which can be drawn on, and to hypothesize the optimal middle ground where new solutions can be sought.

Chapter 4

Cross-Cultural Vicissitudes of Character, Motivation, and Intellect

But where are to be found earnest seekers and inquiring minds? Whither are gone the equitable and the fair-minded?

> Baha'i Faith, Baha'u'llah, [1978] 1988, p. 90

Sincerity is the single virtue that binds divinity and man in one.

> Shinto, Takatomi Senge, in Wilson, 1995, p. 514

"Please, Man of Shakya," said Dhotaka, "free me from confusion!" "It is not in my practice to free anyone from confusion," said the Buddha. "When you have understood the most valuable teachings, then you yourself will cross this ocean."

> Buddhism, Sutta Nipata 1063–64, in Wilson, 1995, p. 489

If I am not for myself who is for me? And when I am not for myself what am I? And if not now, when?

> Judaism, Mishnah, Abot 1.14, in Wilson, 1995, p. 488

In the previous chapter we experienced a glimpse into the texture of life for two highly educated and sophisticated people, both of whom struggle with the same difficulty with frames of moral and spiritual meaning greater than the self. We saw how precarious, yet significant, is the distinction between those who manage to even just begin to resolve this tension in the direction of a greater meaning and those who remain paralyzed in the prison of self. In this chapter, we will deepen our awareness of how this difference plays out in earlier levels of development, namely, in the lives of ordinary, less sophisticated people, who constitute the majority of humanity.

In order to appreciate more deeply the odds against which Ivan and Tom, Finnigan and William, Elliot and Ada, as presented in the following sections, negotiate their lives, we have to adopt a larger historical perspective on the nature of the times. One of the central features of the twentieth century has been its spiritual vacuum, the result of the perversion of religion.

The responsibility for this greatest of tragedies . . . rests primarily on the shoulders of the world's religious leaders . . . those who, presuming to speak in God's name, have imposed on credulous masses a welter of dogmas and prejudices that have constituted the greatest single obstacle against which the advancement of civilization has been forced to struggle. . . . In an age of scientific advancement and widespread popular education, the cumulative effects of the resulting disillusionment were to make religious faith appear irrelevant. . . . [But t]he yearning for belief is inextinguishable, an inherent part of what makes one human. When it is blocked or betrayed, the rational soul is driven to seek some new compass point, however inadequate or unworthy, around which it can organize experience and dare again to assume the risks that are an inescapable aspect of life. (Universal House of Justice, 2001, pp. 59–60)

In Ivan's life in the following section, we will see how this yearning for belief, in the absence of more viable frameworks, was coopted by one of the most destructive ideologies of the twentieth century, communism. In the life of Tom, we will discover how the most simply expressed spirit of a self-sacrificing greater love, even in the context of a pervasive culture of poverty, was sufficient to tip the balance of his choices in the direction of the common good. In the life of Finnigan, we will experience the paralysis of a life unable to find an abiding compass point greater than self, and therefore unable to take on the greater risks of life. In the life of William, we will experience the simple power of faith and moral rectitude. In the life of Elliot, we will see how moral rectitude and social responsibility were the saving grace of a man forced to make his life choices and steer his way in an entangled and highly ideological society. The life of Ada will show us how a person unable to find a frame of reference beyond her self-constructed ideas became entangled in her own opinions and hostilities, and despite her good intentions, lost her way in the same highly ideological and conflict-ridden society.

These stories, in widely varying degrees, capture something about the ways that the mass of humanity has been negotiating the three dominant belief systems of the twentieth century—nationalism, racism, and communism (Universal House of Justice, 2001). The themes of nationalism, and its obsession with real or imaginary threats to national survival; racism, and its obsession with the demonstrably false idea of the possibility of racial purity; and communism, with its perversion of the human yearning for freedom and justice, run like a spider's web through the six following vignettes and illustrate variations of the predominantly materialistic view of human nature and the nature of life characteristic of our modern world. To the extent that some of these six people have managed to discover their deeper spiritual nature and counterpoise it to dominant beliefs, they have been able to find more optimal ways of being.

In this historic context, the vicissitudes of character, motivation, and intellect that these six profiles reveal illustrate the possibility for different choices and remind us of the ultimate power of a human being to exercise free will. In essence, we will be looking here at differences in the strength of the heart to be sincere, to understand directly and be guided by that understanding, even when it cannot rely on the powers of mind to interpret this understanding into coherent systems of meaning. Studying degrees of sincerity is a difficult task, and it is no wonder that psychology has utterly ignored it. Yet spiritual traditions maintain that "Truthfulness is the foundation of all human virtues" (Abdu'l-Baha, ctd. in Shoghi Effendi [1939] 1990, p. 26). It is the goal of this chapter to encourage, through the following vignettes, a deeper exploration of the degrees of truthfulness we live with and of the ways they define the overall quality of our consciousness from moment to moment.

Having already explored the subtle distinctions between CC and its suboptimal counterpart on the postconventional level, we now focus on the remaining two earlier developmental levels characteristic of adulthood—early conformist and fully conventional. As we examine the capacity of earlier developmental forms of consciousness to function with a more optimal CC orientation, we need to remember that people from all walks of life exhibit that capacity. In an age when intellectual sophistication is so highly prized, it is always sobering to remember that the first people to recognize and respond to Christ were not the learned ones of the times, who remained caught in the clutter of their intellectual arguments against him; they were the simple, uneducated ones.

COMPLEXITIES AT THE EARLY CONFORMIST LEVEL

Theoretically, the early conformist level of consciousness is characteristic of early adolescence; but in actuality, it is not uncommon among adults. This level of consciousness relies on some combination of concrete and abstract reasoning as a result of which people can perceive cause-and-effect relationships between self and other, and, in varying degrees, coordinate relations and identify variables, and generalize cause-and-effect chains into a third-person perspective of the neutral other. As Commons and Rodriquez (1990) point out, "when a neutral observer cannot determine which side in a social conflict is correct, the outcome preferred by the largest number of persons is adopted as the most neutral" (p. 330). This level of general cognitive development translates into what Weinstein and Alschuler (1985) describe as situational self-knowledge—a way of knowing oneself through concrete situations described as primarily external, or as "global subjective states" without differentiated nuances, and with "no reported consistencies across situations" (p. 20). The accompanying overall structure of the self typically exhibits a tension between an imperial and an interpersonal self/other organization (Kegan, 1982).

While this level of development is, under normal circumstances, transcended in late adolescence, in particularly cognitively barren or hostile environments, it can become established as a stable level of adult functioning, as we will see in the two following cases. Early conformist consciousness seems to have a higher demographic distribution among lower socioeconomic classes, particularly males, military populations, marginalized populations, inner-city neighborhoods, and similar groupings (Wade, 1996). This means that, given the current conditions of extreme wealth and poverty in the world and the concentration of wealth and resources in the hands of a relatively small percentage of the world population, a large portion of humanity functions at this level and has no real access to more sophisticated cognitive development.

Hence, the question arises, can people living in impoverished circumstances tap into any other internal resources that would allow them to live more optimally, despite their limited cognitive functioning? The contrast between Ivan and Tom in the following section illustrates the possibility of remaining true to one's yearning to "recognize that which leadeth unto loftiness or lowliness, glory or abasement, wealth or poverty" (Baha'u'llah, qtd. in Noguchi, Hanson, and Lample, 1992). We see the contrast between Tom's choice to manifest his spiritual nature in the modest ways available to him, given his arrested cognitive development, and to live with a relative unity among what he knows, what he loves, and how he exercises his will; and Ivan's choice to overlook the yearnings of his heart.

Conformist consciousness is the culmination of a long and defining period in a person's life, beginning in early childhood and reaching into young adulthood—the time of intense development of both mind and heart. Developmental theory (Erikson, 1980; Kegan, 1982) has shown how central to this period is the quality, first, of the family environment and, second, of the wider role-recognizing culture. In the preschool years, the family is the context in which a child's capacity for trust, autonomy, and initiative is negotiated, as she gradually disembeds from and coordinates her impulses and perceptions. During school age, pre-adolescence and adolescence, the larger culture of significant adults and peers becomes the defining context in which industry and a sense of identity are negotiated and the capacity for fidelity is built. To the extent to which both of these environments are intrinsically moral and nurturing enough to foster the successful resolution of successive psychosocial crises of personality development and the formation of ego strengths, the young person can exhibit pre-CC.

This period holds the potential for the early intuitions of the heart to begin to be reinforced by a morally oriented environment. Such an environment rephrases the child's spiritual intuitions in explicit moral terms and begins to engage the child's emerging reasoning capacities into deliberations about right and wrong; guiding but not repressing. Hoffman (1991) calls this moral induction, a specific form of socialization that cultivates an internal moral orientation by enlisting "a motivational resource that exists in the child from an early age, namely, the child's capacity for empathy, defined as a vicarious affective response to others" (Hoffman, 1983, p. 252). This fosters the formation of early moral interest—a tendency to see and understand life in simple right and wrong terms.

This tendency is linked to the existence of intimate models of authentic moral authority in the child's immediate environment; models whom the child intuitively differentiates from other authority figures who may not necessarily represent authentic moral authority. The particular attraction of young children to the models of authentic moral authority in their lives suggests the presence of an intuitive moral sense, which responds to authenticity. This intuitive moral sense is an expression of the human spiritual potential, the inherent spiritual attraction to truth, beauty, and goodness, which gradually takes the form of what Maslow (1959) described as the human striving toward authenticity and fulfillment. This intuitive moral sense is negotiated, however, in a tension with developmental differentiation and ego formation, hence the tremendous significance of authentic moral models early in life.

The child's fascination and unconscious identification with intimate role models can gradually grow into a sincere, trustful, and open attitude toward adults, which allows for explicit moral guidance through moral induction and dialogue. As values are increasingly internalized, children's intuitive moral sense or moral interest develops into moral earnestness. This earnestness is related to the gradual assuming of personal moral authority and responsibility and the development of empathy and concern with relationships. In concordance with the cognitive limitations of this age, the moral concerns are constructed fairly dualistically and in predominantly concrete terms. While complex social-cognitive understanding is still lacking, the intuitions of the heart keep these young people on course and gradually point them toward further differentiation. With the advent of adolescence, this process can snowball into a passionate quest for personal integrity and a preoccupation with character, leading to the formation of conscious internal moral standards. In some particularly idealistic youth, the identity of reformer or champion for positive social change emerges.

The life of Tom illustrates some of these processes in modest but clear terms. Ivan's life illustrates the prominent absence of most of these processes.

Ivan: A Bulgarian Communist Miliatiaman

Ivan is in some ways a unique East European phenomenon of the last fifty years—the product of communist ideology and a representative example of the better version of communist chiefs—not the thoroughly corrupt ones, but those who, at least in their own minds, sincerely adopted the communist idea of social justice and equality. Ivan's case illustrates how ideological consciousness, as the complete opposite extreme of CC, takes root in a person with somewhat arrested development and moral motivational deprivation. He is a less extreme case than a religious fanatic or a fascist, in that he has not lost his compassion and humanity. Yet, he illustrates the same process of the formation of the antithesis of CC.

Ivan exhibits what Wade (1996) describes as egocentric arrests in adulthood as a result of a generally tough, misanthropic, and autocratic social and home environment. Throughout the interview, Ivan did not manifest more than concrete operational reasoning (see Commons and Rodriguez, 1990), with the most generalized, global understanding of others, as well as of social roles. He appeared dualistic and intolerant of ambiguity (Perry, 1968) and seemed thrilled with the discovery of even the simplest linear causal connections, which may account for his fascination with criminology. He also had difficulty describing any complete social patterns, but seemed to drift back every time to concrete situations, as is characteristic of situational self-knowledge (Weinstein and Alschuler, 1985). Finally, he did not seem to have a developed sense of self, but exhibited an alternating imperial/interpersonal self/other differentiation (Kegan, 1982), with a tendency to make others captive of his own goals and point of view and perceive them through a rudimentary, alien other abstraction (Wade, 1996). His optimal functioning seemed to be at the early conformist stage (Wade, 1996).

At the time of the interview, Ivan was a corporal in the criminal police at the Bulgarian Ministry of Internal Affairs, and had held this job for over twenty years. A handsome, well-built man in his fifties, he looked at the interviewer with eyes somewhat blurred by drinking, and had an overall secretive, distrustful, evasive manner. Nevertheless, he was friendly and unassuming, and tried to make the interviewer feel comfortable by offering her a drink "just to relax." Surprised that the interviewer does not drink, he poured himself some Vodka, lit a cigarette, and, after much hesitation and quite a few questions about what the interviewer might want to know, prepared to sign the consent form, which was obviously very disconcerting for him.

He immediately struck the interviewer as a good-hearted, honest, simple-minded, and sturdy peasant, humble, rigid, and hard-working. With the first few words, the interviewer noticed how impersonal and cliché his language was, to the point where the interviewer felt in him a disturbing absence of mind (Arendt, [1958] 1998). It was as though words were being spoken but there were no real thoughts behind them, just a clever computing machine continuously unraveling the sought hidden agenda behind the interviewer's every word. Almost every time the interviewer asked a "why" question, his answer disowned responsibility for any particular opinion, and conveyed a general message of "I don't know; they said it was supposed to be that way." Whenever he expressed a feeling, it was apologetically understated, almost as though he believed he was not supposed to have personal feelings.

Ivan's life story begins rather bleakly: he was born "in a dark cellar," while his parents were fleeing from the bombings during the Second World War. His parents were peasants, each from a large family, and with little education who tried to find a life in the big city. As he says, "they didn't have much to give me or much to teach me, because they had fallen behind on life themselves. But they always told me: "Don't take what belongs to another, be clean and tidy, study hard, be honest." That was the best they could give me."

These basic values of honesty and hard work constitute the most positive rootedness Ivan has. In a more traditional precommunist world, Ivan would have probably found a way to build a simple life around them in dignity. But class injustice and the resulting social mobility and political upheaval tossed him in a direction where other priorities took over. Class identity and class struggle were emphasized by the ideology of the day, while the depth dimension of human existence was not only not drawn upon to sustain people and balance out and humanize the angry social transformations under way but was completely denied by the materialistic Marxist ideology.

Ivan's parents became blue-collar workers in the city, and the family of four lived in a poor urban neighborhood, huddled together in one room and sharing kitchen and bathroom with another family, not an uncommon arrangement at the time. In this marginalized existence, it seems that Ivan did not identify with them or with any other particular figure or place in his childhood. He grew up with very scarce positive values in which to root his sense of identity, with the low self-esteem of belonging to the lower classes. He shows a cold estrangement from himself, problems with self-image and concerns about appearances.

As it turns out, his grandfather had actually been a well-off village land-and-cattle owner and a solid, respectable man. However, Ivan did not dare openly identify with him, because in those early years after the communist revolution, being a landowner was considered politically incorrect, and the village kids teased him when he went to visit his grandparents. So, although he loves and remembers his grandfather, he barely mentions him in the interview. It becomes clear, though, that he loved village life and field labor and greatly enjoyed it, and those moments were among the few grounding experiences in his early childhood.

Ivan had little in the way of holding environment growing up. His mother worked shifts in factories all her life, and Ivan felt for her grueling life. So every time it was his family's turn to clean the shared spaces and the front and back yard, he would make sure he did it on her behalf before she came home from work. He was obviously a compassionate, empathic child, but his stark environment did not support that. His mother never praised him; in his words, she was rather cold, which he believes was "a good preparation for life."

Ivan's stark childhood, and the resulting generally arrested developmental profile, is not unique to the Bulgarian context; he has equivalents in the U.S. context as well. These people, on both sides of the ocean, underwent direct, unmediated socialization into the available mass culture, as a result of not finding something more lasting in which to root their identity. Most have a precarious self-image and sense of identity and are self-absorbed and instrumentally oriented. Some important distinctions arise, however, related to the developmental characteristics of the mass culture into which they are directly socialized.

Sim, Ivan's U.S. counterpart (see Mustakova-Possardt, 1996), was socialized into a gangster imperial (Kegan, 1983) subculture, with an instrumental purpose and exchange orientation (Kohlberg, 1984). However, his subculture was somewhat held in check by the laws of the overall culture of his society, which requires a social law and order orientation (Kohlberg, 1984). Although Sim lost himself more than once, there was also the sobering influence of friends and family, which introduced an alternative conversation into his life.

Ivan's story is different. He was directly socialized into a dominant imperial communist ideology, which operated on the basis of fear, punishment for disobedience, and reward for obedience. The initially idealistic socialist ideas from the turn of the century, which focused on social equality and justice, free education and health care for all, social unity and integration, had been progressively distorted at the hands of angry and oppressed primitive people, who saw in them an opportunity for revenge and access to power. The communist ideology that developed was oriented toward transfer of power from the upper classes to the lower classes and control over the former upper classes. With such compartmentalized justifications of new forms of oppression, and thorough severing from all the positive aspects of past traditions, that ideology became increasingly corrupt and indiscriminate in its ways. Hence, the whole fabric of social life was based on a heteronomous moral orientation (Kohlberg, 1984). The predominant social values were completely arbitrary, rewarding habitual lying and lack of shame and remorse, plotting, pervasive paranoia and suspiciousness, self-centered power struggles for interpersonal advantage and control—the characteristics of egocentric consciousness (Wade, 1996).

This social system filtered directly into Ivan's life through his father, reinforcing the early adolescent boy's instrumental developmental motivation and establishing it as a norm. It not only did not introduce, but also did not allow an alternative conversation. Not having been exposed to any significant figures of authentic moral authority, Ivan had little to counterpoise to the overwhelming influence of the system. He had little experience with empathy and concern for others and no exposure to reflection on life's greater meaning. Thus, Ivan was reinforced in his self-protective and opportunistic (Cook-Greuter, 1990) ego development, while the upper reaches of his moral reasoning show a punishment-and-reward and good boy/good girl orientation (Kohlberg, 1984). Below are some concrete examples of how this developmental process unfolded.

In Ivan's childhood, his father made the somewhat abrupt but typical for the times transition from a shop assistant to work in the Ministry of Internal Affairs. At that time, the party policy was to summon half-literate workers into government loyalty, teach them the dominant communist ideology, give them positions of power, and thus create a new, manageable ruling class of loyal puppets. Ivan's father specialized in criminology and worked for the government for thirty years. The stories he told his family of the struggle of the good policemen against the bad criminals impressed the young boy and became his ideal, while Ivan's character was influenced by the best in his grandfather—a strong, sturdy Bulgarian who cracked walnuts between his teeth, loved his farm animals, had a grounded, earthly philosophy of life, and had a basic integrity about him. The concept of a steady effort to do good, which will be rewarded, got filtered through the simplistic socially dominant idea of fighting the bad guys who disturb social order. This was the closest Ivan came to a moral ideal.

In some ways, Ivan's concrete operational boyish fascination with cops is reminiscent of Tom's, whose life we will examine next, but it took Ivan in a direction much different than Tom's. While this ideal allowed Tom to work for social order and justice in a democratic society, the same ideal led Ivan to protect a social order that was unjust and oppressive.

Ivan's ambition to become somebody led him to pursue a career in law. Nothing in his environment invited a careful, critical, and self-reflective examination of his real capacities. The standards in the family were primitive, and the social system modeled quick opportunities to rise in status through an amoral, expedient combination of ambition and acquiescence. His father was an example of how one could make a career without much education. So although an average student, Ivan applied to university to study law, explained his failure at the exams with circumstances, worked in a factory for a couple of months, and eventually used his father's connections to get a job at the Ministry of Internal Affairs. He says, "I felt that was my place, my hobby . . . no, not that, what's the word, my calling . . . whether it's genetic, or the fact that my father worked there."

These words reveal the ignorance and mindless confusion that accompanied his search for competence and identity and how readily the available political ideology filled that vacuum. At twenty-two, Ivan became a cop, a government agent and a member of the communist party, with the fancy title "criminal expert." He was sent to specialize in Moscow, and began "to grow as a policeman." As he says with great pride, in his two years in Moscow, he read more books (in criminology and law) than he had ever read in his whole life—a disturbing reflection on the erudition required to be a government agent. He became a loyal government servant, to the point where on the way back from the Soviet Union in 1968, he intercepted the Bulgarian army reserves heading in trains to invade Czechoslovakia, and he never asked a single question. Asked how this event impacted him, he says:

To tell you the truth, it was not spoken about nor written about in the press. Or if there were any discussions, they were in the vein of "if it had to be done, then it had to be done." I simply could not discuss it, nor did I think about it too much. I cannot remember discussing it with colleagues, pondering over it. Nothing stands out in my mind, nothing I remember. It was common knowledge that Czechoslovakia had to be saved from capitalism, that socialism was in danger. If that was the judgment of those in authority, that's how it had to be. I remember no comments about it, no thoughts, no interpretations. That was the system. We were not supposed to interpret, plus we were government servants.

The only personally important thing Ivan remembers, associated with the Czech events, was the fact that a neighbor, who was younger, had been recruited to go to Czechoslovakia and was rewarded on returning with free admission to the university, with no entry exams. He studied law and thus got an advantage over Ivan.

Eventually, Ivan got a chance to pursue a degree in law part-time, through a special quota from his job. In his value system, self-reliance and clever and stubborn resilience are central. As he says, "the struggle with life has to be waged like a man, all the way." These individualistic, instrumental values are, in fact, reminiscent of the ones characteristic of U.S. culture. The difference is that because of his geographic location, he put them to service not to materialistic success in a market economy, but to materialistic success within a destructive sociopolitical ideology. He showed no more and no less critical discernment or concern with larger issues than many of the people interviewed in the U.S. sample. His interpersonal morality is equally limited to his family, friends, and familiar others.

Ivan liked helping people, who turned to him because of his high position. Using his connections to procure for others jobs within the system, or helping somebody get out of trouble with the police, or responding to an emergency, was both empathy driven and an opportunity to feel in authority. Overall, Ivan was still negotiating issues of authority, moral and other, which had not been negotiated earlier in his life. Whereas most conventional adults at some point begin to translate authority issues into issues of responsibility and agency, Ivan showed no trace of agency, limited, mostly interpersonal responsibility, and a strong concern with authority.

For example, asked what kind of causes he contributes to, he relates two occasions on which he gave money. One was for an idea that he likes but did not believe could become a reality and did not care to follow up on or even discuss. The other time was on seeing a Red Cross box in some public place. He did not know what cause it was for, nor did he ask. His thinking was: "If it's for the Red Cross, it will be for good."

Ivan is not a man without social consciousness. He resents the careerism and lack of work ethic he sees in his younger colleagues at the ministry. He feels gratified that his own daughter chooses not to use her father's connections but to confront life's challenges with her own abilities and to serve others as a nurse rather than seek an easy job. He cares enough about his job that if he came into a lot of money, he would invest most of it into restructuring the criminal agency he works for, to make it more efficient and leave some improvement behind after his long career there. He feels responsible to help train and teach younger colleagues. He follows social guidelines diligently and will join in the cleaning of the neighborhood, a common practice and somewhat of a requirement under communism, without being asked, because "I can't sit at home when people are working outside."

Through Ivan's uneven developmental profile runs a mindless social adaptability, with no trace of self-reflection or internal moral conversation. His thinking is full of stereotypes, platitudes, borrowed opinions, and unexamined contradictions, whether he talks about the war in Bosnia and the danger of Islamic fundamentalism, internal or external national security, privatization, or other issues. He divides the world into "us" and "them" in a way consistent with the alien other social perspective-taking (Wade, 1996) of communist ideology. "Us" are the fellow party members and government servants; "them" are all the unknown alien others, be they people of different professional or other interests, class belonging, or, even worse, Westerners. Egocentric communist ideology seemed to be his ultimate frame of reference, with a compartmentalized interpersonal humanity with immediate others.

Ivan is a dramatic example of how vulnerable marginalized people from deprived environments are to all kinds of ideologies. He illustrates the easy transition from what Freire (1973) calls "naive transitive consciousness" to "fanaticized consciousness," in the absence of an alternative conversation with sources of moral motivation.

In his childhood and early youth, Ivan's intuitive moral sense, expressed in his spontaneous attraction to his grandfather's qualities, entered into conflict with the "moral" values of his society. At that fork in the road, and typically around the same age (between six and ten), many moral leaders report feeling different, "being in a world not of my own making" (Bembow, 1994, p. 152). Their first encounters with cognitive dissonance, or "catching culture in a lie" (Bembow, 1994, p. 153), lead them to lean on their moral instincts in order to begin to overcome certain forms of socialization.

All of Bembow's (1994) activists report having a sense of core values always having been with them. For example, Jim, one of her interviewees, describes his early moral awareness, love of truth, and intuitive discernment of untruth. He says that at the age of seven his "little antennas went up" because of "the expressions on people's faces and the tone of people's voices and how people just dismissed certain things" (p. 154). Paul, another one of her activists, says he "always felt, even at a very early age, that [I] should not be associated with violence" (p. 175). In another example from the same source, Clara May refuses the Governor award for her essay because it had been modified without her consent to become less challenging to the status quo of racial injustice. Nothing in her socialization experience prepared her for that moment, all the more that she could "hear [my] Mama crying in the back of the auditorium" and she knew her Mama had "caught hell" to be at the ceremony (p. 174).

Ivan, however, chose not to lean on his intuitive moral sense, but to override it for the sake of personal advancement within the status quo. He bought into the communist social ideal, which rejected the morality of his grandfather and required ideological loyalty instead. In the years that followed, he tried to follow that ideal with as much integrity as he could muster, but he remained conflicted and self-justifying, much like Ramina, although on a different level.

Is Ivan a nice person? Certainly. Is he a sincere soul? No. He compartmentalized away all inconvenient questions and fails to take any real responsibility for the violence, humiliation, and betrayal the social system he served inflicted on millions of people. The fundamental difference between being a nice person and being genuinely sincere is elaborated throughout this chapter, on both levels of adult consciousness.

Tom, Ivan's developmental cross-cultural counterpart, to whom we now move, illustrates the capacity for sincerity and more optimal functioning at the early conformist level. Ivan and Tom share the intellectual and spiritual deprivation of the culture of poverty. Their minds were not trained or drawn upon in any significant way. Yet Tom made different choices than Ivan.

Tom: A Small-Town Florist with Civic Responsibility

Tom illustrates the possibility for a biological adult to operate with pre-CC, otherwise characteristic of adolescence. He exhibits a centrality of moral motivation with all four dimensions developed within the structural limitations of a mostly situational social self-understanding, concrete to abstract operational thought, and an interpersonal self (Kegan, 1982). Tom has not reached the structural developmental threshold for CC, and operates out of conformist consciousness (Wade, 1996). In spite of that, he reveals some critical discernment with regard to social realities, tries to act in ways that are consistent with his moral instincts, contributes in meaningful ways to the social life of his town, and is a respected and positive influence.

Tom is a friendly, talkative, simple, honest all-American man who "loves his government," has spent his whole life in his suburban home town, knows everybody's lives and struggles, and lives and breathes through his community. His florist shop is known in town, and he is respected because of his active involvement in the life of the town. In his words, "I've done everything, I was a policeman for seven years, I've been in politics, I ran for office, and I worked for the mayor of our city for thirty-five years."

He is full of stories, and he makes sense of all his experience through specific situations. No prompts were able to obtain any descriptions of patterns of social self-understanding from him, and every "why" question brought out another long, detailed, and sometimes jumbled, stream-of-consciousness story. However, at the heart of all his confusing accounts were unfailing kindness, humility, and love for people.

Tom came from a poor family, with seven children and limited horizons on life. He is conscious of appearances, and self-image is a central issue. He was a sickly child with low self-esteem. He "felt like a failure in school," "hated school," and wanted to prove that "one doesn't have to be smart to be successful." An adolescent at heart, Tom is still caught in a quest for social identity in his fifties.

Tom's early family environment lacked any character-building moral tension, and fostered direct socialization; however, it was warm, empathic, accepting. Tom dropped out of high school, and went into the Navy at seventeen under minority enlistment for two and a half years. Before that, he managed to get himself into the National Guard at thirteen because he "liked weapons and guns and so forth, you know." His reasons consistently show impulsiveness and naive sincerity. He takes pride in having been "a special state police officer for seven years." He liked the job because of his childish fascination with authority and all institutional forms of power. In spite of his self-image issues, however, his predominant motivation is not self-interest. What he really likes is "working with people." His idea of a cop is "smart looking, respectable; compassionate." He has intuitively found a deeper source of identity, that of a helper.

The better impulses of Tom's heart seem to have been fostered by the significant presence in his life of a stepfather, whose love, generosity, and dedication made him a role model for Tom. This man married Tom's mom with her seven children and cared for them, gaining Tom's lifelong love, respect, and gratitude. Tom responded to the gift this man gave him with a remarkable level of loyalty and commitment.

When his stepfather was terminally sick, Tom, himself a "hypochondriac" with obsessive fears and constant health problems, rose to the occasion with surprising strength. He quit his job and devoted himself to his stepfather's care, refusing to give him up to a nursing home. "He worked too hard for the house we're in, so I says, well I'll take care of him home." After his stepfather underwent a lung cancer operation, Tom was afraid to leave him in the hospital lest "somebody would try to end it for him, and I didn't want that; I wanted him to have whatever life he had to have, that's the way it should be, anyway." This choice speaks of Tom's intuitive life philosophy and respect for life. He learned how to give his stepfather the daily shots he needed, "how to aspirate and so forth with a syringe," and "used to shave him every morning . . . do his hair, men's things . . . he would look forward to it." In spite of his "hypochondriac" fears, Tom did not shrink away from accompanying his stepfather through the last stages of cancer.

He was getting worse and worse, and it was harder to shave him, because he was getting away to just the bones; he only weighed sixty pounds when he was buried. I could pick him up myself. . . . When he died . . . that was really tragic for me . . . he wasn't my blood-father, he was the only father I had since I was six months old.

Tom's stepfather's self-sacrifice seems to have stirred in the boy's heart the capacity for idealism and the desire to reciprocate. That relates to the moral imperative we see in Tom.

Tom's loyalty and commitment to his stepfather carried over to his mother, because just before he died, his stepfather said: "take care of Mom; so that's what I've been doing, since he died, taking care of my mother, who's very sick, she's eighty-seven years old." Although Tom reports himself to be "spend-free, an impulsive buyer," he kept the house together and manages his mother's limited resources with great care so that she could be financially secure for the rest of her life. He took that responsibility in the same generous spirit, alone from among seven siblings, some of whom became alcoholics like his biological father and contributed nothing to the family. This fact highlights once again the element of free will beyond all contextual influences, the capacity of every human being to make a choice to listen to the deeper calling of the heart.

Tom's bond of loyalty and love to the man who adopted and raised him translated into a lifelong, empathic response to all the unloved, struggling ones. His levels of empathy appear much less restricted and more expansive than those of Finnigan or Ada in the next section, although Finnigan and Ada are developmentally more sophisticated. Given Hoffman's (1989) claim that the development toward higher levels of empathy is essentially the result of development in social-cognitive perspective-taking, the contrast among Tom, Finnigan, and Ada reveals once again the neglected and poorly understood power of an activated depth dimension of existence.

If Tom sees a boy with ripped, worn out shoes in the street, he calls him over, buys him a pair of shoes, and sends him on his way, feeling rewarded by the happy look on the child's face. These acts of selfless love and compassion and desire to give run through everything he does. He says if he were to win the lottery, he'd give it all away to charities. One of his favorite charities is "the poor farm . . . for indigent old people." For years, since he has been a florist, every Mother's day he sends a bouquet to every old lady (he says there are thirty-six of them!) and a red carnation to each of the men on that farm. He also does jobs for free for the farm, or tries to buy them something to make their lives there more cheerful (for example, a TV).

They never met me, and I've walked up there and gone right by, and nobody's even said anything, and I feel prouder about that, I wouldn't want them mauling me, you know. I just have that feeling that I know that I did that; they don't have to know who I am, it's not important.

Tom sponsors a child in Africa, and gives to a lot of charities, "to almost anybody that comes through the door if they are wearing a collar," poor priests or nuns who "feed the homeless." In one breath he expresses his complete and naive trust in the institution of priesthood, as well as in many other institutions; in the next sentence he tells a story of how he once asked the priest to identify himself and show Tom his papers.

Tom clearly struggles to differentiate authentic moral authority, and fluctuates between naive trust and suspicion in a dualistic and undifferentiated way characteristic of adolescence. But in his decisions, giving seems to take precedence over not being cheated, and the standards he uses to orient himself reveal both simplicity and a level of critical discernment. For example, "Salvation Army is always a favorite for my heart," because when he was in the National Guard during Hurricane Carol in 1954, during the public safety operations, the Salvation Army offered all the officers on duty coffee and doughnuts for free, and the Red Cross came later and charged a dollar for the same. In these simple, first-hand experiences Tom shows a tendency to observe people and distinguish purity of motive.

His empathy extends to concerns with social justice and equity, although understood interpersonally and with minimal abstraction: "there's some people that I'd like to see have something, that have nothing, you know." Tom's humility, kindness, sharing, and respect for other human beings illustrate the potential of the impressionable naive consciousness (Wade, 1996) of a young child as fertile ground for the development of both empathy and truthfulness with proper guidance and moral induction.

Ma used to give us a dime to go to church, or a quarter to go to church, we'll put it that way, probably fifteen cents. So we go out to church and put a nickel in, and keep the dimes, and now we go to the theater, we had thirty-five cents, but the other kid only had fifteen cents, so we gave him a dime, now we both got twenty-five cents, that's the way it was.

Tom's intuitive moral sense extends into every realm of his life, integrating the public and private domains into one inseparable whole. He is politically involved. "I'm not one to stand back, if I see an issue that I'm against, or for, I go and fight it, or support it." He talks about social justice: "I don't like the rich to get the breaks, and the poor to pay for it." He protests the political corruption, as illustrated by the big government salaries State representatives vote for themselves. He sees the political bashing on TV as the source of negative attitudes.

I used to listen to Rush Limbaugh, but I'm sick and tired of hearing him bashing Democrats. Why should anybody bash anybody? Why don't they let Bill Clinton try to do the best he can, even if he is the stinkiest President we ever had, let him do what he can. Why are we constantly bickering between them two, they get nothing done over there, in Washington. And you get guys like Rush Limbaugh that are constantly, constantly turning the people against government.

He sees the bombing in Oklahoma as an outcome of "warmonger" attitudes, sparked by such TV shows and political bashing. His personal philosophy comes through again, as in the case of his stepfather's death: life is about kindness, working together, giving people a chance. He cannot name his beliefs or talk about how these principles are to be ingrained into social life, but his heart responds to the plight of innocent victims of all this political fighting.

The bombing in Oklahoma will stand out in my mind forever. . . . I saw the little black kid there with glass embedded into his face, and I'll never get over that in my life. I felt so much hurt in my heart, that this is America. How could anybody do this, what was he thinking about?

Contrary to the general assumption in developmental theory that cognitive decentering precedes affective decentering, in Tom affective decentering leads the way. His case supports Allport's (1959) claim that affective provincialism, as well as its opposite, affective decentering, depends on attitudes one learns. Fostering the capacity to respond with one's heart is an important aspect of spiritual education.

Tom's environment, however, did not foster his ability to fully understand that which his heart responded to; hence, his lagging cognitive understanding, which accounts for some of the contradictions in his thinking. For example, despite his compassion for people, he makes blanket racist statements like: "I don't like the Japanese . . . probably Pearl Harbor is within my mind . . . I treat them respectful, I just ignore them." "I'm against open borders, I'm against all these aliens coming into our country."

However, Tom grapples with his contradictions. He loves his next-door neighbors who are also "aliens," and whom he volunteers to help in every way he can, because he believes they are nice people. What comes in his way is his inability to summarize his specific situational experiences with "aliens" into pattern understanding and his resulting reliance, although with discomfort, on ready attitudes.

The failure of Tom's environment to challenge him cognitively amplifies the many cracks in a materialistic capitalist system, in which people are left to themselves. Both Tom's parents came from barren backgrounds. His stepfather was "from the home for little wanderers," and his mother was "a barmaid." Despite his integrity and good heart, Tom did not develop much sense of agency but feels somewhat helpless and inadequate. Asked how he deals with difficulties, he says he goes to the doctor and has a pill prescribed. Nevertheless, his strong civic sense made him work hard to receive permission to dedicate a square to the name of a police detective sergeant whom he admired and to organize its execution. He always votes because "it is a right and a privilege." At one time he chose to work for the same amount that he would have gotten through unemployment because he had no better job options and would not feel right to collect unemployment benefits.

In spite of his cognitive limitations, Tom exhibits intuitive critical moral discernment in virtually every situation he confronts. He is a connected human being who functions from a relative unity of his spiritual capacities to know, to love, and to exercise his will. Table 4.1 uses Danesh's (1994) model to contrast the overall development of Tom's capacities with those of Ivan (Ivan's are marked with one asterisk on the left; Tom's with two asterisks on the right), highlighting the differences between optimal and suboptimal consciousness on the early conformist level.

Table 4.1
Ivan's and Tom's Powers and Concerns

Primary Human Concerns	Main Human Powers		
	Knowledge	Love	Will
Self	Self-experience *Self-discovery** Self-knowledge	Self-preoccupation *Self-acceptance** Self-development	Self-control *Self-confidence Self-responsibility**
Relationships	*Sameness of people** Uniqueness of people Oneness of people	*Acceptance of others Empathy with others** Unity	*Competition Cooperation and equality** Service
Time	*Present (here and now)** Mortality Immortality	Primary union *Separation Secondary union**	Desire *Decision Action**

The contrast between Tom and Ivan shows that pre-CC is superior to ordinary early conformist consciousness in its powers of love and will, in its sincere attraction to truthfulness and responsible action, which prompt the person to use to the fullest their current capacity for reasoning. Pre-CC highlights a significant omission in contemporary education—the failure to fully appreciate the importance of cultivating the qualities of heart in education. Chapter 6 will return to this problem.

In the next two sections of this chapter, we will examine the complexities of conventional adult consciousness, which is still predominant in the world of the twenty-first century. Therefore, it is particularly important to understand the fine line between transitional CC and conventional consciousness and to appreciate more fully how education and social contexts can support the distinctive characteristics of transitional CC. Since this level of consciousness is particularly sensitive to social convention, we will examine separately an American and a Bulgarian pair.

How is conventional consciousness different from the conformist level discussed earlier? While conformist adults rely predominantly on concrete operational reasoning and function out of some configuration of imperial and interpersonal self/other differentiations, conventional adults exhibit predominantly formal operational thought and function out of a mix of interpersonal and institutional self/other differentiations. In that sense, conventional adults are much more able to think through contradictions, to manifest social consciousness, and to discern and deal with patterns in their social experience with a degree of agency. In the following four profiles we can recognize many of the common tensions of adult experience, as most of us know it.

The two pairs also represent two stages in transitional CC. A study of the evolution of critical consciousness in the life of Mahatma Gandhi (Mustakova-Possardt, 1996), identified eight chronologically ascending psychosocial themes in the lifespan unfolding of his moral consciousness. They group around three levels of moral consciousness: pre-CC, transitional CC, and CC, and represent the specifically moral elaborations of the more general psychosocial tasks of ego development (Erikson, 1980). Table 4.2 summarizes the successive ascendance of content themes in the evolution of critical consciousness.

In Tom's profile, we saw the negotiation of moral authority, and ultimately moral responsibility, as the specifically moral elaborations of the general psychosocial task of adolescence—identity. Transitional CC embraces two stages, expanded moral and social responsibility and sociopolitical consciousness, which are the specifically moral elaborations of the general psychosocial tasks of adulthood—love and generativity.

Transitional CC continues to negotiate the earlier themes of moral interest, authority, and responsibility in the context of growing critical discernment, moral introspection, and moral agency. The establishment of meaningful and wholesome relationships within an ever-expanding social radius becomes central and develops in the direction of the formation of a social consciousness concerned with social justice and equity. The first stage of transitional CC is characterized by a not yet fully developed formal operational thought and a distinct fluctuation between an interpersonal and an institutional structure of self. It is represented by William in the American pair below. The second stage of transitional CC, which manifests full formal operations and an established institutional self, is represented by Eliot in the Bulgarian pair.

Table 4.2
Successive Ascendance of Content Themes in the Evolution of CC

Ascendance of tasks (themes)

				Historical and global vision
			Philosophical expansion	
		Principled vision		
		Sociopolitical consciousness		
	Expanded moral and social responsibility			
	Moral responsibility			
Moral authority				
Moral interest				
Pre-CC	Transitional CC		CC	Lifespan development

Transitional CC adds a critical moral dimension to the egoic struggles characteristic of ordinary late conformist and achievement/affiliative consciousness (Wade, 1996). As a result of self-transcending moral motivation prevailing over other primary motivations (such as power, mastery, and prestige), these egoic tensions between mind and heart are negotiated at the optimal capacity of respective stages. The person operates within conventional sociocultural frameworks and tries to redefine different aspects of them, while lacking the systemic ability to encompass and conceptualize the transformation of the whole. The outcome is a distinctive, yet limited, moral agency for positive social change.

Transitional CC increasingly sustains a critical moral dialogue with individual aspects of social reality; that is, we see the birth of problematizing, a fundamental characteristic of Freire's (1973) definition of CC. In problematizing, individual energy may be invested in moral leadership around specific issues. The person defines a cause, identifies sociopolitical choices, and makes decisions about degree and character of involvement. Allegiances with others within social activism are carried beyond affect and increasingly critically examined. Work is often geared toward community empowerment.

Transitional CC, as represented by William and Eliot, is characterized by embeddedness in conventional realities and efforts to operate morally and responsibly within them. Its limitation is the lack of systemic understanding, due to which social patterns may be experienced as overwhelming when one is committed to bringing about positive change. What sustains William and Eliot in their efforts to become agents of change is, in varying degrees, an activated depth dimension of existence, which has not yet been fully integrated with their structural understanding.

COMPLEXITIES ON THE CONVENTIONAL LEVEL: AN AMERICAN PAIR

Finnigan: The Passionless, Casual Life of a Liberal Relativist

Finnigan is a compassionate person, with special empathy for helpless children, young people, and the elderly, with regard to whom he expresses concerns with justice and some social consciousness. However, these concerns remain peripheral to his life, which centers around private interests and priorities. Whatever larger understanding he has gets compartmentalized away because of presumed helplessness to induce positive social change. Finnigan's profile allows us to deepen the important distinctions between what the general cultural norm may consider a "nice" person and a CC person.

Finnigan is a pleasant, relaxed, and friendly man in his late thirties, with an intelligent, attentive, and gentle manner. He seems composed, in no hurry to accomplish anything, and somewhat prematurely aging. His humble and cozy environment indicates a close-knit, loving family, in the physical maintenance of which he is quite engaged.

For the past twenty years, Finnigan has worked with kids eight to eighteen in an afterschool day care program. His sees his work as a calling and sees himself as someone who is always ready to help people. He loves helping children to "find the person within themselves," steering them "in the right direction." He invests extra hours talking to young people about their personal and family problems, making sure they have safe rides home, and doing what he calls "outreach" as a self-defined part of his job. He takes personal responsibility to love and support all the young people he works with "through the growing up process." In his own words, he considers all the kids that walk into his building his own. His reward is "watching a kid, so to speak, going from being a wiseguy into a good, responsible person."

Finnigan has patience, understanding, and respect for children. He extends his caring, nurturing nature to friends, neighbors, and family. He feels for the helpless:

Well, as far as the elderly and kids go, when those two groups get preyed upon, I wish the laws were different for the fact that, you know, mugging an 80-year-old person or molesting a child, they're helpless to an adult. . . . There are people that need medical attention, and they're denied it because they don't have health insurance. . . . I think we'd be better off, maybe, with a socialized medical system, only for the fact that it would reach people that haven't been getting reached and would offer services to those that are denied that for the sake of what their economic situation is.

Yet, Finnigan does not go beyond expressing those concerns in the manner of general wishes. He makes it clear that if he had enough money, he would not be working at his job, but would, perhaps, open a CD store because of his love for music, and because he "would become bored . . . hanging around the house." There is no strong sense of purpose, life commitment, or moral imperative. His social concerns are peripheral to his life and are mainly recognized because of personal contact with the issues.

if issues on a person by person basis affect you directly, then, you know, it's going to be more prevalent in your mind. I mean, there's probably thousands of issues I could bring up, but they don't pertain to me individually at this moment. . . . Plus I think part of it too is you get caught up in your day to day routine.

Asked about his social and political involvement, he explains that he doesn't really follow up on issues, "cause then you have to become active." He offers his disillusionment with the political system and its corruption as the reason for his withdrawal and skepticism. What comes across, though, is a general dissociation from larger life, not because of a lack of critical discernment, but because of the absence of larger commitments and sense of agency and a tendency to compartmentalize larger social reality. Finnigan's critical discernment verges on negativity as he discusses the rottenness of the legal and medical systems, the bureaucracy at all levels of government, and the overly liberal tolerance of all kinds of excesses in society, including violence. He expresses ambivalence in trying to make sense of social reality and, despite his moral instincts, reveals the lack of clear moral frames of reference: "How do you determine what's right . . . morality itself is just a person's values, and everyone's values are different. . . . People think differently. Unless someone infringes on you, then you might have to say, hey, wait a minute."

Unlike the CC individuals who, regardless of their developmental level, always seemed to "know what that fine line is," Finnigan seems at a loss. He recurs to basic "common sense moralism" as he calls it, or conformist interpersonal morality.

For me to be a good person is to respect and be responsible for your own actions. I would not go out and physically harm anybody. I would respect another person's viewpoint, whether it be different from mine or not. Moral judgment, in terms of, you know, I'm not going to go out and sell my kids. You know, people do things like that. . . . I come from a Catholic background. I don't even remember the ten commandments. I can't name them. But that's what I grew up on, and that's what I would say I believe in, so to speak, in terms of day to day life.

These words capture his laid-back and rather un-self-reflective utilitarian approach to morality. He expressed no intense self-searching efforts at internal or external consistency. In the moral dilemmas he describes, his ultimate frame of reference is not so much particular values but rather the outcome or how people will see it. He is not willing to fight difficult causes or engage in defense of justice even around the most specific decisions in his daily work. For example, giving a kid a ride home in the evening and running the risk of being accused of molestation is not something he would be willing to do because it would be difficult to protect his reputation afterward.

Finnigan's moral, social, and political ambivalence is related to his individualistic frame of reference. Asked why it is important to support what one believes, he explains that "if you don't, then you're not an individual . . . you're just a sheep following the rest of the sheep." He considers himself an individual and believes

there's probably maybe something beyond, but I look more from the idea of Darwin, which we're just another animal on this earth, and when we die, we go into the ground and feed the worms, so to speak, if you want to call it that. I just think we're a more intelligent animal than most of the rest. But you can look at it two ways. Are we actually that more intelligent? We're the ones that are destroying the environment and everything else. For people that have faith, I think it's great for them. I have a tendency to—I believe in myself more so than a God or anything along those lines.

Finnigan's critical discernment remains crippled by a narrowly individualistic and materialistic frame of reference, which he shares with many people in the Western world. Suspended in his own small world, he takes pride in standing by his wife and adopting and loving his stepson as his own. Apart from that, he admits that he "was never, you know, a devout, devout anything. . . . I believe in individuals."

Finnigan's case leads one to ponder why an intelligent man with such a good heart and empathy for human beings has not developed CC. He exhibits empathic concerns with relationships, with justice and equity, with not hurting others, and some measure of social consciousness. His work to help educate good, responsible people is essentially work for the betterment of society. However, despite his commitment to supporting the positive growth of young people, his social consciousness is not central to his way of being. He takes only limited responsibility, even within his calling. It is striking that the extent of what he took responsibility for in his own life matched the scope of the moral authority of the only significant authority figure of his childhood—his mother.

Finnigan had a close relationship with his mother (his father died when he was a baby, and his mother raised him and his siblings). He describes her as "God's gift," because she was very loving, understanding, and supportive and met her life's challenge of raising three children as a widow with scanty means with quiet dignity and kindness. He does not remember ever having any real tension with his mother; the only punishment that stands out in his mind is when she wouldn't talk to him after he tried to steal a magazine and got caught. She believed in him and trusted all of his choices, allowing him to grow "happy go lucky," an average student, with reasonably mature judgment and ability to protect his self-interests; an overall nice person who generally stayed out of trouble.

There seem to have been no strong passions in his childhood; always a decent middle ground in a safe, protected environment. He feels that things may have been different had his father been alive because he was "very religious," and "I would have been brought up a little bit differently, a little more rigid." As it was, there were no strong frames of explicit moral reference beyond basic niceness, although his mother was a genuine Catholic.

Finnigan's older brother became a father figure, teaching him to excel in sports and be performance conscious. Finnigan learned the distinction between playing "the better people" rather than the "lousy kids," and did not question the distinction, but focused on finding a niche for himself in the system of things. His interests centered around overcoming his own insecurity by developing competence and helping other kids do the same. He did not have any big dreams, or, as he says, "I never took myself too seriously" but had what he calls "that reality check." In the place of adolescent inspiration and search for ideal models, a certain casual, relaxed attitude set in. He repeated in his life the relaxed, honest, intimate, casual relationship he had with his mother: "I'm very easy. My wife thinks I'm so laid back that I'm asleep sometimes, but I don't let—If I cannot change something, I don't let it affect me, or at least outwardly affect me. I've enjoyed my life."

Finnigan's case exemplifies the dual nature of the construct of agency—both a structural developmental and moral motivational. As a structural developmental phenomenon, agency is related to the degree of differentiation of the self. In this respect, Finnigan is not lacking; he manifests a formed institutional self. Nevertheless, he tends to remain a skeptical, helpless, passive observer. His life, along with a number of other cases, suggest that the scope and degree of authentic moral authority in early life may have to do with the scope and degree of personal moral authority, responsibility, and agency that the young person develops as an adult.

Finnigan's life lacked figures who might introduce tension around responsibilities and stimulate the development of broader responsibilities and agency. To the degree that his mother modeled virtues of character such as honesty, fidelity, constancy, kindness, patience, and compassion, he developed some moral character and moral identity. However, the absence of critical moral discourse as an organizer of experience and of values that require a higher level of engagement, such as earnestness, righteousness, high standards, courage, and active love, left him prone, like many other American youngsters, to a direct socialization into sports and peer groups.

Finnigan's rootedness in relativism does not offer a basis for enduring commitments beyond the self. His concerns with right and wrong seem to balance out with his concerns with self-interest. He has no framework for thinking about community in the context of larger society, no sense of purpose in common with other people. His moral understanding is self-referential and does not have the power to fuel a strong inner sense of imperative; rather, it vacillates between normative and instrumental concerns.

Overall, in spite of his mother's spirituality, the depth dimension of Finnigan's existence appears unactivated. No idealism stirred his successful social adjustment. Problem solving took the place of problematizing. His motivation tends to be predominantly expedient.

Finnigan's case is extremely symptomatic of the prevailing culture in the United States, as it reflects a utilitarian, relativistic morality and a limited individualistic materialistic worldview quite common among the interviewees for this study. The dramatic absence, both in the overall culture and in people's educational experience, of a recognition of the spiritual potential of a human being and of life as an opportunity to rise to one's potential and seek for and actively embrace beauty, truth, and goodness has left its imprint on every level of discourse and every domain of human activity.

Variations on the theme of Finnigan surround us on all sides, sometimes more sophisticated, yet essentially the same. Academe, which sets the general moral and educational tone, is frequently an example in that direction, as Wilshire (1990) poignantly shows in his *The Moral Collapse of the University: Professionalism, Purity, and Alienation*. Moral intensity and passion are confused with fanaticism and fundamentalism and therefore feared and distrusted. They do not easily fit into a corporate consumer establishment, where the most fundamental collective human enterprises—education, health care, and the justice system— have become the most lucrative businesses.

On an even larger scale, Finnigan's ambivalence illustrates the dilemmas of secular individualism, as it stands in opposition to religious fanaticism and intolerance worldwide. Our world is divided and torn apart by those two extremes. The newly emerging interreligious dialogue, initiated by the World Parliament of Religions, is now seeking to restore a balanced approach to human life that recognizes and honors the rational soul.

In contrast to Finnigan, William has found in the same casual, laid-back culture a reason to resist easy solutions. He lives with moral imperative and a sense of awe, which is not found in any area of Finnigan's life. William's story helps one understand the murky area of transitional CC in its earliest form, expanding moral and social responsibility.

This is a time when horizons are first beginning to expand beyond one's personal life, and questions are increasingly seen as consequential in the wider world. Full-fledged moral agency has not yet emerged, and the sphere of interest is still limited to more immediate interpersonal group loyalties. It is possible to remain stuck for many years in this place, as is the case with Finnigan. That seems to happen in people whose ego strength is not sufficient to overcome the security and attraction of conventional life, yet whose sense of truth and justice keeps pulling them beyond. This is a developmental place fraught with contradictions and limitations, yet the feeling left by such a person's way of being is one of integrity and potential for growth.

William: A Life of Integrity and Awe

A man in his sixties, William belongs to the generation of our parents, when for many conservative people from lower middle-class backgrounds like himself and without a particularly progressive education, firm social rootedness was very important since the world was a less dynamic place than we know it. Hence, William's life story is very traditional. He is the father of six children, worked for many years as a service representative for IBM, divorced, and later remarried. Nothing in his story strikes one as an example of radical openness to growth. Yet, he is generative, healthy-looking, filled with awe of life, poised and ready for new growth, and eagerly looking for ways to serve others and help redress social imbalances. Despite all his contradictions, William is strangely empowered.

William took this opportunity to reflect on his life with readiness. He spoke with a clarity and coherence which revealed a habit of self-reflection. He was open and forthcoming with his personal understanding, without being profuse in either words or emotions.

William's sense of responsibility to others is a dominant theme throughout his life. In his young years, it was coupled with a sense of limited agency and external locus of control. He dropped out of school, joined the Army, got married while in the service, had children, and had to go to work instead of continuing his studies.

His married life was dominated by relationships. He describes himself as someone who is "more sensitive to people . . . I like to satisfy." Both his family and his job gave him an opportunity to do that. They also gave him a valued sense of familiarity, solidity, rootedness, predictability, accomplishment, and control. Asked how his family life contributed to his sense of who he is, he turns the question around: "How did my family life contribute? I think, how did I contribute to my family life, how did I contribute?"

This is a theme that runs through everything he has to say: I am what I can give, what I can share with others! His habitual morality is expressed in the sense of satisfaction of giving to his six children and grandchildren both financial assistance and understanding, love, support, and shared experience. In the same way that he gives to his family, he also gives to others. Through his lodge, he volunteers in a VA hospital where he spends time with the veterans, distributes food baskets for holidays, gives blood, raises funds for charities. He does not see his own contributions as anything extraordinary because, in his understanding, the veterans have given to their country amply and deserve some reciprocity. He speaks about his volunteering at the VA hospital with humility: "It's nice to give back—you know, if you've gotten a little, it's nice to give back something. It's a good feeling. It's a sense of sharing. Doing what you have to do to help others."

William's fundamental moral orientation becomes most evident when he talks about raising his children. He talks about "the times we had together and the love we had together, from the times when they were small." Even though he and his wife could not afford to do many exciting things with six children, it was the togetherness that mattered. He also speaks with a lot of love about his lost seventh child, a girl who was born severely retarded, started having grand mal seizures at one, and died at two. "It was a joy to have her. It was a very innocent child, had a start in life, and was taken away. She just didn't have a chance."

William's love for his children was combined with a strong sense of moral responsibility to teach his children some moral values and standards to which he believed the children needed to be held.

You give the kids a sense of value at home, and then they went to school, and it seems like whatever you gave the kids, they'd come home and say they don't have to do that. We're our own boss. You can't tell us what to do. Kids weren't disciplined. I guess they don't believe in that any more. . . . It's entirely different than the situation I was brought up in. I went to a parochial school, where they had discipline, taught a sense of values, taught to respect authority. Authority was your parents, anyone older than you were. You could question authority, but you had to respect it too. And I think that all that started to go in the sixties. Everything started to change, and I don't know if it's for the better or not. . . . And you can be a friend, but you have to be a parent also. There are times when you got to make some decisions.

In spite of some ambivalence about his own agency, William draws important distinctions not heard in too many other interviews for this study. William was among only four out of the nineteen American parents spoken to, who identified a need and felt a strong moral responsibility to resist the cultural tide and teach his children alternatives to prevailing values. His discerning understanding of the surrounding cultural pressures allows him to differentiate between being a loving and appreciative parent and trying to please one's children by becoming their friend and peer, relinquishing authority and the responsibility that goes with it. He met the resistance of his wife who "just wanted to be a friend instead of a parent," and he had many self-doubts; nevertheless, he did not give up what he felt was his responsibility to uphold.

He also differentiates between respecting authority and being able to question authority; he questions the dominant cultural tendency to couple critical questioning of authority with an unwillingness to respect any authority. He does not exhibit absolutist thinking and does not reject the changes that came with the sixties, but contemplates them with some fundamental concerns. These concerns reveal the presence of a internal moral standard in spite of his multiplistic reasoning (Perry, 1968).

When William talks about how his children came out as adults, he defines successful adulthood with having a sense of responsibility and accomplishing things. With love and sadness he recognizes that some of his children became truthful, respectful people with the integrity to go through hard times with dignity, work hard, and teach their own children right, whereas others were rebellious and untruthful and had all kinds of problems. He does not come across as judgmental or self-righteous; rather, he feels responsible and struggles with self-doubts about whether he did all he could have done to help his children find their way.

Altogether, William strikes one as a man trying to be in touch with his feelings in spite of his generational difficulties with that; he comes across as self-reflective, caring, morally responsible, with integrity of character. He also strikes one as a connected human being. All the moments of supreme joy he describes are moments of being at one with himself, nature, a team. The very language he uses to describe his happy moments is markedly different from the even-keeled, low-keyed, pragmatic, and slightly indifferent cultural norm we heard in Finnigan. He talks without inhibitions about being "elated" when his first son was born, about "having produced this beautiful looking baby," having produced "life that could mean something to a lot of people, to the world!" He describes a comparable feeling of elation when watching the sunsets over the mountains of Tucson, the scenery, "seeing what God has wrought," the "amazing, amazing sunsets and the beauty." He reveals an ability to be inspired, to marvel at beauty and harmony. What comes across in all these examples are William's faith in the ultimate meaningfulness of life and his sense of awe and oneness with it. His life is a consistent effort to align himself with that meaning.

The significant people William describes unite the two aspects of his character: love and caring, and the ability to go against the cultural tide, make difficult moral decisions, and operate out of character and internal moral standard. From his second wife he says he learned "a lot of love and caring for people." They had both of their mothers living with them for a couple of years before they died and took care of them. That didn't seem to have been a difficult decision, rather a natural outcome of habitual morality: "That's just the way we were brought up. You took care of your parents. And that's what we did. We felt that was our responsibility, and so we welcomed them in our house. That's social welfare at its best, you know; it was our responsibility and we did it."

William's circle of friends is composed of people who, like himself, have sought and found within the social system an institutional way (the lodge) to help others, share, and address social needs. The routes chosen for social activism are conventional and do not involve challenging the system. They rely on traditional roles and appeal to conservative men like William, who have always worked hard and are responsible people but have a difficult time exploring their inner experience and making dramatic changes in their ways. These routes offer an opportunity for interpersonal identification: in William's words, he enjoys "the camaraderie of the social life too" because "we have a sense of a social organization."

William displays the characteristic limitation of transitional CC: the inability to understand the social system and have a coherent guiding vision of positive change, as well as the inability to include one's own institution in a similar critically discerning examination. As a result, he has many contradictions. Having struggled all his life with self-doubts, lack of self-confidence and agency, William is drawn to people who give the impression of strength. He doesn't question the emotional price paid in some of those cases; introspection and intimacy with others are clearly issues he compartmentalizes. He respects men who have the courage to make difficult decisions and who resist invitations to reexamine those decisions.

Roosevelt was a good man and did what he had to do to bring the people out of the Depression . . . to solve the problem. . . . Whatever his policies were, but he was a leader. He led us during the Second World War. . . . Started some social policies. I don't know if they are good now or not, but he started them and they were good for the times. And Truman, the same thing. Him and MacArthur. MacArthur went in Korea . . . tried to place himself above everything else, and Truman kind of was a man for the times, says you can't do that. He was the guy that successfully brought the Second World War to conclusion. Gave the ok to drop the atom bomb. He had to make the tough decision. . . . They were the right decisions for the right time. Now people try and revise history and I don't know how you can revise that. They did what they had to do for the times. They seemed to make the right decisions. Guys who were willing to make the tough decisions are the guys that stick out in my mind. The real leaders. Tom Watson sticks out in my mind. . . . Here again, started a company from scratch, made the company into one of the greatest companies in the world at the time. . . . They weren't afraid to make the decisions. And they stuck by their decisions.

William's multiplistic reasoning cannot reconcile the contradictions in his thinking. Manifesting a clear achievement orientation (Wade, 1996), he admires these tough and successful self-reliant individuals. Yet, he values cooperation, teamwork, and team accomplishment. In his work in IBM, as well as in his current lodge commitments, he loves working with his peers.

Going to your peers, getting some knowledge from them, getting their experience, kind of working together, I enjoyed that. I do that now. I'm retired, but I work in a fraternal organization. We do the same thing . . . working with people, getting a job done. . . . Bringing a not so successful business operation in line and making it successful. . . . And the profits we get out of the business, we disperse to charity. That's a good feeling.

In William, we see a constant struggle between wanting to maintain open communication with people and wanting to be permeable and actively receptive, and his inner resistance and need to protect his institution. His political beliefs reflect that: he does not express empathy with social groups other than the veterans with whom he has personal contact.

He studies issues closely and draws an interesting distinction between the ideological significance that's placed on practically every issue and its common-sense value. Although his position can easily be categorized as conservative right, his judgment defies such simplifications:

We have to get back to basics and common sense again. I think we've lost that. Everything has become too politicized. You have to do what's good for the country and what's good for the world, what's good for us. . . . The budget issue is common sense, and yet we're trying to make big politics out of it. . . . And one party won't give in to the other because it's not their issue. They've taken over an issue.

William reveals the same moral imperative and unity-and-common-sense-above-ideology approach when he shares his thoughts about international issues such as the war in Bosnia.

Let's stop the fighting. Let's get together. What are the issues here? There's no sense in

what they are doing. . . . The nonsense that's going on in the world. . . . Killing of innocent people. What? Just a political thing—'cause I'm right? You don't believe in the other
person, what they're doing is right? They're just as right as you are. Or that your faith is a
little different than somebody else's faith? People have been killed in the name of God,
it's ridiculous. It's terrible. I'm sure God didn't want that.

William does not use words as cliches, but takes the responsibility to examine
the meaning behind the words. When he talks about the leadership responsibilities of the United States, another mainstream conservative preoccupation, he
takes it to a deeper level: "We have to be serious about our role as a leader in the
world. And show leadership in this world—whether it be the ebola virus,
whether it be Bosnia, whether it be South Africa. Don't shirk your duty if you
are a leader. . . . We have to be consistent in the roles we take in the world."

His suggesting that the United States has not really acted as a leader does not
come from partisan loyalties; his focus is more on the sense of seriousness itself.
The same critical discernment comes through a seemingly conservative position
on welfare:

I think we've gone overboard in welfare. People lost sense of their work ethic because of
welfare. . . . We have to have common sense in that, because I think welfare is just a gift
from people to another group. It's a way of redistribution of the wealth, but it's actually a
gift. . . . Talk about Roosevelt at the time. He instituted some type of welfare, social security, but the welfare he instituted, as I remember, was a civilian conservation corps, the
public works projects, where he gave people jobs, and that wasn't welfare because they
worked, they were given jobs so they could exist and pull themselves up. Now you don't
have to work. We've lost that work ethic. . . . It's great to give, but you got to be careful.

William is consistent in applying the same principle with his own children: he
loves giving, but is careful not to undermine his children's sense of responsibility. Asked to define his own understanding of morality, William describes it as
"a sense of honesty, a sense of religion, a sense of good, bad." He elaborates:
"religion should give you probably a sense of what's good and bad in life, a
sense of spiritual goal, and how you attain that spiritual goal . . . a sense of values."

William struggles with his religious commitment to the Roman Catholic
Church.

I think there's the same God for all denominations, no matter what they are. I feel sorry
for the people that say there's a difference between your God and my God. They have to
fight because there is a difference. I think there's one God, and in your heart, if you believe that, and he's a loving God, I don't think he wants us to suffer. I don't think he wants
us to go to war. And whatever the ritual is . . . I'll go attend . . . where they say you con-
gregate to honor and adore this God. . . . And I'm not going to change the religion I was
brought up in. I still hold some of those truths.

In summary, William is a compelling example of both the strengths and the
limitations and contradictions of transitional CC in its first stage, expanded
moral and social responsibility. He combines personal integrity with some

prejudices and contradictions that he is unable to fully reflect on, while manifesting typically limited agency. However, he defines his own conventional balance between understanding and observing the norms of his society while maintaining his independent investigation of truth and personal freedom of self-definition. He questions his social environment, makes active efforts to redefine his relationship to social realities in congruence with his morally defined understanding, and seeks an alternative vision of how things should be. This is the hallmark of transitional CC.

The one central presence that stands out in William's life, otherwise caught in the American cultural context of individualism (Bellah et al., 1985), is his deep faith in God. It amplifies his strong moral sense and clearly activates the depth dimension of his existence. It counterbalances his vulnerable sense of self and proneness to ego defenses such as his taste for toughness and allows him to live happy, self-fulfilled, inspired and hopeful, hungry to learn more about life. Table 4.3 highlights the differences between optimal and suboptimal consciousness on the early conventional level, by summarizing the contrast in the overall development of William's capacities with those of Finnigan (Finnigan's are marked with one asterisk on the left, William's with two asterisks on the right).

Table 4.3
Finnigan's and William's Powers and Concerns

Primary Human Concerns	Main Human Powers		
	Knowledge	Love	Will
Self	Self-experience *Self-discovery** Self-knowledge	Self-preoccupation *Self-acceptance Self-development**	Self-control *Self-confidence Self-responsibility**
Relationships	Sameness of people *Uniqueness of people** Oneness of people	Acceptance of others *Empathy with others** Unity	Competition *Cooperation and equality Service**
Time	*Present (here and now) Mortality** Immortality	Primary union *Separation Secondary union**	Desire *Decision Action**

As we can see, transitional CC in its first stage, expanded moral and social responsibility, shows a clear developmental advantage over its non-CC conventional equivalent in the degree to which it manifests its spiritual powers around central human concerns. It is more attracted to goodness and committed to the development of the self and exercises its will accordingly. With a comparable understanding and orientation in the area of relationships, it is yet more whole-hearted in the exercise of will—committed to service. It thinks more deeply about life, is more attracted to creating meaningful relationships, and is less prone to excessive deliberation and more able to act wholeheartedly. Altogether, as was the case with pre-CC, moral consciousness on this level is superior to its developmental counterpart in the activated powers of love and will, or the presence of heart.

COMPLEXITIES ON THE CONVENTIONAL LEVEL— A BULGARIAN PAIR

In the pair below, both Ada and Eliot appear to exhibit, at first glance, the second stage of transitional CC, sociopolitical consciousness. They both have a clear sense of institutional self and well-defined relationships with their socio-political milieu based on fully formal operational considerations. A closer examination, however, reveals an expediency orientation in Ada slightly predominant over her moral motivation. As a result, when we meet her, she appears more on the side of conventional non-CC.

Ada: A Moralistic, Conservative Pro-Communist Bulgarian Doctor

Ada was the most difficult Bulgarian case to analyze in terms of CC; she showed such a mix of moral responsibility, intelligence, and impermeability in her strangely unquestioning acceptance of communist ways. The ability of the components and dimensions of CC to help explain her way of being in itself constitutes evidence of the feasibility of the construct.

Ada is a committed Bulgarian pediatrician in her fifties, who takes pride in her profession and for whom medicine is no less than a lifelong calling. A person of high educational standards, she took her father's legacy of solid commitment to the medical profession (he was a well-respected veterinarian), made it her calling, and worked her way up from a small village deep in the country, through all the hurdles of a rigid totalitarian social and educational system, to a prestigious position in the Medical Academy in the capital of Sofia.

Ada resembles William with her pervasive sense of moral values of honesty, loyalty, responsibility, hard work, righteousness, truthfulness, constancy, perseverance, and knowledge. Her values made her withdraw from what she saw as unsatisfying social contacts throughout school and limit herself to her love for books, becoming an honors student. The same values did not allow either her or her father to use political privileges, which her family could have taken advantage of due to the earlier contributions of an uncle to the communist idea. In a society where political privilege was the surest door to good education and career, she took pride in working her way through a series of competitive contests for progressively better professional opportunities. She never entered the communist party although prompted to do so in order to be considered more reliable in the more and more responsible positions she held. She spoke her mind and did not compromise her understanding and principles, but worked hard to earn her own professional standing in spite of interpersonal conflicts with authoritarian superiors. She distrusted the pompous sloganeering and ulterior career motives of open party meetings in the workplace and remained ideologically aloof. Altogether, she spoke of consistent concern with normative issues.

Ada's personal and professional integrity made her condemn careerism. As a result of the restructuring of the Bulgarian Medical Academy after the fall of communism, she had to choose between remaining within the Academy and enhancing her career but abandoning her commitment to prophylactic pediatrics, since that clinic had to be moved outside the academy, or accompanying her clinic at a new place where she would not be able to take a higher position. She chose the second. She felt committed to defending the importance of prophylactic pediatrics through her own work and personal reputation; she also felt a loyalty to her colleagues in prophylactic pediatrics who were working toward the same goal. Ada did not feel it would be professionally ethical to move to a different clinic within the academy and take a higher position than that of people who had worked within that clinic for many years, in spite of the fact that the Board of the Medical Academy was willing to offer her that. In her professional choices, she appears guided by normative rather than instrumental concerns.

Ada's work ethic, high standards, and sense of personal moral responsibility within her own context parallel William's. She is also a devoted and self-sacrificing parent and daughter who responds to every need in the family regardless of how great a load for her that entails. Her greatest reward is the success of her children and the wellbeing of her parents whom she deeply appreciates. Within her much more communal and interconnected culture, she extends herself, just like William, beyond her immediate responsibilities and offers her medical expertise and other forms of help to a network of colleagues, old and new friends, and neighbors. An institutional self with clear boundaries, she juggles all her self-defined responsibilities remarkably successfully, with self-respect and without bitterness.

Yet, a closer evaluation showed that her questioning of social relations is rather selective and out of a more self-aggrandizing than genuinely moral motivation. Although she takes responsibility to redefine her relationship with social conditions in congruence with her understanding, she does not appear guided by a search for an alternative vision of how things should be on grounds of explicit concerns with issues of justice and equality. Instead, she shows a tendency to rely on self-righteous, negative criticism, and remains impermeable to social influences.

Ada is an individualist who does not identify with any community, not even her professional community to which she is loyal. She feels morally superior to people around her and exhibits a warrior hardness, a lack of humility, and a self-righteous tendency to dismiss other points of view. In her interview, she spoke patronizingly of her fellow students at school and later of her husband, and she exalted herself over colleagues who had different political convictions. She condemned the student movement during the fall of the communist regime in 1989 because, in her opinion, the students had no reasons to protest. Asked to elaborate on how she reached that conclusion, she said that the students at her university did not strike, which was supposed to be evidence that there were no serious grievances. Other sources reported that, in fact, some students at that university did go on strike.

Ada shared that she asked her students what they thought of the strike, and they said it was nonsense. However, in Bulgarian universities, professors have a lot of power and authority over their students and, more often than not, represent the establishment and enforce its expectations and strict limits. The students' choice to speak their minds to their professors is not a simple matter and may have grave consequences. During the events in question, the faculty was as polarized as the rest of society between supporting the democracy movement, and supporting the communist party line and dismissing student concerns. The pro-democracy professors suspended classes and went on strike with their students. The pro-regime ones continued classes. Hence, Ada had every reason to know that by actually teaching during the strike, she was making her position clear to the students who chose to remain. Yet, she seemed willing to use her power and authority to obtain from the students the answer she wanted and was not entertaining any discomfort in retrospect.

In the same vein, she refused to recognize the legitimacy of the political discontent of many people with the communist regime, continuously pointing out how courageously she had been able to work her way up and that other people could have done the same instead of complain and cause havoc in society. Since she appeared to be such a socially responsible person, with a social law and order orientation (Kohlberg, 1984), it appeared that she may be aware of some of the issues involved but may disapprove from a moral point of view of the methods used by the democracy movement during the transition from communism. However, it became clear that her seeming critical discernment disguised a tendency to rationalize her own emotional needs for safety and security in a way described by Wade (1996) as characteristic of conformist consciousness. Ada seemed intolerant of ambiguity and tended to rationalize her reactions.

As she criticized the social changes during the current attempts at democratization and idealized the secure and familiar communist past through a semblance of reasonable arguments, Ada increasingly demonstrated that she was guided by self-interest predominant over moral motivation. For example, she objected to the restitution of government-appropriated private land on the grounds that the grandchildren of the owners whose land was once taken away should not have a claim on it now, because had it not been taken away, it might have been squandered by the family itself. The semblance of logic was that if we want to start from a better place now, we should all start equal and create better social structures. On closer questioning, it became clear that she was bitter that she had no land to gain from the restitution and would be falling behind and losing hard-won social status as a result of that law. Ada's sense of identity proved to have a stronger class component than she was willing to admit. Having adapted to the repressive ideological society and having found a way to be successful, she expressed frustration with the way the democratization process tried to revert a lot that had been done in the last fifty years of communist rule and its insistence on making public all the human abuses of the communist regime before any reconciliation could occur. In her view, so much had been accomplished during the years of communism that these things needed to be left alone as things of the past.

Ada carries the same impermeability and self-protective closedness into her family life. Since the political changes of 1989, her growing resentment toward the social chaos of the transition to democracy has led her to become a staunch supporter of the Communist party and the old social order. She understates the social and political injustice of the communist regime, refuses to discuss controversial issues, and criticizes her husband and older daughter for supporting the Democratic party. With her friends, she avoids political discussions and refuses to draw any connections between professional medical and social issues. Her choices and decisions come from an inner place that does not include others and the outer world.

In trying to understand the way of being of this intelligent, responsible, and otherwise caring woman, the interviewer went back to her family experience growing up. Ada's sense of identity was formed in a profoundly ideological and polarized environment, where beliefs and ideas were defining, and contrasts between moral and amoral choices were clear-cut. She came from a family that united high ideals and education, and a prominent social profile on her father's side, with simple working class honesty, warm-heartedness, generosity and work ethic on her mother's side. Some of her father's brothers were political figures—one of them close to the king, another a close collaborator with one of the prominent Bulgarian socialist thinkers before the communist revolution. Because of this mixed heritage, after the revolution her father was forced to leave the capital and go deep into the countryside, as was the practice with many intellectuals who were considered of questionable allegiances. He made the choice to remain there for the rest of his life and, like many other professionals at the time, adopted a neutral political stance, buried family history in silence, and focused on family and personal values.

Ada grew up rooted in an idyllic country life amid the goodness and hardworking generosity of villagers and their genuine respect for her father. She was "the daughter of the vet and the school teacher," the two most prominent figures in a village. She was influenced by books, the strong moral authority figure of her father, and her mother's warm, self-sacrificing love. However, like Ramina, she made certain choices in what became defining in her life. She identified most completely with her father, a respectable, uncommunicative, unempathic, righteous man. He raised her with clear moral values and standards, but they were one-sided and upheld in an authoritarian moralisitic manner rather than used as explicit organizers in an ongoing moral discourse around daily life.

Ada's father's patriarchal moral standards reveal characteristic limitations and contradictions. Although he was an honest, hard-working, and dignified man, his strict norms did not prevent him from having an extramarital affair which eventually ruined his marriage. He taught his children work ethic and self-reliance, rewarded silence, and made Ada his favorite because she never confronted him on his choices, while penalizing financially her brother for speaking out and condemning his behavior.

Ada's environment did not stimulate critical moral discourse or self-reflection. Even the father's banishment from the capital to a village by the communists was never discussed in the family, and Ada only found out later. In this philistine patriarchal environment with its characteristic inconsistencies, in which the security and well-being of the immediate family required observing conventional social mores, Ada learned not to question, as long as she could find a niche for herself. She was encouraged to study and excel and developed an achievement orientation with no dominant search for life meaning larger than the self. She remembers no significant quests, and her definition of happiness constituted a reasonable level of comfort and freedom. Asked about her personal philosophy or spiritual beliefs, she translates that into observing concrete rituals and traditional Bulgarian Orthodox Christian holidays. Altogether, Ada dealt with her shame around her father's extramarital relationship in a small village where everybody knew the family by developing strong class identity and stereotypes, moralisitic self-righteousness, and emotional estrangement, reminiscent of Ramina's. Neither one operates with more than minimal self-reflection. Both exhibit a predominantly fear-based orientation to morality, which often borders on moralism. Both illustrate the importance of subtle motivational orientations to the overall quality of consciousness.

Ada's case is a compelling illustration of the need to understand CC in specific contexts. Without understanding the highly ideological nature of former communist societies, one can easily mistake the prevalence of normative concerns in her conversation for moral motivation. However, in communism, the public model set before people by sociopolitical leaders was one of disguising crude self-interest behind moralistic ideological language, quite similar to contexts of religious fundamentalism. Ada's case shows that authentic moral motivation is a much more complex phenomenon than the overt embracing of a moral standard. Analyzing her motivational structure through the expanded motivational template, offered as an assessment tool in chapter 3, reveals the preponderance of self-interest in a motivational profile of mixed motifs.

The cases of Ramina and Ada show that while the youthful idealistic love for books and education and the striving to excel are important in the formation of moral character, in some cultures where that is the norm for intelligent people, as was the case for East Europeans, for whom learning was the way to resist the oppressive regime, such an inclination does not necessarily indicate an authentically discerning mind. Authentic moral motivation is what people call "a pure heart." That is not a heart free of tensions, but a heart that genuinely loves truth more than anything else and propels the mind to keep up with that quest. When all the possible analysis of environmental conditions has been done, it remains impossible to say why some people manage to preserve the purity of their hearts into adulthood and others in similar conditions are moved to make other choices.

Eliot: A Bulgarian Dentist and Early Sociopolitical Activist

Eliot's story parallels Ada's in many ways, while illustrating her CC counterpart within conventional consciousness. He also grew up in the countryside, in a strong patriarchal family. Similar to Ada, Eliot is committed to his profession as his life calling. Along with his family, it represents the main axis of his life. Also like Ada, he describes a patriarchal family culture dominated by the authority of strong male figures; an environment in which women have a secondary role. However, unlike Ada's childhood, his life seems populated by significant adults in the extended family, each of whom contributes in an important way to his sense of moral identity.

Education is very important in the family, and there is a tradition in the professions: Eliot's father and brother are dentists, one of his uncles is an architect, the other a chemistry professor. His mother is semiskilled. An accountant with "only" secondary education, she was not allowed to pursue college education with the advent of communism but was penalized with physical labor instead for the fact that her father was considered well-off. Two generations back, Eliot's grandfather had a trade—he had a store for books and stationery, and his grandmother was a housewife. The family tradition and pride had a material expression in the beautiful old Bulgarian house of his grandfather, which had traditional Bulgarian Renaissance architecture and was situated in the center of town. The town itself is a cultural and historic center, which preserved the best Bulgarian spirit and tradition of over ten centuries. Eliot's childhood is inseparably associated with that house and what it represented. His sense of moral identity is securely rooted in a rich patriarchal culture and family tradition.

Eliot's story captures in succinct ways the recent history of the country. After the communist revolution in 1944, the house was knocked down by the populist totalitarian government, and an ugly apartment building was raised in its place. Eliot has never quite forgiven this violation of his family pride and tradition. Nevertheless, he chose to remain in the town of his grandfathers and established a professional standard in dentistry there, which is his family's particular contribution to the town. Every decision Eliot describes, every detail of his life, seems morally colored and a reflection of his family's resistance to the political and cultural changes that came with communism.

Eliot speaks about the history of his family as it intertwines with the history of the nation. He identifies with the political convictions of one of his grandfathers who was a member of the House of Representatives before communism and supported a prominent Bulgarian political leader with a Western orientation. Given the general Russian orientation and the rise of communism, that was a brave and unusual stand at the time. Overall, Eliot reveals impressive knowledge of the history of Western civilization and rootedness in time and place. In this sense, he is a typical representative of the Bulgarian intelligentsia, with both its solid historical understanding and its conservative bent and stereotypes.

Every member of his extended family had to deal with some form of social injustice, oppression, and persecution, because of the ideological distrust of communism for educated professional people. Each stood with courage and dignity, preserved his or her values and beliefs, worked hard to survive and educate himself or herself, and transcended the sociopolitical circumstances. The family is rich in examples of how character is built and grounded in virtues, examples of high personal moral standard.

Eliot remembers his grandmother, who was "a very religious woman of refined character" and remarkable composure, and who would never blame anybody for life's misfortunes but always took responsibility herself. Although the family was victimized, none of these significant adults in his life acted like victims; each was a moral agent in his or her limited environment. The family found a sense of community with other families in the neighborhood also struggling to preserve their integrity against the tide, and their children grew up together, sheltered into a carefully protected, loyal, interconnected, and morally aware environment.

Eliot is the epitome of this familial, cultural, and historical background. He has a strong underlying sense of moral identity. His commitments, like those of his family, are primarily limited to an interpersonal circle, and noticeably less permeable to the rest of the world. The meaning of life is limited to adhering to one's family and class values and remaining true to oneself regardless of circumstances.

This form of individualism, which we saw in Ramina as well, is typical of East European existential resistance. It is colored by an implicit faith in a meaning and wisdom of life larger than the self, a higher truth to which one has to remain faithful. This faith is the motivational source of the continuous elaboration of connections between right and wrong, good and bad, true and false, which serves as a vantage point for critical discernment and self-reflection.

Here are some examples from Eliot's life. He remembers schooling as his first direct encounter with the repressive political system that created rigid educational structures to socialize children into the mainstream ideology. At the time, he resisted intuitively, internally comparing school requirements with the authentic sources of moral authority that he knew in his life, and found those requirements wrong and morally lacking. Thus, he gradually developed critical discernment. As he entered adolescence, freedom of speech and convictions became an ideal, and he stood up for it openly for the first time when he was thirteen, running serious personal risks for his future.

As he looks back at how he negotiated the repressive regime, Eliot talks about the oppression on a systemic level—another important characteristic of the Bulgarian sample. People who grew up in morally grounded political resistance learned early to discern systemic ideological manipulation. Hence, their moral choices in those circumstances seem to have provided an optimal challenge to their cognitive capacities. As a result, although most may still operate as primarily conventional thinkers, they show a level of systemic understanding, which Wade (1996) describes as the upper cognitive reaches of achievement or affiliative consciousness.

Eliot learned early to separate education from schooling into the establishment; he valued education and worked hard to gain the knowledge that he was raised to believe was his only legitimate path to freedom. He did not identify with prevailing standards but developed an idealistic personal moral standard, linked to the family's tradition.

He chose a profession which could provide relative independence from party politics. Like Bembow's (1994) activists, he was always different: earnest, serious, determined to not just get by but to become an outstanding dentist. And with the professional help of his father and brother, he did.

Eliot's professional life is a story of taking on greater and greater challenges against big odds: insufficient current professional information, inadequate material conditions, absence of laws that support and foster private practice. But he wanted to be an innovator in his field; he wanted to change the low public standard that had come to be the unfortunate outcome of socialist free medical service and low-paid medical professional work. He acts out of strong convictions about what medical service should and should not be about and puts his and his family's well-being at risk to be a path-breaker. Here are some examples of his thinking:

In 1992, I decided I had to break away from government medical service and start private practice. I was the first person in the town . . . who left a government job, and many colleagues couldn't understand. Today, 5 years later, there are only 5 of us dentists solely on private practice, and 60 who hold both government jobs and private practice. Personally I cannot justify the decision to combine the two. Morally speaking, this is a prerequisite for corruption. Most of my colleagues practice transferring patients they get through their government jobs into their private practice by convincing them that the service they need cannot be done in the government clinic. In addition, they steal materials from the government clinics. I do not want people talking behind my back that that is what I do. I want my clients to come to me because they want my service. . . . Also, if I have to serve 30 people today in the government clinic, I cannot do it up to the standard I want. I don't believe one should work that way.

Eliot's professional standards are colored by normative concerns. His professional approach requires a lot of sacrifices and is financially uncertain in an inflation-ridden economy. However, he is not intimidated, but positive, grateful, and appreciative of the experience he is gaining. The lowest point in his life was when he graduated stomatology before the fall of the communist regime and saw no hope for real professional development in the stigmatizing social system.

His professional motivation is not free of self-interest. Eliot is self-reflective and honest enough to recognize that his sacrifices mostly revolve around his family, and he is not really eager to extend himself beyond his own private practice. He is a dedicated father of two young children and a husband who works hard to support his wife's professional development as a dental surgeon herself. Beyond that, he admires people who give freely of themselves to others, and knows he is not that way.

In France, my wife introduced me to a man, extremely intelligent, extremely good-hearted, a man who does everything with love. Such people are very few and I'd love to be like him. But I cannot even understand how you can do something that you are in no way obliged to do, and perhaps that's how it should be in life. Not to do things by obligation, but because you feel you have to do it and help the other person. This is what I admire in that man. And there are others I admire, who are ready to help and give all of themselves. But I think in Bulgaria such people are few.

In this excerpt, we hear a level of skepticism characteristic of the Bulgarian intelligentsia he represents and reminiscent of Ramina. The sources are several. First are the individualism and limited family loyalties and life purpose with which he was raised. Second is the middle-class caution in the treacherous political environment, with moral agency limited to personal choices and tempered with self-interest. In this climate of distrust beyond one's family and friend, others are seen not as part of a larger humanity but as a potential threat. Third is the lack of spiritual frames of reference explicitly sustaining faith in humanity.

There are parallels between Eliot and William in their developmental and cultural limitations. Developmentally, both exhibit wholehearted commitments, limited to an interpersonal range, and are somewhat suspicious of others that are different. They also share fairly conservative cultural allegiances, traditional loyalties, and impermeability to other ways, which tend to limit rather than facilitate developmental vision. Both cases suggest the importance of the balance between moral loyalties and permeability in transitional CC in order for it to be able to grow in the direction of a fully developed mature CC.

Eliot shows the characteristic for conventional thinkers' tendency to be dualistic, easily disillusioned with people, and self-protective. Like William, he also reveals some stereotypically male conventional limitations: seeing himself in the role of the bread-earner, he is too busy working to be in touch with his feelings. He is not very communicative and open, does not tend to share himself, does not recognize interconnectedness, and is boundary and goal oriented.

In spite of his guardedness, Eliot has been very politically active since the fall of the communist regime. He had the courage to participate in the first demonstrations, which the still powerful communist network video-filmed in order to track down participants. He offered his organizational competence in the first democratic elections and took on responsible tasks. He contributed financially to the election campaign, something very unusual in Bulgaria, given the limited means of most people, Eliot included. He devoted time and enthusiasm and was disillusioned when re-communization began. Now, he has found new ways to continue his involvement, bringing political and organizational vision to the task of building new democratic structures.

Eliot relies on the personal respect he commands in his town to encourage people to vote for democracy. However, when offered the opportunity to run for mayor and to become the enlightened leader that he has the potential to be, he declined. He felt his dental practice was more important to him than a political career. Devoting his life to service was not really an option for him. He has maintained a steady commitment to supporting the democratic process, as well as substantial financial contributions. Overall, his public work reveals an ongoing tension between courage, commitment, and competence on the one hand and skepticism and a sense of being overwhelmed with the multiplicity of the social situation on the other. He grapples with this tension between self-protectiveness and true commitments, in a way characteristic of transitional CC.

Eliot takes a perspective on the country's political and cultural heritage and national character in important ways and shows critical discernment in the tasks he takes on. For example, he tries to educate people that communism as a political system is outdated. He tries to help others see their own learned helplessness as a result of their political experience and break the inertia in thinking. He interprets media information to others in intelligent, independent-minded ways. Through his own professional example, he tries to model the feasibility of the democratic way. In spite of his skepticism, he is a leader, generally positive and operating on faith.

Eliot talks about international issues with a mix of understanding, stereotypes and contradictions, similar to William's. Discussing the war in Bosnia, Eliot shows an ability to see through the international power-and-interest dynamics involved. Yet, he tends to interpret the war as "a Moslem versus Christian issue," and practical concerns about the potential ambitions of Moslems in Bulgaria seem to dominate over his humanitarian concerns. He searches for solutions within the international status quo, sharing stereotypical popular beliefs in a world conspiracy of Masons and Jews and expecting solutions from the Western big powers. However, invited to share his more personal experience with the Bulgarian Moslems as a medical practitioner, he shows empathy, fair-mindedness, and respect for their humanity and positive qualities.

Eliot's moral motivation shows well-developed dimensions 1 and 2, moral identity, and moral responsibility and agency. His motivational limitations have to do with his limited empathy and permeability (dimension 3), as well as with his not particularly spiritual, mostly individualistic frames of reference (dimension 4). He believes in a higher power of goodness and justice, and in that sense clearly operates from a moral frame of reference larger than the self. He says that in his daily life he is guided by a value system which corresponds to the Ten Commandments. He does his best to align himself with these principles, and he believes that if all people were to do the same, there would be peace on earth. However, he seems fairly satisfied within his individualistic personal philosophy. Overall, he parallels Danton in his predominantly secular individualistic morality, which leaves him not fully empowered, with a partially activated depth dimension of existence and significant tensions between mind and heart.

In spite of his limitations, Eliot reveals a consistent generativity, unlike Ada's. The contrast between the two helps understand how CC is differently expressed in different contexts. In a totalitarian context, the ability to resist and consistently question, without allowing self-interest to obscure one's sight, becomes particularly central to CC. While both Ada and Eliot are intelligent, moral, and independent-minded people, the difference between them is mostly in the consistency with which they resist the tide. This consistency is related to their motivation. Eliot's primarily moral motivation, strengthened by his family tradition, underlies his *principled resistance*. Ada's mix of self-interest and moral motivation accounts for her reactive resistance to only some social aspects as a way of gaining identity.

In contrast, in the more democratic and multifaceted U.S. context, life offers an infinite variety of possible pathways. Unless a person belongs to an oppressed group, as is the case with Jim, choices are not so clear-cut, and consistency and resistance acquire different dimensions. Although resistance to the mainstream cultural tide is still crucial, as William's case shows, it is primarily the inclination to seek broader meaning than pragmatic self-interest which becomes distinctive, as we saw in the case of Finnigan.

In the strength of Eliot's moral resistance to the tide from the vantage point of a continuous elaboration of right/wrong, good/bad, true/false distinctions, Eliot is the Bulgarian counterpart of William. As pointed out earlier, the comparison between the two of them reveals an important characteristic of transitional CC version: its difficulty with permeability. Since permeability comes fully with the movement toward postconventional consciousness, transitional CC always seems to raise the question of whether the individual exhibits enough of a balance between moral identification and permeability, to be developmentally alive, rather than too set in his or her ways.

In exploring this particular limitation of transitional CC, it helps to look at one of Colby and Damon's (1992) moral exemplars, Suzie Valadez, who is also a conventional thinker. What makes her permeable enough and tips the balance in the direction of life-long growth is her activated spiritual potential, which requires compassion, humility, tempering one's tendency to judge, forgiveness, and acceptance of others and of differences. It may be that, to the degree that a person with transitional CC has that activated spirituality, it counterbalances more rigid identifications, and allows for growth and expansion.

Table 4.4 highlights the differences between optimal and suboptimal consciousness on the advanced conventional level, by summarizing the contrast in

Table 4.4
Ada's and Eliot's Powers and Concerns

Primary Human Concerns	Main Human Powers		
	Knowledge	Love	Will
Self	Self-experience *Self-discovery** Self-knowledge	Self-preoccupation Self-acceptance *Self-development**	Self-control *Self-confidence Self-responsibility**
Relationships	Sameness of people *Uniqueness of people** Oneness of people	*Acceptance of others** Empathy with others Unity	Competition *Cooperation and equality Service**
Time	Present (here and now) *Mortality** Immortality	Primary union *Separation Secondary union**	Desire *Decision Action**

the overall development of Eliot's capacities with those of Ada (Ada's are marked with one asterisk on the left; Eliot's with two asterisks on the right).

As we can see, transitional CC in its second stage, sociopolitical consciousness, shows a clear advantage over its non-CC conventional equivalent in the consistency of its choice, that is, in the exercise of will. In the next chapter, we will revisit mature CC in order to gain a fuller appreciation of the range and expansiveness of its exercise of free will.

Chapter 5

Degrees of Courage

Heaven and earth contain me not, but the heart of my faithful servant contains me.

> Islam, Hadith of Suhrawardi, in Wilson, 1995, p. 544

All that which ye potentially possess, can however, only be manifested as a result of your own volition. . . . How lofty is the station which man, if he but chooseth to fulfill his high destiny, can attain!

> Baha'i Faith, Baha'u'llah, [1952] 1983, pp. 149, 206

Where there is no vision, the people perish.

> Judaism and Christianity, Proverbs 29.18, in Wilson, 1995, p. 538

Without faith there is no knowledge, without knowledge there is no virtuous conduct.

> Jainism, Uttaradhyayana Sutra 28.30, in Wilson, 1995, p. 536

In chapter 2, the profiles of critical consciousness began with the story of Jim, a remarkable yet very ordinary African American activist. This chapter completes the profiles of ordinary people with the story of Emily, a Bulgarian single mother who confronts with courage sexism, classism, and ablism in a society which has no such awareness to speak of yet. Emily is a path-breaker, every bit as much as the moral leaders studied by Bembow (1994), Colby and Damon (1992), and Daloz et al. (1996), on some of whom the later part of this chapter draws as exemplifying degrees of courage and spiritual integration. The purpose of this chapter is to help the reader appreciate the many degrees of mature CC, of the marriage of a strong heart with a strong mind.

EMILY: A BULGARIAN SINGLE MOTHER'S
CONFRONTATION WITH SEXISM, CLASSISM, AND ABLISM

Emily lives with a fully activated depth dimension of existence, with a profound sense of the wisdom of life. Despite her many battles, she hardly dwells on "evil." Instead, she takes on difficult tasks with quiet equanimity and lives with faith in the universe.

Emily reflects the transition to the intellectual, moral, and spiritual integration of authentic consciousness. She exhibits an autonomous 5 (Cook-Greuter, 1990), interindividual (Kegan, 1982) structure of self and metasystemic thought. Emily maintains a critical moral dialogue with her sociocultural environment—a society caught in the midst of a turbulent transition, painfully emerging from under the economic, social, and psychological rubble of fifty years of communism, with very little to offer women like herself. She continuously redefines her relationship with this society in congruence with her understanding; and she lives out of an alternative vision of what constitutes justice and equity.

Emily is an unemployed single mother of three children, a thirteen-year-old girl, an eleven-year-old girl with Down syndrome, and a baby. She lives on social security in a social environment in which being a single mother automatically makes a woman an outcast; the social network is inadequate, hostile, and prejudiced; and retarded children are considered a source of shame and are usually abandoned after birth. With her choices, Emily has challenged practically every social norm and has brought on herself a double stigma. Yet she carries herself with quiet dignity and does not see herself as a victim of society. She left the interviewer with the impression of a happy, fulfilled person on a path of life-long growth and expansion and at one with the world.

Emily grew up on the fringes of society and struggled with her self image. Her parents' home was on the outskirts of Sofia, small and very poor, although arranged with taste by her mother, according to Emily. Her parents were somewhat of an outcast couple themselves—her father, an intellectual in exile; her mother, with only elementary education. They did not fit any particular class in terms of education and occupation. Emily was ashamed of inviting friends to her home, and she did not overcome that until she was eighteen. Her life is the story of a beautiful, intelligent, and courageous woman who took many years and many blunders to find herself.

Like Jim, Emily grew up with an activated spiritual potential, and like him, although coming from an ostracized social class, she lived with a sense of inner dignity and pride. Emily's environment was materially poor and spiritually alive; she describes it as "awesome." Her mother was a "naturally intelligent, warm-hearted woman with a sense of humor," and her father was artistic, intellectually searching, morally driven, and "solid." Her mother's "highly developed sense of beauty and harmony" dominated the home. Her father's courage and love and understanding of nature gave her a rich outdoor experience of the world.

It was not only her father's outdoor adventures that expanded Emily's horizons; he was also an idealist on an independent search for meaning. In her words, he read thinkers not widely known at the time: Hegel, Feuerbach,

Engles' *Anti-During*. He read science fiction to his young daughters at bedtime, at a time when people in Bulgaria had not even heard about that genre yet. Because of his intellectual devotion to the communist idea, and his critical approach to its early realization in the 1950s, her father was expelled from the communist party for independent thinking and lack of submission to the party rules. However, he continued to teach his daughters his beliefs, not giving signs of heart-brokenness because of his marginalization. Emily has internalized a lot of his spirited resilience and detachment from social power hierarchies.

Overall, even in her early life, the theme of being different, outside the norm, dominates, just like in Bembow's (1994) activists. She relates intense moral self-reflection around identity issues and a continuous search for meaning and redefining of belonging. For example, she relates an incident in kindergarten, when a boy who liked her was given the task to supervise whether the other children washed their hands well and observed the required discipline. When the time came for him to report, she knew he was going to point her out as the best child, and she also knew she did not deserve that because she sprinkled water on the other children and broke the discipline rules in front of him. She was selected and got a reward, a little bag of sea shells, which she put into her locker. During afternoon nap, she snuck up to her locker to check on her bag of sea shells and found it missing. She remembers that as her first encounter with two things, theft and the realization that fully grew on her much later, that "undeserved things do not happen."

Emily has a strong moral sense, reminiscent of Gandhi (Gandhi, 1927). Later in this chapter, we will look at Gandhi's account of growing up and at how this inherent moral sense grew into intense self-reflection and search for meaning. Like Gandhi, Emily lived as a child in a contemplative, magical world of her own and describes beautifully the synchretic oneness with the world that her naive consciousness (Wade, 1996) at the time allowed her to feel.

There are things that I have just always known. I don't know how, but I just knew. And I had a calmness inside. I also knew that other people did not know those things. I saw the world full of magic, magic that is not beyond people's reach. And I felt very surprised that people did not seem to understand that.

Emily's inherent moral sense and spiritual potential were not consistently fostered by regular spiritual practices, but grew on the fertile ground of authentic models like her parents. She seems to have imbued those models into her own strong moral character. She struggled for years with gender and class-related low self-esteem, but her sense of inner dignity prevailed.

Emily remembers being always hungry for attention and seeking it through artistic self-expression and rebellious leadership. As a child, she set out to prove that girls are no less capable than boys, played soccer, which was very unusual for the time, made swords and pistols from sticks, and commanded the respect of the boys in the neighborhood. Her strong character reminds one of the formidable willpower of human rights activist Virginia Durr, described by Colby and Damon (1992). She was an excellent student, ambitious and independent-minded. She had the courage and the strong sense of justice to confront teachers with what she believed was wrong, running personal risks, and was everybody's favorite.

In preadolescence, she was increasingly attracted to the kids who fell outside the norm and, on retrospect, considers that period the beginning of her personal philosophy of understanding, accepting, and learning to value people's differences. Like Gandhi, Emily shows a lifelong elaboration of some moral principles central to her way of being. In her case, it is the belief that differences have to be respected as part of the richness of life, because they actually represent alternative pathways and thus offer a better understanding of the human potential.

Her adolescence is populated with significant relationships, each elaborating further the theme of growing in acceptance and understanding. Her descriptions of significant people include teachers and friends, as well as family, and show high personal standard and discrimination: she appreciates nobility of character, good taste, and meaningful engagement with life.

Around thirteen, she became progressively disillusioned with the social system and broke away from the role of the favored student, becoming a social rebel instead. She became aware of the "falseness of social norms and feigned ideals" and of the existence of social classes in the supposedly classless communist society. This was her first experience of what Bembow (1994) calls "catching culture in a lie," and it spurred Emily's struggle to transcend class distinctions in her own friendships. Another significant development of that period is the intellectual quest that her alert searching mind set out on, from Nietzsche's concept of the superman to films and all-night conversations with other young people, "exploring new worlds of meaning."

For the next ten years, individualistic rebellion, social life, and self-image became central, leaving academic achievement and college admittance by the wayside. When she was eventually admitted to study for school teacher certification, she quit halfway through, realizing the rigidity of the educational system within which she would have to teach.

From that point on, Emily's life was a series of tests, as she herself sees it, and also much like Jim's; she came out of each one strengthened and with a deepened understanding of life. Her ability to view life's challenges as spiritual tests reflects two important qualities: a remarkable permeability and openness and an activated depth dimension of experience. These two qualities are clearly related, as they appear in a similar configuration in Jim and in moral leaders from various studies (Bembow, 1994; Colby and Damon, 1992; Daloz et al., 1996; Gandhi, 1927).

Emily gave birth to a girl with Down syndrome and a distorted spine. The doctors prepared her that the child would die. She refused to think that way, putting all her faith with God instead. When it became clear that the child would live, the hospital staff pressured Emily to leave the girl behind. Emily refused. She speaks of her retarded daughter with deep appreciation and gratitude:

I knew very well that the child had chances. I had also seen enough in the homes for abandoned children that I wasn't going to leave my daughter there. Whatever chance she had, I would use it. . . . Never mind the doctors' expert opinion. I have intuition. I never even thought twice whether to leave her or take her. . . . Everything significant in my life has come through her. . . . The way I thought at the time, nobody can know the real potential of a child when they are born. Everybody has their life path. I could not leave her behind. She was born to me, and it was my job to see her through.

Emily refuses to even use such strong words as personal moral responsibility. She is quick to add that if somebody else, faced with the same dilemma, decided to leave their child behind, she would be the last to judge that act as immoral. She believes that nobody is in a position to understand another person's life journey. Again, we hear the same theme of respect for life and its mystery in each person's path, a richer and more complex developmental elaboration of the theme we saw in William.

If I had the opportunity and the means, I would take all these abandoned children from the homes, and create a wonderful environment for them to help them develop. . . . I can undo somebody else's decision to leave their child behind, if I think I can do more. But I have no right to judge.

Another typical theme of mature CC, which recurs in Jim and Danton, is that of Emily's personal growth shared with others. She saw her retarded daughter not as sick but simply as different, and learned to help her develop. She shows a remarkable capacity to take her daughter's perspective and work with it as normal, with wisdom and common sense, without falling victim to the doctors' scary conclusions. Emily thinks that her retarded daughter's great needs provided a wonderful opportunity for her other daughter to learn to manage her own egoism, help her sister, and accept differences in people rather than see herself as a victim.

Emily shows both compassionate understanding of her own children, without extremes of guilt or indulgence, and a deeply spiritual personal philosophy, in which learning to give to others with an open loving heart, regardless of differences, and without self-pity, is the highest value. As a young mother, she used to feel bad about not being able to provide nice material things for her children, but she considers it one of her lessons to become detached from those ambitions and help her daughters understand that one cannot have all one wants.

Emily's intellectual quest for meaning sets her apart from Jim and makes her markedly more philosophical and self-aware. She articulates a profound spiritual understanding of interconnectedness and energy systems, when she talks about how every child's unwanted reaction is only a reflection of what the parents still need to work out in themselves.

If I lose control over myself sometimes, or feel irritable, perhaps not right away, but 10 minutes later one of my daughters starts talking to me with irritation or aggressiveness, without even a visible reason. I know where it comes from, it comes from me. So I try to calm down, and then they calm down. . . . The egoism of every child is only a reflection of the egoism of the mother. They observe and learn from the mother. At least until adolescence, they are one single energy system.

The whole conversation with Emily was suffused with intense introspection as she makes sense of what she sees as her spiritual tests. She shows an intelligent, thoughtful engagement with every aspect of her reality. When she relates her marriage to, and divorce from, a physically and emotionally abusive alcoholic, she contemplates her own part in that, and her responsibility in helping healing happen. She is fair and clear-minded and refuses to be manipulated. As a divorced woman and single working mother in a science lab, she relates experiences of institutional sexism and discrimination. She stood her ground and finally lost her job. Then began the humiliation of trying to receive social security. She confronted extreme social discrimination against single mothers, and even more so against retarded children. Emily weathered all that, and fought her battles with remarkable common sense and equanimity.

In the meantime, Emily's living conditions in her father's house faced her with a different kind of challenge. Her mother had died, and her father, who had undergone an overall degradation in his later years, in Emily's words, brought in his girlfriend with two daughters and even a granddaughter, to coexist in a tight space with his daughter's family. It was a severe humbling experience that Emily relates: "I had nothing in common with those people, in terms of inner life, way of thinking or way of living. I learned to accept other people and to live with them in good will, without irritation, without extremes . . . for the common good."

Amid this challenge, Emily offered to take care of an old single aunt who had undergone an operation and had nobody to care for her. Since the house was so full, she took her into her own bedroom for a couple of years, until her aunt died. She says the decision was easy to make; what was hard was learning to live with the old woman, who was a difficult, opinionated, controlling character. Emily describes the caring straightforwardness and firmness with which she managed the old woman's egoism and rigidity of character. In the same spirit of empathy, compassion, understanding, personal responsibility, and habitual morality, Emily took care of her aged grandmother, and her first husband's grandmother, and relates these things as "little things, not worth mentioning." She takes no credit, does not like to talk in terms of sacrifices, and does not see herself as a helper. She operates with a level of unity of self and morality comparable to that of Colby and Damon's (1992) moral exemplars. "I don't think a person has to make sacrifices for anybody else, in the sense that, if you are not doing something out of an inner conviction, there's no point in doing it. You have to do it with conviction, not as a sacrifice. When I do things, it's because I believe it's important to do them."

Emily sees all the relationships in her life as "quality relationships," as she calls them. She reads a lot, moves with ease and critical discernment in the world of ideas, and shows no compartmentalization between ideal and real, between intellect and spirit. The teachings of Christ, the Christian Master Beinsa

Douno, and Carlos Castaneda are part of the way she lives, with faith, positivity, strength, and serenity.

You asked me how I managed with practically no means and no job. Well, this is how. I have searched all my life to gain a better understanding of myself and the things that happen to me. Now I know that this is not the only world, that there are many worlds and many lives; and everything that happens is what we need in order to gain understanding. . . . So now I can take things which would crush me otherwise. . . . I have learned about mental health—if we can see things positively, and discover the learning potential in every situation, we are OK. When a person is angry or in crisis, she or he cannot understand what's happening to them. They can only sink, although that's not bad either. Through it, one can come closer to oneself, find one's own inner support down there, at the very bottom, and rebound.

Emily is by far not a fully integrated human being. Side by side with her spiritual understanding, she grapples with bitterness and frequent irony of both herself and men. Like Jim, who had to negotiate racism in his life, she had a lifelong struggle with sexism in a patriarchal society and went through many painful stages of growth, including alcoholism and helplessness. She challenged and confronted men and took the anger and revenge that came back at her. As she emancipated herself first from men, then from institutionalized sexist morality, and finally from her own sense of inferiority, she began to understand that if she can fully accept herself, men will learn to accept and respect her too. Gradually, she found out that confrontation is unnecessary; that the real battle is within. As she told her story, her graceful, thoughtful presence alternated with proud bitterness and irony, commanding awe and respect.

We should not confront people. We either accept a person or we don't. If we can fully accept ourselves, why wouldn't we be able to accept others? A man may not become intimate with you, your lover or husband, but the very fact that he exists means his existence is necessary. . . . My conflict with men was that I refused to act as they expected me to. I sought that conflict because I wanted to prove that women are equally worthy in their way of being as men. . . . I was a fighter, and men do not like to be fought. . . . I thought I could accomplish something by fighting outside circumstances. The real fight is within.

Emily is a courageous moral agent in complex and unusual ways. First of all, she takes responsibility to clear up the negative energy within herself. Then she helps others, with no self-righteousness or personal expectations attached; and afterward, she forgets what others would call help.

To every person I have ever hurt, I have tried to make up in some way. Even if just to apologize within myself. For example, the drastic way I separated from my husband, with two little children on my hands, left him with a deep sense of guilt that he had to heal for a long time. . . . Later, I realized that there were other things I could have done if I had been calmer and stronger. I could have worked on myself, and in this way he would have changed too. I judged him very severely. In our much later contacts, I found a rare moment when we were able to talk without bitterness, and apologized to him. . .

When others turn to me in need, I do what I believe is right. I don't know if I want to call that help. It's more of a mutual thing, they learn from me and I learn from them. These relationships are gifts. . . . I share what I know about waters and feeding and mental health. . . . I try to help others not feel like victims of their lives. . . . But I cannot talk about volunteering help, because I cannot remember. For me, to do something good, and then to remember it and talk about it, is already about something else; it's about your ego, not about others. I simply engage with the other person's world, and it is something beautiful and enriching for both of us.

The way Emily turned around the question about volunteering shows that she lives her life with no compartmentalization of private and public. Jim was the only person from all the interviewees for this study who came close to her way of thinking. With her extended family, who still consider her a hopeless rebel, as well as with friends, and with every person who crosses her path, she practices unconditional love and acceptance, honesty, and personal transformation. She sees herself as an agent of positive social change through her personal example of courage, tolerance, and understanding in an intolerant and fear-driven world.

The measure of the development of a country, or a civilization, is precisely its social sphere, that is, how it relates to different individuals. People like my daughter, and other invalids, or people who are different. . . . I participate in this process of educating and civilizing through my neighborhood, the attitude of my neighbors to me and my daughter. I do not fit into their concepts; I am different. Yet, they do not act differently; those who communicate with me do it genuinely; the others, who don't, are also genuine. Nobody is aggressive to me, and that's in itself progress, especially in a neighborhood like this, where people are not very sophisticated. I believe that my behavior, my approach and way of thinking are reflected in others; everybody can feel when a person is calm and has accepted herself. I am open, and they are open, and approach me with a small comment, conversation, advice, or just to enjoy the baby, and exchange a few kind words.

Emily transcends fears of destitution and anxiety over material things in an impoverished environment, profoundly shaken by a large-scale sociohistorical transition, and driven by misery, materialism, and fear.

In my opinion, a person has to be truly mature spiritually to be ready for money, to use it wisely, and not become its servant and forget that one's real task is work on oneself. Few people have remained unscathed from having money. . . . I have no fear of destitution. I believe that if I act according to my best understanding, it will somehow reflect in the material world. Logical, isn't it?

Emily has difficulty committing, whether to a job or to a sociopolitical cause. She defines herself as a free spirit, who "cannot be made to fit into the boundaries of one family, one country, one planet." She does not consider herself politically engaged at this particular point in time. When the communist regime first fell, she saw an opportunity for people to release the accumulated tension of fifty years and open up to change. But soon she saw things begin to repeat themselves and realized that there is not yet a readiness for real change, which requires an internal transformation. So she chooses to view things more philosophically, in contrast to the general context of politicizing and extreme polarization. Nevertheless, her sociopolitical thinking is engaged and responsible, showing complex social perspective-taking:

> In order to judge a particular political line or group, I have to understand and feel the thinking of the whole nation. The current state of things is the outcome of the whole complex of people, with all its groups. Nothing happens accidentally. What we have is what we need at the moment. That's how it is with everything in life. It's another question how I see the future, a future without fear. Fear is at the core of all human misery. In order to do away with fear, we have to all understand who we are, where we are going, what life is about, and that life does not end here. Then we will have global change. Global change will mean that things are done without self-interest, that international help is given for the right reasons and in the right way. . . . Every nation has its values, and the help given has to respect those values.

Emily's emergent global vision brings together political, historical, and spiritual understanding. She sees the purpose of both individual and collective life as transformation and progressive unification with the source of life. She is acutely aware of the interrelatedness of all spheres of human activity, emotional, social, material, spiritual, universal, as well as of the limitations of our current paradigms of thought. She lives with awe of the beauty, strength, and harmony she sees reflected in the universe, and with a strong sense of spiritual responsibility. She believes the sense of well-being comes out of acting out of her real values, a theme recurring in Bembow's (1994) interviews with activists. Morality, in her definition, is the sense of beauty and harmony with oneself and the universe, a reverberation of the eternal theme of moral discourse of the unity of truth, beauty, and goodness (Sorokin, in Maslow, 1959). Although she does not yet exhibit broad social concerns with justice, she operates out of an emerging holonomic understanding, which includes paradoxes, and stands in dialogue with history.

Emily's story of spiritual emergence has deep and illuminating parallels with the story of Gandhi (1927). It is important to see that figures of such world magnitude as Gandhi are on the same continuum of the CC pathway as ordinary people like Emily, or Roberta Guaspari, the divorced U.S. mother of two children who created in the late 1980s and early 1990s the East Harlem violin program for inner-city children. The difference among them is only one in degrees. How can we, then, more fully describe the range of potential expansion of mature CC?

THE RANGE OF MATURE CC

The level of mature CC elaborates the themes of principled vision, philosophical expansion of understanding, and a growing historical and global vision (see Table 4.2). While we saw principled vision illustrated in the profiles of Jim and Danton and early philosophical expansion in Emily's profile, the late stages in Gandhi's life will give us more of a sense of the infinite degrees of potential expansion of mature CC.

The cognitive threshold for mature CC is the establishment of postformal thought. As the individual is able to coordinate hierarchically social patterns, variables, and laws into a fully postconventional understanding of the system that binds them together, the individual begins to dereify social phenomena, as we saw Jim do; that is, to understand them as products of a particular social organization of power and knowledge and not as absolute realities. With the movement from systematic to metasystematic operations (Commons and Rodriguez, 1990), people become able to compare systems, as we saw in Danton. That brings about a growing emancipation of the individual from sociopolitical conditions.

Social perspective-taking progresses to a new level of relativistic reasoning (Perry, 1968), as the contextual nature of a person's epistemology and social experience is understood, without it paralyzing one's capacity for moral judgment. Emily is a good example of the full development of this capacity. With the understanding of systemic realities comes a new awareness of one's own social conditioning, as we saw in Emily's struggles with sexism; a sustained effort to transform begins. Empathy for others increasingly recognizes the common human condition, as we saw in Emily.

This personal liberation gradually leads to the formation of a new sense of community with fellow thinkers, each of them value originating, system generating. This had not yet occurred for Emily when she was interviewed for this study, but we see it happening in Gandhi's life. Philosophical expansion progressively transforms into an evolving spiritual vision, which transcends the illusory intellectual concept of individual freedom in isolation (Bellah et al., 1985). The social system or culture is deconstructed and understood not in a vacuum, but within an unapologetic spiritual frame of reference. The knower is truly brought into the process of knowing, and both social reality and individual consciousness are dereified from the point of view of explicit moral and spiritual values.

Individuals functioning at this level of CC will manifest what Colby and Damon identified as a "paradoxical mix of lasting commitments and sustained capacity for change" (p. 184). Within a variety of personal styles, all exhibit a striking openness to moral change and active receptiveness to particular social influences. Interactional continuities which reinforce the individuals' "open, reciprocal, generative, truthful and self-reflective" personal styles spur lifelong moral growth and "establish open systems of feedback between the self and others" (Colby and Damon, 1992, pp. 196–97). These individuals also exhibit a faithfulness to the "overarching original values, which endured the flux of frequent change and growth, and in a fundamental sense contributed to the shape of that change and growth" (p. 185).

Collective dialogue and permeability are no longer the ceiling of social achievement, nor is postmodern cultural sensitivity considered the most progressive possible form of social consciousness. Moral commitment brings about a vision of a future. Existential skepticism is transcended. The secular/spiritual, reason/intuition, mind/soul dualities are increasingly reconciled.

People examine past, present, and future from the point of view of moral principles and with an understanding of the relativity of one's sociopolitical role within a larger historical process. The sense of history brings about unlimited agency and creative leadership, characterized by a historical perspective and an understanding of epochal themes, fundamental to Freire's definition of CC. Self and morality are fully united into a way of being which involves standing in responsible relationships with oneself, family, friends, nature, calling, society, culture, country, history, the world, and God.

In order to appreciate more fully the common themes of spiritual emergence across cultures and historic contexts, we will now look briefly at the life of Gandhi, drawing on his autobiography (Gandhi, 1927).

When we think of Gandhi, we think of a moral and spiritual leader of world magnitude. We remember the Hindu philosopher of nonviolent resistance in the name of social and political justice and a nation's right to self-definition. Few of us know that Gandhi began his life as a very ordinary child and average student, not marked by any exceptional endowment. Gandhi's (1927) autobiography, *An Autobiography or the Story of My Experiments with Truth*, on which the next section of this chapter draws, illustrates how this simple, contemplative child slowly grew to become a world leader. The very title of his autobiography clearly speaks to the one prominent theme in his life—his love of truth and his commitment to putting his understanding of truth to practice.

Of course, we sophisticated and skeptical postmodern thinkers quickly jump: What is truth? Whose truth? As defined how? But for Gandhi this was no theoretical question. It was the instinctive knowledge of the heart which, with the years, he grew to understand better and articulate in increasingly all-embracing and unitive ways. Every time he experienced the tension between mind and heart, he brought himself back to his heart's knowing and stretched his mind to comprehend more deeply the mysteries of his heart. Then, with unfailing energy, he put his understanding to practice, so that in his life there was no gap between learning, understanding, and wise practice. Gandhi's path of steep lifelong growth illustrates the tremendous power of an awakened spiritual potential. His early life story of a harmonious development and expansion of his capacities to know, to love, and to act accordingly contains many valuable lessons for contemporary education.

GANDHI AND THE LIFESPAN EVOLUTION OF CC

Pre-CC

Moral Interest. Gandhi's childhood is dominated by an intuitive moral sense that continuously interacted with a morally oriented environment and gradually grows into a passion for truth. Below are some examples of those interactions.

Gandhi's early environment seems to have particularly fostered the truthfulness and permeability to and fascination with authenticity characteristic of the level of naive consciousness (Wade, 1996). His mother made a lasting impression on the imagination of the young child with her deep spirituality, which

Gandhi remembered as "saintliness." Her uprightness and seriousness, whether they were about the different vows she occasionally took in the context of her Hindu practice and always carried through with equanimity or the way she conducted her daily affairs, seem related to Gandhi's truthfulness. This quality of the young Gandhi later grew into one of his strongest characteristics—fidelity and passion for truth. Here is how he describes her moral character:

The outstanding impression my mother has left on my memory is that of saintliness. She was deeply religious. She would not think of taking her meals without her daily prayers. Going to the Vaishnava temple was one of her daily duties. As far as my memory can go back, I do not remember her having ever missed the fast during the four months of the rains. She would take the hardest vows and keep them without flinching. Illness was no excuse for relaxing them. . . . During one fast she vowed not to have food without seeing the sun. We children on those days would stand, staring at the sky, waiting to announce the appearance of the sun to our mother. Everyone knows that at the height of the rainy season the sun often does not condescend to show his face. And I remember days when, at his sudden appearance, we would rush and announce it to her. She would run out to see with her own eyes, but by that time the fugitive sun would be gone, thus depriving her of her meal. "That does not matter," she would say cheerfully, "God did not want me to eat today." And then she would return to her round of duties. (Gandhi, 1927, pp. 2–3)

This authentic model of moral character and authority left an imprint on the little boy's imagination, which translated, with the advent of concrete operational thought, into a moral earnestness and a passion for melodramatic devotion. A shy and reticent child, he lived in an idealistic world of his own, with clearly differentiated rights and wrongs, in which "to follow truth and to go through all the ordeals" (p. 4) inspired him as an ideal.

Young Gandhi shrank instinctively from what he perceived as wrong, and believed literally in what to him seemed right, with the evaluation happening somewhat unconsciously. For example, on one occasion his class was taking a spelling test in the presence of the educational inspector, and Gandhi had misspelled the word *kettle*. The teacher subtly prompted him to copy it from his neighbor's slate. Gandhi could not believe what the teacher was suggesting. He remained in denial of the teacher's act, until it turned out later that everybody else had copied in order to represent the teacher well in front of the educational inspector.

Gandhi's intuitive moral sense was strengthened by the presence of moral discourse as an explicit organizer of the daily life around him. The young boy's life was populated by men of significant moral authority. The men in his family were prime ministers in several states for three generations, and were all "men of principle." His father was "a lover of his clan, truthful, brave and generous," known for his "impartiality in the family as well as outside", and for his loyalty to the state. Despite the subservient position to the British of all Indians in the British Empire, Gandhi's father combined loyalty with dignity and did not allow himself to be treated with disrespect by the British political agents. In contrast to many corrupt officials, Gandhi's father had no "ambition to accumulate riches" and left "very little property" but lived a life rich in experience in practical affairs and commanded the respect of people.

Hence, moral values and moral induction practices and ongoing distinctions around duty, right, and wrong appear to have been extremely prominent in Gandhi's family and cultural environment and led to Gandhi's lifelong habit of evaluating what's "right, proper, and pleasing." These moral voices, authoritative but not authoritarian, maintained in the young child an optimal empathic arousal (Gibbs, 1991), which allowed them to be effectively internalized.

Gandhi's moral earnestness, his habit of subjecting every experience or encounter to careful moral examination, gave birth to the next major theme in his life—the negotiation of external and internal moral authority. On the one hand, within the context of his time and culture, his moral interest began to be expressed as the desire to serve his parents, which later expanded to the idea of sacrifice in devoted service. On the other hand, with the advent of abstract thought, he began to carefully scrutinize the moral authority in the decisions of adults around him.

Moral Authority. One has to understand the developmental nature of this period in order to appreciate how it played out differently in Gandhi's life. Early adolescence is characterized by tension between a hedonistic, instrumental purpose and exchange orientation, characteristic of egocentric consciousness (Wade, 1996), and the first signs of personal moral authority found in "structured self-identification through the member role and intra-group relationships," characteristic of early conformist consciousness (Wade, 1996, p. 119). In the fairly materialistic Western context, which often reinforces instrumental purpose and exchange, this tension becomes translated into the all-too-familiar "disease of adolescence," when most adults feel manipulated by their teenagers, who pretty much reject all authority and seem to grow only very slowly beyond an egocentric view of life.

In Gandhi's account, even self-centered power struggles were morally redefined, and out of the struggle with remorse, internal sense of moral authority developed. A good example is his attempt to challenge the authority of the cultural norm of vegetarianism by running away at night with friends to experiment with meat.

Under the influence of other children, he had arrived at the conclusion that "the Englishman is bigger and rules over the Indian" because he eats meat. So he concluded that reform was needed to give a fair chance to his countrymen to be free. We can hear in the birth of these first abstract ideas the moral imperative in his reasoning: "I wished to be strong and daring and wanted my countrymen also to be such, so that we might defeat the English and make India free." (p. 15) Here is a sample of his thinking as it reveals the birth of principled decisions:

I said to myself: "Though it is essential to eat meat, and also essential to take up food reform in the country, yet deceiving and lying to one's father and mother is worse than not eating meat. In their lifetime, therefore, meat-eating must be out of the question. When they are no more and I have found my freedom, I will eat meat openly, but until that moment arrives I will abstain from it." This decision I communicated to my friend, and I have never since gone back to meat. (p. 16)

This illustrates Hoffman's (1991) emphasis on the importance of moral self-attribution and empathy-based guilt in the evolving of genuinely moral motivation. In this developmental period of image building, Gandhi took the age specific concerns with reputation onto an explicitly moral level. He developed a passion for personal integrity and for building character, which was so intense that "the least blemish drew tears" (p. 10).

Young Gandhi's critical awareness of authentic moral authority in adults seems to have a lot to do with the models of integrity and substantive life meaning that significant adults provided around him. Also, in colonial India, he grew up in a political environment replete with acute contradictions. Gandhi was exposed daily to conversations among adults who were trying to negotiate oppressive social and political reality with a measure of dignity. Much like the contemporary Americans described by Daloz et al. (1996), he was socialized into critical social awareness, in the context of a strong family unit which protected him from the direct influence of the outer world. This seems to have strengthened his critical faculties and built resilience.

Daloz et al. (1996) have identified similar themes as part of the gradual formation of lifelong moral commitments in the people they studied. Some of them are (a) a home with open doors which provides glimpses into the larger sociopolitical world, (b) a public parent, (c) exposure to and learning to discern justice and injustice, and (d) the gradual expanding of the meaning of "home" to include increasingly more encompassing spheres of trust and agency (pp. 28–37).

In this period, Gandhi's preoccupation with character leads to aloofness from peer group activities and entertainment and a tendency to develop his own standards through lonely endeavors. Gandhi begins to evolve a strong sense of the authority of personal decision, an example of which is the authority he attributes to the vows he takes throughout his life, be it of vegetarianism, celibacy, or some other practice. He also examines carefully the authority and moral integrity of the words and actions of others. This leads initially to a self-righteous, dualistic understanding of the moral role he defines for himself—that of a reformer.

The young reformer Gandhi feels a need to exercise authority over others where he finds them lacking. In the early treatment of his wife (according to the Hindu custom of child marriages, he was married at thirteen), that tendency makes him a tyrant unable to recognize her right of choice. With time, the desire to control gives way to active love, and the moral demands that active love places on Gandhi eventually counterbalance self-righteousness. He does not lose his passion to reform, but he learns to respect the freedom of those he seeks to reform. He redefines authority and power as the moral authority of service and a sense of mission: "He who would be friends with God must remain alone, or make the whole world his friend" (p. 13).

Hence, in this period, the socially conformist developmental task of structured role identification is negotiated in Gandhi's life in profoundly moral ways which have a lifelong significance. The death of his father marks the turning point from which the theme of personal responsibility predominates.

Moral Responsibility. While early adolescence negotiates the central theme of moral authority, in late adolescence and young adulthood the question of personal moral responsibility becomes central. This period negotiates the tension between responsibility to community standards and responsibility for personal self-definition. In Gandhi's life, it gives birth to a unique Gandhian blend of respect and freedom of choice.

Gandhi's decision to go to England marks the beginning of his gradual emergence from embeddedness in his environment and culture, and the early establishment of his self-contained, institutional self (Kegan, 1982). Gandhi's encounter with his caste's refusal to allow him to go to England and his firm decision to make the trip are a good example of an evolving new sense of self and responsibility still struggling with the pull of shared realities. Once in England and extricated from the embrace of his kin, Gandhi takes responsibility to live up to his own decision and not be disheartened by the estrangement he feels in a discriminating foreign culture. Instead, he begins to apply to it his critical discernment and defines his own relationship with the surrounding milieu.

As Gandhi negotiates fitting into English society, where he chose to study, he gradually defines his own standards. Having undertaken "the all too impossible task of becoming an English gentleman" and compensating "for my vegetarianism by cultivating other accomplishments which fitted one for polite society" (p. 37), he eventually realizes the questionable character of the concept of a gentleman. Discovering that he "was pursuing a false idea," he commits to simplicity and humility instead. This philosophical commitment illustrates, in contrast with the unexamined underlying assumptions of his social milieu, his adolescent quest for a life based on principles.

Gandhi's discovery of vegetarianism is yet another example of his growing sense of self. He had been vegetarian by force of the standards of his own community. But after reading Salt's *Plea for Vegetarianism*, he becomes "a vegetarian by choice" (p. 35)—he redefines the idea until it becomes a broad concept. This importance of ideas in his life path is a recurring theme in the lives of other moral leaders (Bembow, 1994; Colby and Damon, 1992).

With the maturing of Gandhi's sense of personal moral responsibility, his critical perception expands from immediate personal and interpersonal to social concerns, which marks the period of transitional CC.

Transitional CC

Expanding Moral and Social Responsibility. Gandhi's focus shifts progressively toward larger social reality, as he begins to examine and redefine current social tastes or prevailing concepts. A good example is his view of the Eiffel Tower, which cuts right through the general consensus on this marveled architectural object. Gandhi calls the Eiffel Tower "the toy of the Exhibition. So long as we are children we are attracted by toys, and the Tower was a good demonstration of the fact that we are all children attracted by trinkets. That may be claimed to be the purpose served by the Eiffel Tower" (p. 58).

At this point, we see in Gandhi critical consciousness comparable to William's: he engages in an ongoing critical moral conversation with himself and the world around him and feels implicated in the moral realities he perceives. The difference is one of scope. Gandhi's agency and range of experience is much more expansive. While William dialogues with the cultural mores of his society, Gandhi begins an independent inquiry into religion in an effort to understand the fundamental principles of Christianity and Hinduism. These investigations lead him to find common patterns between the Bible and the Bhagavad Gita and to think further about unifying principles such as nonviolence as the highest form of spirituality. He studies the lives of religious teachers, compares theism to atheism, and embarks on a lifelong effort to define his own relationship to God.

Like William, he is increasingly preoccupied with the life of service to others. He begins with a systematic effort to bring his inner and outer life into harmony, building for himself a life of economy, hygiene, and simplicity. "As I searched myself deeper, the necessity for changes both internal and external began to grow on me" (p. 41). Then, he begins to turn toward leadership in the public sphere. He is "elected to the Executive Committee of the Vegetarian Society" and has to face his first public challenge in the form of a responsibility to speak out and side with what he sees as the right cause, even though it is a losing battle. With time, Gandhi's conviction in the power of truth to prevail strengthens, and his life path becomes that of a tireless champion of truth in increasingly complex social battles.

Gandhi takes it on himself to "resist the canker of untruth" (p. 49). He initiates new projects which foster in others a deeper understanding. Gandhi describes these endeavors as led not by an outstanding mind, but by a love of simplicity and moral earnestness. This is a period of dynamic interaction between leadership and learning from others, the beginning of the kind of open and receptive social dynamic and subsequent developmental transformation of goals which Colby and Damon (1994) and Daloz et al. (1996) identify in their exemplars.

Although Gandhi finds many soulmates in this process, he never finds a guru: "in spite of this regard for him (Raychandbhai) I could not enthrone him in my heart as my Guru. The throne has remained vacant and my search still continues" (p. 65).

This is the climax of the theme of responsibility—throughout his development, Gandhi remains fully responsible for his own process. He names moral earnestness as the great passion of his life and the criterion through which he selects the people he trusts most. This passion is so great that no guru can satisfy it completely: "Infinite striving after perfection is one's right. It is one's reward. The rest is in the hands of God" (p. 64).

With his return from England into the messy political and social reality of India, Gandhi develops fully his social consciousness and, like Eliot though on a different scale, embarks on social and political work.

Sociopolitical Consciousness. Gandhi was born in the family of a minister and exposed to a life without the extremes of deprivation or spoil. Basic family virtues, spirituality, and stern traditions reinforced in him a middle-class tendency to see things in predominantly individual moral terms. It took several clashes with social realities before he expanded his causal understanding of the social world beyond individual moral principles. Although he experienced many clashes with the abuse of power in India, his journey of initiation into systemic prejudice was his trip to South Africa. There, he gradually realized the all-embracing nature of the problem.

Forced to submit to humiliating class rules, Gandhi begins to subject the existing social system to careful analysis and performs his first act of civil disobedience. This marks the beginning of his evolving strategy of social opposition within socially accepted boundaries. Subsequent class abuse prompts Gandhi to distinguish between social protest for the sake of personal gratification and social protest as a result of a well-thought-out systematic approach to a chosen social cause.

The hardship to which I was subjected [denied his first-class seat and thrown off the train] was superficial—only a symptom of the deep disease of color prejudice. I should try, if possible, to root out the disease and suffer hardships in the process. Redress for wrongs I should seek only to the extent that would be necessary for the removal of color prejudice. (p. 82)

An interesting subtheme of the mature period of Gandhi's life is that of synchronicity. Both support and challenge seem to come his way when he is ready to take them. For example, the opportunity to work on the Bill of Indian Franchise in South Africa comes at a time when he has completed his other obligations and has been contemplating for a while the opportunities for broader action. He is mentally ready, as well as at a crossroad. His Pretoria experiences and his studies of Christianity have prepared him to evolve a clear political vision.

In Pretoria, Gandhi makes his first effort to organize the community as an educator and leader. His method of public work takes shape. He approaches the Indian community in Pretoria directly, states the problem clearly and simply, and lays the major decisions in the hands of the community. At the same time, he offers a broader vision that helps unite people and points to a common goal. Gandhi both empowers the people he works to help and brings an understanding which bridges the distinctions maintained within the group, helping overcome differences and separateness. For example, he insists that even the poorest Indians in South Africa legitimately constitute the Indian community and cannot be excluded.

In the fight to empower the illiterate and disunited Indian community in South Africa, Gandhi develops further his political vision. He does not accept the offer of the community to support him financially, but chooses his battles carefully, with larger responsibilities in mind. His political vision soon expands beyond specific group interests and into a growing understanding of the political and social system he is dealing with. This marks the transition into CC and the progressive elaboration of his principled vision.

In this process, he continues his religious exploration in an effort to see a larger spiritual picture and its implications on social and political justice. Gradually, he becomes the Mahatma (which in Hindu means "saint") that India reveres.

Critical Consciousness

Principled Vision. As he comes to understand the social power and knowledge networks which maintain oppression in South Africa and compares them with two other sociocultural systems (India and Britain), Gandhi develops a principled understanding of power and knowledge networks. This is the beginning of what Bembow (1994) refers to as dereification, that is, an ability to see through the hegemonic sociopolitical dynamic between power and knowledge and to overcome its grip on consciousness. At this point we are reminded of Emily, who also deconstructed her social system and the Bulgarian historical experience.

The scope of Gandhi's agency, however, is of a different magnitude. He begins to open up and place before the disempowered specific alternatives for action, creating a political body to represent his group (the Natal Indian Congress), with subdivisions (Colonial-born Indian Educational Association) and a specific agenda (regular meetings, fund-raising, propaganda, etc.). Gradually, Gandhi includes in his representation the poorest and most disenfranchised, taking political action beyond class interests and into principled issues of equality, loyalty, trust, and unity on a national level.

Gandhi's day-to-day public and political work with people stimulates his evolving contextual thought. His understanding of service deepens, and the concept of universal love evolves. It unites into a consistent spiritual framework his political work and his religious understanding of morality on all levels. Gandhi defines the service to India as his particular form of self-actualization.

Philosophical Expansion. This expansion of thought to broader concepts and principles was long coming, and in a certain way, the potential for it was always there in Gandhi's introspective approach to life. But once his political activity in South Africa becomes channeled, Gandhi's restless mind embarks on a new reexamination and reformulation of the basic truths that guide him, informed by his experience in political work. It is noteworthy that this period sets in when Gandhi is in his early thirties.

Out of his extensive studies of religion and contemplating life in England, South Africa and India, his concept of Western civilization emerges as one which unlike the Eastern, is "predominantly based on force" (p. 142). About this time he begins to evolve his fundamental principle of nonviolence, and shortly after he demonstrates it during his lynching by the mob in Natal.

This is a period of evolving theories around every particular issue that emerges. An example is his thinking about the education of his own children in South Africa. As a "student of the history of civilization" (p. 150), Gandhi sees existing academic options both in South Africa and in India as part of a system of segregation and oppression, meant to prepare individuals to fit into the system. To him it becomes a choice of liberty or learning.

Had I been without a sense of self-respect and satisfied myself with having for my children the education that other children could not get, I should have deprived them of the object-lesson in liberty and self-respect that I gave them at the cost of the literary training. . . . The youths whom I called out in 1920 from those citadels of slavery—their schools and colleges—and whom I advised that it was far better to remain unlettered and break stones for the sake of liberty than to go in for a literary education in the chains of slaves will probably be able now to trace my advice to its source. (p. 151)

The next long period in his life is rich in redefinitions of earlier ideas after they have been put to practice. The universal principles that evolve as a result are grounded in what Gandhi calls his own "experiments with truth." Gandhi challenges every established pattern of thought both in himself and in others. One of the dramatic examples is his inclusion of the Indian caste of the untouchables into the communal living arrangement he establishes, a decision which challenged centuries of rigidly established social distinctions. Perhaps the most profoundly spiritual redefinition, which reflects the Mahatma's deep integration of mind and heart, is that of freedom. Gandhi moves from an emphasis on freedom of choice guided by moral imperative to freedom from self. He discovers the liberating effect of the vow to observe celibacy, lets go of possessiveness, and frees himself of the passions of the self. Gradually this helps him free himself from attachment to family life to explore the dimensions of communal living. He also explores the freedom from the slavery to the senses and the "joy of vigilance" (p. 156), as well as the powerful potential in the cooperation between mind and body.

All of these and many others are examples of the explosion of patterns that Gandhi identifies all around him. He increasingly brings those patterns together into systems of thought, whether about "the simple life" (p. 159), or about social oppression, or about India's "poverty and subjection" (p. 174).

Gandhi offers a brilliant analysis of autocratic versus democratic methods of public government and of their sources in political structure. He examines the role of journalism in social life. He turns Ruskin's utopian vision of community into reality by patiently introducing democratic and deeply innovative social reforms. He develops a holistic approach to body and health through critically examining hydropathy and allopathy. He develops further his principle of nonviolence by making an important distinction between a person and his deeds and the principle of resisting the second but not the first.

> It is quite proper to resist and attack a system, but to resist and attack its author is tantamount to resisting and attacking oneself. For we are all tarred with the same brush, and are children of one and the same Creator, and as such the divine powers within us are infinite. To slight a single human being is to slight those divine powers, and thus to harm not only that being but with him the whole world. (p. 206)

The political and spiritual complexity of this vision does not need discussion. However, the intellectual faculty remains, until the end of his life, more prominent than his capacity for love and compassion. This humanness and fallibility of Gandhi's has been subject to much writing and has been interpreted as questionable authenticity (Erikson, 1969). It is very important therefore to differentiate between developed moral consciousness and the idea of a perfect moral being.

Historical and Global Vision. It is remarkable to trace Gandhi's progression from the understanding of social injustice to a historical understanding of the global roles of nations. Since it is impossible to do justice to that transformation in this limited format, the following quotes give just a taste of that vision:

> A nation that wants to come into its own ought to know all the ways and means to freedom. (p. 285)
>
> My South African experience had convinced me that it would be on the question of Hindu-Muslim unity that my Ahimsa (non-violence) would be put to its severest   test. (p. 334)
>
> Before one can be fit for the practice of civil disobedience one must have rendered a willing and respectful obedience to the State laws. . . . A Satyagrahi (a person practicing passive resistance) obeys the laws of society intelligently and of his own free will, because he considers it to be his sacred duty to do so. It is only when a person has thus obeyed the laws of society scrupulously that he is in a position to judge as to which particular rules are good and just and which unjust and iniquitous. (p. 357)
>
> To safeguard democracy the people must have a keen sense of independence, self-respect and their oneness, and should insist upon choosing as their representatives only such persons as are good and true. (p. 380)

The many continuities that the reader has noticed between Gandhi's life and some of the profiles in this book illustrate the common themes of spiritual emergence. The degrees of courage and expansion of CC seem to reflect degrees of development and integration of the spiritual powers to know, to love, and to exercise one's free will. Figure 5.1 offers a snapshot of the relative positions of all the people discussed so far on the CC/non-CC continuum. Each person is indicated by their first letter, and Eliot appears with his first two letters to distinguish him from Emily.

In the next chapter, we look at why contemporary education falls short of cultivating critical consciousness as an attainable goal of adult development. We examine the specific ways in which educational vision needs to expand in order to develop more consistently the full range of human powers and become more conducive to the large-scale activation of the human spiritual potential in the direction of the formation of empowered moral consciousness and global citizenship.

Figure 5.1
Position of All Profiles on the CC/Non-CC Continuum

	Motivation	Pre-CC			Transitional CC		CC	
		A	B	C	D	E	F	G
CC Pathway (Moral Motivation)	Unity of self and morality							xG
CC Pathway (Moral Motivation)	Moral concerns dominant over self-interest			xT	xW	xEl	xJ xE xD	
Non-CC Pathway (Expediency Motivation)	Self-interest dominant over moral concerns			xI	xF	xA	xR	
Non-CC Pathway (Expediency Motivation)	Immoral people							
	(Structural dev.) →	Preconventional			Conventional		Postconventional	

Key:
A: Moral interest
B: Moral authority
C: Personal responsibility
D: Expanded moral and social
E: Sociopolitical consciousness
F: Philosophical expansion
G: Historical and global vision

Chapter 6

Education for Critical Consciousness

Upon the reality of man . . . He hath focused the radiance of all His names and
attributes. . . . These energies . . . lie, however, latent within him.
Baha'i Faith, Baha'u'llah, [1952] 1983, p. 65

Make every effort to supplement your faith with virtue, and virtue with
knowledge, and knowledge with self-control, and self-control with steadfastness,
and steadfastness with godliness, and godliness with brotherly affection, and
brotherly affection with love.
Christianity, 2 Peter 1.5–11, in Wilson, 1995

A trail through the mountains, if used, becomes a path in a short time, but, if
unused, becomes blocked by grass in an equally short time. Now your heart is
blocked by grass.
Confucianism, Mencius VII.B.21, in Wilson, 1995

This book started with a central question: What kind of overall educational shift
would constitute an adequate collective response to the developmental readiness
of people in the twenty-first century to be educated toward critical
consciousness? How can diverse cultures and historical contexts incorporate into
their public education a consistent understanding of the dimensions of optimal
human consciousness?

The construct of critical consciousness, understood as a consciousness that
brings systemic thought and an engaged dialogical relationship with reality from
a place of unity of mind and heart, of integration of knowledge, love, and will,
provides a normative framework for rethinking education. It allows us to
examine the strengths and limitations of current educational models in the
historical context of an emerging global society and to explore possibilities for a
new level of educational integration which can meet the challenge of our world,
discussed in chapter 1.

The most central finding of this work has been that empowered, resilient moral consciousness is a function of the extent to which the individual's spiritual capacities to know, to love, and to exercise free will are fully awakened and harmoniously developed. We saw in the earlier chapters that optimal moral consciousness is a complex phenomenon and cannot be reduced to any single dimension, be it moral reasoning, character or values, critical discernment, caring, social responsibility, or agency. We saw sophisticated people like Ada and Ramina, who clearly had character and some moral values of caring and uprightness guiding their choices yet did not exhibit the overall quality of empowered moral consciousness. We saw Ivan's definite sense of social responsibility, which also did not amount to moral consciousness. We saw that despite his empathy and caring for the helpless, Finnigan is not truly engaged with his world.

What is distinctive about empowered moral consciousness is that it is guided by love. Love for truth, beauty, and goodness is the missing link that brings together moral values, character, sincerity, moral reasoning, critical discernment, responsibility, empathy, and compassion into a qualitatively different consciousness—empowered, resilient, and authentically moral. Love is the depth dimension of human existence. Love for truth, beauty, and goodness is a powerful motivator, a deep resource that, when tapped into, allows a human being to become all he or she can be.

Love for truth, beauty, and goodness is what allowed Jim, Danton, Emily, Eliot, William, and Tom to transcend their limitations and the limitations of their environments and to embrace the human condition with understanding and agency. In contrast, in Ada, Ramina, Finnigan, and Ivan, who are all decent, caring people, fear dominates over love and despite the inclinations of their hearts does not allow them to become truly themselves.

Empowered moral consciousness understands and transcends its fears. It is a consciousness in which the spiritual yearning for truth, beauty, and goodness has been amplified to such an extent that the love-knowledge and attraction of the heart and the understanding of the mind have entered into synergy. Through this dialectic of heart and mind, CC people continuously face, understand, and redefine fear as an inescapable part of the human condition, while they are moved by expanding circles of love. They are not guided by fear and all its by-products—prejudice, rationalizations, skepticism, hostility. Their powers to know and to act are fully released. They are what Freire calls subjects of history.

Of course, in each CC person, there is a different configuration of knowledge, love, and level and degree of agency, linked to the educational impact of life experiences. All of these variations, along with the general characteristics that run through them, contain significant implications for education.

In Tom and William, we saw moral consciousness led by a sincere heart, attracted to beauty, truth, and goodness, and choices that reflect that attraction. In each of them, the power to know lags behind, and both men struggle, on their different intellectual levels, to reconcile these contradictions. In Elliot and Danton, we saw mind leading the way. Both these intellectuals' hearts seem to be struggling to keep up with the implications of personal convictions, and their choices are a little bit, though not too far, behind. In Jim and Emily, we saw the highest level of integration of mind and heart and some correspondingly courageous life choices. In Gandhi, we saw the limitless capacity of the harmony among knowledge, love, and will to expand to world-embracing levels of agency. In all these people, we saw a way of being dramatically more wholesome, positive, and resilient than in their non-CC developmental counterparts.

Hence, these life stories reveal the powerful potential of tapping the human spiritual yearning for truth, beauty, and goodness in cultivating the sincerity of both mind and heart, the synergy of the structural cognitive capacities of mind, and the discernment and the moral motivational capacities of heart. There are, evidently, multiple developmental pathways of CC. For some people the mind leads the way, for others the heart. But generally, the developmental profiles in which heart led the way seem better integrated and more expansive. This finding converges with the conclusion of Daloz et al.'s (1996) study of 100 lives of "sustained commitment to the common good in the face of global complexity" (p. 244): "committed lives have a heart—not mere sentimentality, but rather the strength and grace of a seeing heart that, joined with an open and informed mind, can apprehend reality in a manner that seeks not to deny but rather to engage central challenges of the twenty-first century" (Daloz et al., 1996, p. 131).

To what extent, then, does education as we know it not only develop the rational capacity but also cultivate sincerity and earnestness, moral passion and self-reflection, the power of the heart to be attracted to beauty, truth, and goodness, and the willingness to act accordingly while continuing to rethink one's understanding of beauty, truth, and goodness? A serious consideration of this question reveals that dominant educational paradigms do not explicitly recognize as an educational goal the cultivation of the spiritual powers of the heart in harmony with the cultivation of minds, but define a much narrower rationalistic focus, the heritage of the materialism of the Enlightenment. To the extent that good education happens, it is the result of often unappreciated individual educators going far above and beyond their defined goals and objectives and setting out to cultivate hearts through love and personal example.

Recent educational innovations have begun to overcome the long-standing primary focus on the development of logico-mathematical and linguistic intelligence, on the power to analyze causality and to understand and work with the relational logic of linguistic structures. Ever since Gardner's (1983, 1993) work, there has been a growing effort to redress the imbalance and to develop a more harmonious whole-person approach to education, cognizant of different intelligences that work in concert. However, the cultivation of interpersonal intelligence, as well as of aesthetic, musical, spatial, and bodily-kinesthetic intelligence, is still somewhat peripheral to the educational enterprise, while intrapersonal intelligence has remained almost completely outside the realm of public education.

There have been recent calls to education to cultivate intelligence understood as "a dialectic of the intuitive and the analytic" (Hart, 2000, p. 15). Hart (2000) suggests that young people need to learn to "see through the eye of the heart" and to develop "wisdom which blends insight into what is true with an ethic of what is right" (p. 15). However, such educational goals imply as a unifying center a moral understanding which is still profoundly absent in educational vision.

Our current educational enterprise continues to reflect the prevailing ontology of materialism and the philosophy of relativism. Different innovative pieces, such as emphasis on critical thinking, story-telling, and experiential writing, as vehicles for the development of intra- and interpersonal intelligence are loosely held together by an overall attitude of expediency. Even efforts in new interdisciplinary areas, such as global studies and human rights education, and requirements for a service component in many fields, remain piecemeal and colored by expediency. (For example, for European Union or Global Studies majors to be approved by Boards of Regents at different universities, the general rationale still has to be economic benefit or advantage in international power dynamics.) Lacking is a coherent, integrated, historical vision of the nature of individual and collective human potentiality, which would integrate all educational efforts into a larger purpose.

PARADIGMATIC REASONS FOR THE ABSENCE
OF EDUCATIONAL VISION

The paradigmatic reason for this absence of vision is best understood when we remember that education, in every society, reflects the structural relationships between the main social sectors. According to Malaska (1993), member of the Club of Rome and secretary-general of the World Futures Studies Federation since 1990, society can be seen as consisting of three human "orders," or sectors—the economic, the sociopolitical, and the spiritual orders. These three sectors interact with one another, and "society as a whole is harmonious, or inharmonious, according to the quality of relations and interactions between its three parts" (p. 45). To the extent that one order dominates, the imbalance "ruins the autonomy and optimal functioning of the subordinate orders" (p. 46).

As discussed in chapter 1, Malaska finds that most societies currently represent examples of such an imbalance, which would explain why education for critical consciousness is, at this time, a vision rather than a reality in any part of the world. The preponderance of the economic order in Western industrialized societies accounts for the high prevalence of individualistic expediency motivation found among the U.S. interviewees, as well as for the dominant view of education in the United States as the path to better jobs and more prestigious careers. Out of twenty U.S. interviewees, twelve exhibited non-CC, two exhibited pre-CC, three exhibited transitional CC, and only two exhibited mature CC (see Appendix). Materialism and relativism dominate U.S. consciousness and are reflected in a paralysis of will and a deep split between mind and heart. Education in the United States and most of the Western world is still fundamentally materialistic, reflecting capitalist market values.

The preponderance of the sociopolitical order in former communist East European societies accounts for the highly ideological thinking of the Bulgarian interviewees and their tendency toward reactive intellectual individualism. The greatest obstacle to the development of CC in the Bulgarian sample seemed to be either totalitarian ideologies or idealistic individualistic reactions, still totalizing in nature. In some interviewees, such as Ivan, this totalizing tendency fossilized into ideological consciousness, the antithesis of CC. In others, such as Elliot and Danton, it sought philosophical elaborations but still had difficulty opening up into an explicit spiritual dimension. Recent changes in East European societies have begun to deconstruct somewhat the ideological and totalizing quality of education and to adopt increasingly the Western model.

The preponderance of the spiritual order in many countries in the Muslim world explains why, to the extent to which public education even exists, Islamic education based on the Koran is not adequately counterbalanced by the cultivation of the critical analytical faculties of mind. Also, fear seems to dominate over love in the traditional Islamic education of hearts. In more economically developed Islamic societies, Islamic education enters into an uneasy relationship with the other two subordinate social orders and generates further tensions, as we have realized ever more acutely since September 11, 2001.

This author's experience living and teaching in Zimbabwe confirms Malaska's (1993) view that a number of African societies "illustrate what happens when none of the sectors makes an adequate contribution to the societal whole" (p. 47). No society in the world at this time represents an optimal resonance among the three social orders. However, Western industrialized societies, despite their imbalance, come closest to resonance in Malaska's view. Since the Western educational system, with its focus on developing the critical faculties of mind, comes closest to attempting to cultivate critical consciousness, it is important to examine its current limitations.

The Limits of the Current Educational Paradigm

Ever since the Enlightenment, Western civilization achieved an official separation of science and religion, which opened the door to the emancipation of modernity (Wilber, 1998) and allowed human intelligence to thrive and explore. As Western civilization became the modern cradle of math and science, which it inherited from the Arab world, where science and religion originated as a direct aftermath of the Islamic revelation in the eighth century, Western civilization progressively began to emphasize materialistic ontological assumptions about the nature of reality, the nature of life, and the nature of a human being. This separation of science and religion in the West can be understood as a developmental step in the collective evolution of consciousness—from a fascination with the multiplicity of concrete forms as expressions of the divine to a more purposeful pursuit of the abstract logic behind material reality. However, what was a developmental, and therefore a relative, step has since then become absolutized and reified, so that it has now become unthinkable for serious science to revisit this split between matter and spirit, between science and religion. Contemporary Western education bears the stamp of this split.

The evolutionary necessity for rethinking is staring us in the face. The problem is that science in the last century and a half has insisted on testability in order to prove or disprove a theory. In the area of matter, up to a point, that approach was productive. It took us to the moon, allowed us to explore the cosmos, brought about a technological revolution in our daily lives, began to decode the human genome, and significantly extended the average human life expectancy. For a while, it looked like we had every reason to assume the ultimacy of this approach.

Two things have happened recently that have shaken us out of our comfort zone. One is that the same positivistic approach that brought about all these phenomenal scientific achievements has increasingly generated more ecological, social, and psychological problems than it seems to be able to address on a global scale if we continue to treat life in this compartmentalized manner (Lanza, 2000). The other is that the rigorous application of the scientific approach led physicists to a recognition of its limits: at the subatomic level of matter, our illusion of scientific control explodes, as we are left struggling to grasp the full implications of the Heisenberg Uncertainty Principle.

We cannot continue to absolutize control and predictability any more than we can afford to absolutize hypothetical constructions of the infinite. There needs to be a serious, open, and unfolding dialogue between that which can be tested and that which can be only inferred or hypothesized. It is very likely that in the synergy of this dialogue human understanding will attain a qualitative shift.

Ancient and more recent religious traditions have used a range of metaphors, before each of them fossilized into dogma, to point humankind toward an understanding of psychospiritual laws and the way to align human life with them. Out of these traditions have developed remarkably effective systems of psychological understanding (Buddhist psychology), social organization (Confucianism), and medical treatment (yoga, acupressure, acupuncture, herbal medicine, etc.). To continue to ignore the validity of these systems because they do not fit into our current scientific paradigm is not only psychologically immature but also scientifically and socially irresponsible.

Hence, productive as the materialistic view has been, it needs to be relativized in view of the growing understanding that matter is not ultimate and may need to be understood as an expression of spirit. While not every scientist has to believe this, it seems only fair and responsible to entertain this view and to seriously study its implications. What cannot be studied directly can be corroborated or rejected as a viable understanding through a study of how its implications play out in the observable world of matter.

Such an ontological shift would fundamentally change the quality of education, which is currently defined by its materialistic assumptions about human nature as basically instinctual and selfish. Educational practice is split between behavioristic socialization and an emphasis on the development of skills, where intelligence is reduced to brain development. Lacking are significant models of authentic moral authority or any truly integrative spiritual conversation. An illustration of that is the reductionistic treatment of altruism in modern social science (Sober and Wilson, 1998), and the accompanying compartmentalization of rare altruistic individuals and examples of expansive human moral consciousness, such as Gandhi's, as more an exception than the rule of the human condition. However,

As the ethicist Alasdair MacIntyre has observed, the notion of "altruism" developed only in the eighteenth century in the wake of the ascent and triumph of the "ego-centric self." Since "human nature" was declared to be, at bottom, selfish, altruism became at once both necessary and impossible. Thus, "altruistic" behavior came to be seen as exceptional or even aberrant behavior.

In a similar vein, those who work steadfastly in the public arena—particularly if they are committed to fundamental change or a single pressing issue—may be labeled "activists." This description is often reserved for people who appear to have stepped beyond conventional political tribes and norms and are perceived as dedicating themselves to a cause outside of the mainstream of society. (Daloz et al., 1996, p. 14)

This tendency to dismiss critical moral consciousness reveals the legacy of individualism and materialism. An education that can foster the graded sequence of progressively more complex and expansive moral ways of being described in this book as the CC pathway of optimal development has to begin with accepting that CC is not an exception, but the fulfillment of the human spiritual potential. It has to reexamine its ontological assumptions about the nature of reality, the nature of life, and the nature of a human being. As Daloz et al. (1996) conclude, we need to examine the images and symbols which "elicit and instill the strength and grace that characterize the quality of citizenship needed in the twenty-first century" (p. 131); because "the quality of a society is dependent upon the strength of its imagination of the world and the meaning of citizenship within it" (p. 133).

Opening up Education: Recognition of the Human Spiritual Potential

The question is, how can education both preserve and develop further the remarkable successes in developing the rational mind since the Enlightenment, and yet acknowledge that faith in reason alone has been insufficient to help humanity transcend its "entrenched patterns of conflict" and politics as usual (Universal House of Justice, 1985) and to move toward a truly harmonious, peaceful, and ecologically sustainable global society?

Education for critical consciousness recognizes the human spiritual potential and engages in cultivating a balanced relationship between mind and heart. It is an education that neither represses nor absolutizes the material nature of a human being, but guides it into becoming an increasingly adequate reflection of the spiritual essence of a human being. Such an education has to begin by recognizing the spiritual resources of the child (Coles, 1990; Lewis, 2000; Robinson, 1977; Wade, 1996), which have historically been greatly underestimated in both East and West. What do we mean when we speak of the spiritual nature of the child?

As J. Lewis (2000) points out, the term *spiritual* is often used in conjunction with other terms such as moral, religious, ethical, and even cultural, and has been accused of being an empty category (Lambourn, 1996). J. Lewis (2000) provides a coherent analysis of why such a view is an artifact of a reductionist methodology, which fails to recognize that the whole is greater than its parts, and that while "the spiritual may well be involved in the personal and social, yet [it] cannot be reduced to it" (p. 265). As clarified in the previous section, when spiritual is understood as the essential nature of reality, that is, pure potentiality, it is easy to see how it informs all manifest dimensions of being but is greater than each of them as well as greater than their mechanical sum total.

Recently, there has been a growing recognition, particularly pronounced in Britain, of the need to include spiritual development as an educational goal. The British School Curriculum and Assessment Authority recognizes spiritual and moral development as important dimensions of school performance (SCAA, 1995, 1996). Accompanying it, there has been a growing academic debate about what constitutes spiritual education and what its relationship to religion should be (Best, 1996; Blake, 1996, 1997; Carr, 1995, 1996a, 1996b; Lewis, 2000). In this debate, there are three generally opposing tendencies.

First, there is the position that for spiritual education not to become an empty term, it needs to be placed in the context of participating in an existing religious tradition, thus giving structure and purpose to spiritual inquiry and preserving its intellectual integrity (Carr, 1995, 1996a, 1996b). This position recognizes that spiritual development involves more than the practice of religion and therefore needs to include the cultivation of artistic sensibility. Second, there is the position that since spirituality is so intricately connected to religion, it cannot be the goal of a secular curriculum, which needs to limit its goals to moral education and the cultivation of political sensitivity (Blake, 1996, 1997).

The third position views the interpretation of spiritual education in terms of religious or moral education as reductionist, since, according to J. Lewis (2000), spirituality should be seen as a characteristic of all phenomena, and the psychological fact of spiritual experience is not limited to any particular domain. People have the capacity to experience feelings of awe and wonder, gratitude, transcendence, unity and wholeness, love and serenity across content areas, and it is this human sensibility that needs to be fostered and enriched through education across the curriculum. In this sense, "the moral, aesthetic, religious or just simply educational all include, not exclude or oppose the spiritual" (Lewis, 2000, p. 4).

According to this perspective, morality is both the outcome of spiritual education and its condition, since as Lewis points out, drawing on the Buddhist tradition, living in nonhurting ways is a prerequisite for the ability to have calm concentration and insightful wisdom, while it is also the outcome of spiritual practices. Such an understanding is supported by observations of critically conscious people, who consistently stand out by virtue of the sincerity of their motives. As we saw, an examination of that purity of heart shows its relatedness to some form or other of spiritual education, which has activated the depth dimension of human experience.

J. Lewis also draws a distinction between spiritual education and religion, seeing religious traditions as attempting "to give the spiritual a holding form, but in so doing necessarily ignor[ing] the essential ineffability and dynamic flux of the spiritual," and establishing ultimately repressive hierarchies which end up defeating spiritual awareness (p. 271). Hence, J. Lewis proposes a spiritual education as a fundamental orientation to coming to know ourselves and to understanding our relations with all things, relying on a range of spiritual practices that quiet the mind, tap creativity, and allow for gentle experiential exploration of the human experience. Ultimately, he sees spiritual education as cultivating qualities of mind and heart through practices that invite authentic investigation.

The goal of truly spiritual education is balance; balance between mind and heart, between honoring material realities and not indulging excessively in them but being guided by a deeper understanding of life. In the minds of many people who have experienced the moralistic turning away from the pleasures and joys of life embedded in many Judeo-Christian and Islamic practices, the mention of spiritual education resurrects historical associations with repression and imbalance and with a hypocritical or a quasi-ascetic approach to life. There are real reasons for that, because religious indoctrination and spiritual education have for too long been used interchangeably.

However, authentic spiritual education can always be recognized, because it is about balance as a fundamental principle of all life. Equilibrium, as Confucius taught in 500 B.C., is "the great root from which grow all the human actings in the world, and this Harmony is the universal path which they all should pursue" (Bryson, 1999, p. 2). Lack of harmony and reactive self-indulgence, which are so much at the heart of all the suffering and paranoia in our world, need to be overcome through enlightened and balanced education, which, as the Buddha suggests, "trims the lamp of wisdom, and keeps our minds strong and clear" (Bryson, 1999, p. 6).

There are reasons to believe that the world religions are right when they claim that a child brings a soul into the world and that soul is naturally attracted to goodness, truth, and beauty. When a parent or an educator looks into the eyes of a child from the very beginning with that understanding, they draw on the child's deep intuitive resources and inherent moral sense, helping to make her increasingly conscious of her resources through engaging the unfolding powers of her mind and heart.

Education for critical consciousness is a good mix of spiritual guidance that prunes the young tree and allows it to grow tall and sturdy and the child's organically unfolding inner constructions of both her own intuitive spirituality and the internalized adult voices of authentic moral authority. Such education helps the child curb her other primal urges toward aggression, rage, jealousy, and destructiveness, which otherwise gradually fuse with the developing ego, make it swell beyond its balanced function, and become the sources of what we have come to know as evil. To learn to curb one's more primitive urges is not the same as to repress or deny them. It means to develop self-knowledge and self-control, so that one's thinking changes and a more serene understanding of life gradually takes the place of what George Pransky (1992) describes as excessive expectations and chronic resentments. While the complete attainment of such personal integration is certainly a phenomenon of advanced adult development, children and young people have much more capacity to stretch in that direction than we currently give them credit for.

In the stories of the CC people we explored, we saw again and again how these children gradually learned the power of their own minds by being continually redirected inward through wise guidance. They were encouraged to seek answers in the silence of their hearts, and prayer was often an important part of that. At the same time, they were exposed to a dignified (rather than hectic and erratic) way of living, modeled by the surrounding adults; a way that truly honors the human spirit. They were also exposed to a discourse which gives a name and a principled explanation to living life from a moral and spiritual center. In this way, mind and heart never grow apart, but strengthen each other through an ongoing synergistic interplay.

Daloz et al. (1996) also found in their interviews that the two most salient sources of positive images were family and authentic religion, the same that we saw in our seven examples of CC. One of their interviewees clarifies "that religion as much or more than any other institution can shape attitudes—attitudes about love and justice and who counts in the world" (p. 129). She makes clear that she is not referring to religion that "operates off the artifacts of the faith" but to "the real, vibrant stuff. The church is too often frightened and operates out of a lot of artifacts" (p. 129).

When religious artifacts are separated from the religious spirit, it becomes evident that self-knowledge and self-control have always been at the heart of the teachings of world religions. Below are some excerpts to that effect, drawn from various traditions, as quoted in Bryson (1999, pp. 50, 88–90):

Learn to distinguish between Self and Truth. . . . Seek not self, but seek the truth. If we liberate our souls from our petty selves, with no ill to others, and become clear as a crystal diamond reflecting the light of truth, what a radiant picture will appear in us mirroring things as they are, without the admixture of burning desires, without the distortion of erroneous illusion, without the agitation of clinging and unrest. (From the Teachings of the Buddha)

Who hateth nought of all which lives, living himself benign, compassionate, from arrogance exempt, exempt from love of self, unchangeable by good or ill; patient, contented, firm in faith, mastering himself, true to his word, seeking Me, heart and soul; vowed into Me, that man love! (From the Teachings of Krishna)

Thine eye is My trust, suffer not the dust of vain desires to becloud its lustre. Thine ear is a sign of My bounty, let not the tumult of unseemly motives turn it away from My Word that encompasseth all creation. Thine heart is My treasury, allow not the treacherous hand of self to rob thee of the pearls which I have treasured therein. . . . Be as resigned and submissive as the earth, that from the soil of your being there may blossom the fragrant, the holy and multicolored hyacinths of My knowledge. Be ablaze as the fire, that ye may burn away the veils of heedlessness and set aglow, through the quickening energies of the love of God, the chilled and wayward heart. Be light and untrammeled as the breeze, that ye may obtain admittance into the precincts of My court, My inviolable sanctuary. (From the Teachings of Baha'u'llah)

While J. Lewis (2000) correctly points out that religious and spiritual education are not the same thing, his understanding of religion is somewhat historically limited. The role of religion in spiritual education might be seen somewhat differently if we understand religion itself as a historical process of progressive revelation, in which the rise of each new religion in the world has brought about a tremendous spurt forward of human civilization, while its later progressive fossilization into power-oriented hierarchical structures has eventually become the source of repression, coercion, corruption, and disillusionment.

As Pitirim Sorokin, professor emeritus of sociology at Harvard University and the first professor and chairman of sociology of the University of St. Petersburg, pointed out (Maslow, 1959), "the longest existing organizations . . . the great ethico-religious organizations—Taoism, Confucianism, Hinduism, Buddhism, Jainism, Christianity, Mohammedanism," have lasted for millennia, in contrast to the relatively short-lived different kinds of other organizations over the centuries. The impact of religious and spiritual teachers such as "Lao-Tze, Confucius, Moses, Buddha, Mahavira, Jesus, St. Paul, St. Francis of Assisi, Mahatma Gandhi and other founders of great religions, discoverers of eternal moral principles, and living incarnations of sublime, unselfish love" has remained without comparison amid monarchs, conquerors, revolutionaries, and other historical figures (p. 10).

If we do not understand the human tendency to reify relative truths as part of the process of a slow historical maturation of collective human consciousness, which has resulted in the corruption, in time, of every human institution, we would have to conclude that institutions themselves are inherently evil and need to be discarded—a line of thought far too prevalent in contemporary thinking. Each religious institution that emerged around the world provided, for a while, important and much-needed structure and direction to daily living. Eventually, each became corrupted and was replaced by other, new religious institutions that corresponded better to the needs of the times.

Every historical religion has contained both the dynamic and the static forms of quality that Pirsig (1974, 1991) differentiates, and practitioners within every religious tradition in the world have expressed awareness of both the impossibility to capture the ineffable and codify it in form (hence the relativity of all codified forms) and the importance of conceivable forms which give structure to the human experience and in that way contribute to it, rather than detract from it, as long as they are held openly. Hence, the current tendency to identify religion with failed institutions, and thus dismiss it, is both myopic and historically incorrect and does not take into consideration the existence of newer religions which have evolved contemporary forms of democratic institutions, not yet corrupted, functioning in positive and constructive ways.

Therefore, it seems important not to counterpose religion and spirituality but to reclaim the importance of both in a person's life. Our inherent moral sense and intuitive attraction to the good, the true, and the beautiful need a context that fosters them, especially in the earliest formative years. Authentic religious and spiritual practice (as opposed to dogmatic, repressive, hostile, and invasive religious practices) provides that context, as we saw in the lives of CC individuals.

The challenge of the family is to find and commit to a spiritual path and to model for its children steadfastness and faith. In education, children need to study and be exposed to the beauty and wealth of a range of religious and spiritual traditions so that they can learn how various traditions spoke to the progressive unfolding of the human spiritual potential throughout life. They need to see how the same virtues have been cultivated by widely diverse traditions (Taafaki, 1986), how people are guided in negotiating birth, family life, work, aging, and death. In this way, children develop critical discernment instead of intolerant absolutistic frames of reference and learn to appreciate early in their lives the beauty of unity in diversity. That is what it means to grow with an open mind and an open heart, not lost in ambiguity or, worse yet, anomie, but grounded, yet open to continuous learning.

There are schools that already recognize and respond to that need. This author experienced firsthand the impact of one such school, Maxwell International Baha'i School in Canada, on her son. He spent two years there, having come from an excellent public school system in Amherst, Massachusetts, which had greatly fostered his intellectual and artistic development but had also faced him with the anomie that plagues most young people in public schools today.

Important as the Western emphasis on ethics is, it has not been sufficient to engage the full moral and spiritual potential of young people. This author's son had seen his best friends, intelligent and talented children, sink deeper and deeper into the grip of moral disorientation and a pervasive sense of vacuum created by the absence of authentic moral authority in their lives. Their rebellion against despair took increasingly drastic forms—alcohol, sex, drugs. None of these children seemed to know that they carried an inherent nobility that needed to be developed, nor did their teachers have the authority to offer them a more engaged moral and spiritual guidance, due to the prevailing individualistic climate of ethical relativism.

At Maxwell, the author's son entered a completely different climate. Despite the growth tensions of Maxwell as a relatively new school, children there were seen primarily as spiritual beings who need a great deal of mature guidance to learn to consistently manifest their potential. Adult authority and respect for children as a sacred trust created a whole different breed of teachers—fully empowered educators.

For two years, in seventh and eighth grade, along with his regular curriculum, this author's son studied world religion. Each semester he was required to choose from the full range of world wisdom traditions one tradition to study in depth. Side by side with his studies in history and world literature, his studies of Islam, Buddhism, Christianity, and the Baha'i Faith opened his mind and heart to such a level of appreciation and respect for the human spiritual journey in this life that he came home transformed. The seeds planted have continued to transform him ever since. In the most conflicted and also the most idealistic of ages, adolescence, he found sustainable ideals that embrace the world; he faced and learned to overcome his own prejudices; he developed a frame of reference much larger than prevailing standards of peer pressure; he learned to resist, yet to love and accept; and he began to understand what it means to live as a noble human being and a global citizen in service to humanity in a turbulent age.

This kind of education should be possible for every child, provided the adults in this world are more committed to cultivating critical consciousness and educating global citizens than to their personal and ideological attachments and fears. The recognition of the human spiritual potential has been a fact in the lives of CC people from different ages, but not for the majority of people. The shift we face in the sciences and in education is part of a process of global spiritualization, which world leaders already recognize (see chapter 1; also see Fifth Annual State of the World Forum, 1999), but which needs to be acknowledged, and actively supported in education.

Serious Integration of Science and Religion

If we continue to believe that only science develops the mind and that religion simply speaks to some emotional needs and is therefore a completely different enterprise, then we cannot move forward and bridge the current unhealthy compartmentalization of life. We have begun to hear voices that point to the faith of science (Kuhn, 1970), and the method of religion (Aull, 1988), and to an organic process of gradual integration of science and religion as part of a new level of understanding of the cosmos in its four aspects: exterior-individual (behavioral), exterior-collective (social), interior-individual (intentional), and interior-collective (cultural) (Wilber, 1998).

When we study the outside of the individual, we study the behavior of the components of the universe, from atoms all the way to the neocortex. When we study the inside of the individual, we study interior awareness, from simple irritability to external stimuli, sensation, and perception, all the way to creative vision. When we study the outside of the collective, we study the social organization of communities, from galaxies and ecosystems to nation-states and planetary civilization. And when we study the inside of the collective, we study cultures and worldviews, from protoplasmic and vegetative all the way to enlightened human cultures (Wilber, 1998, pp. 63–72). Different ways of knowing are most adequate for each quadrant, and none needs to be absolutized, while they all need to enter into an interdisciplinary dialogue.

Religion, as well as science, has some important understanding of all of the above domains. When absolutized, religion has proven incompatible with science; but when viewed as a progressive revelation, it is quite consistent. And in all of the above, it is the human mind that attempts to know the universe and itself, via the potentialities and limitations of its consciousness.

Some serious rethinking is in order along a number of points.

First, religion as an understanding of the nature of a human being and the nature of life has to be separated from the history of the rise and decline of various religions, while both their rise and decline have to be equally acknowledged. As an understanding of the primarily spiritual, energetic, and relational nature of life, of which material life is one important expression, religious insight has been with humanity since the beginning of human civilization. It has been consistently reiterated in every next tradition and is currently increasingly supported by the advances in the physical sciences. Each time this understanding has been brought to the fore by the emergence of a new world religion, it has engaged the most progressive and authentic minds, has spoken to the deepest wisdom buried in the hearts of the mass of ordinary people, and, in spite of much resistance from fossilized earlier views, has brought about a new spurt of growth in human civilization.

To not acknowledge the civilizing impact of early Hinduism on the tribes inhabiting the Hindu valley, or of Buddhism on the whole far East, or of early Judaism and early Christianity on Western culture, or of early Islam on the Arab tribes, is to breed ignorance. Though perhaps no educator would openly deny the above, our actual education shows a heavy disbalance in the direction of emphasizing the degradation and fall of different religious traditions, their fossilization into irrational myths and intolerant and repressive dogmas, and their tendency to inhibit human progress.

Second, neither science nor religion should be absolutized; both need to be viewed and taught as progressive revelation; and their mutual contradictions need to be seen as indications that either one could be wrong on a particular question and a careful counter-examination is in order. If we stop confusing the historical corruption of religious practices and the ensuing decline, in due time, of their respective religious establishments, with the essence of religious knowing and understanding, we clear the field for an open examination of that understanding.

Religious understanding is based on reflection and insight; direct ways of knowing predominate in it, although rational-analytic understanding has its place too. Scientific understanding also relies on reflection and insight, as all the major discoveries in science show, but it is primarily grounded in rational-analytical procedures. Hence, while both, in their optimal versions, include the full range of human ways of knowing, they emphasize different aspects, and as such are quite complementary.

For example, the study of consciousness and human behavior solely as recent endeavors of neurobiology and psychology respectively is an impoverished enterprise that does not really foster critical thinking and discernment, since the study of consciousness and behavior is as old as human civilization. We are beginning to see that what science and religion contribute to the understanding of consciousness and behavior are not necessarily incompatible truths, but rather are mutually complementary different aspects of a greater picture which we do not yet understand.

Hence, both science and religion have much to learn from each other; they both engage the human mind and heart in important ways. In dialogue, they protect the mind from arrogance and ignorance and the heart from fanaticism and fear. Therefore, both need to be part of a balanced, well-rounded education that cultivates integration of minds and hearts. People educated that way are more able to be part of a respectful and equitable dialogue between East and West, and North and South, as we saw in the life of Gandhi. They also develop the capability to move us toward less compartmentalized basic and social science and social institutions harmonious with our best understanding.

Centrality of Universal Moral Values

What is the relationship between spirituality and morality? As J. Lewis (2000) points out, "[I]n many spiritual traditions the notions of spiritual practice and moral behavior are inextricably linked," but this "does not mean that they are co-terminous." (p. 270) Rather, "they develop or evolve alongside each other" (Lewis, 2000, p. 270), amplifying each other. To quote St. Paul, as quoted by J. Lewis, "The harvest of the spirit is love, joy, patience, kindness, fidelity, gentleness and self-control" (Galatians 5.22–24, qtd. in Lewis, 2000, p. 270). Cultivating the spirit leads to a "disposition to behave morally," while this disposition in turn strengthens "openness to the spiritual" (Lewis, 2000, p. 270).

If we recognize the human spiritual potential from the beginning of life, we have to build on that potentiality by making it a top priority to cultivate the child's natural proclivity toward earnestness and empathy. That means that core moral values have to become explicit and central to the public discourse and all educational influences (including the TV industry). The current state of public discourse is one of an uneasy and precarious balance between relativism, which can only sneak moral values into the conversation under the guise of expediency, and polarized political and ideological moralizing. Very little in all this is truly guided by core moral values.

A recent epitome of the current state of public discourse has been the debate around Clinton's personal moral choices as U.S. president. What would have been a morally appropriate way to deal with the consequences of Clinton's choices in a way that turns the whole situation into an opportunity to learn and teach young people a bigger lesson, instead of to preach, argue, and moralize? Many of those who claimed to oppose on principle Clinton's moral choices felt justified to follow them up with a mean-spirited, self-righteous, and politically manipulative public bashing, even placing the report on the gruesome and titillating details of Clinton's acts on the Internet for every young person to read, while campaigning against him. How many of the men involved in that public bashing stopped to reflect on their own personal mistakes and brought a measure of humility, generosity, moderation, and forgiveness to the public conversation? Or are we to believe that in an age where sexism is still so rampant in the public sphere, none of these men, most of whom represent an older generation for which sexism was in the very fabric of male socialization, had anything in their own lives to stop and reflect about that could temper a bit the self-righteous outrage? Was the practice of public humiliation by each and every means what Christian morality is about, or was it more reminiscent of the eighteenth-century burning of witches in Puritan New England? And on the other side of the camp, was there a way to own with integrity the full ramifications of a president's personal choices, without arguing over legal details and half-truths? That is the kind of stark contrast and spiritual vacuum that our children and young people have to negotiate as a public model for moral adulthood. Is it any wonder, then, that they have come to be known as Generation X?

If we choose to see ourselves and our children as primarily moral beings, struggling to understand more fully morality as a balanced and respectful approach to all life, then we do not have to limit ourselves to either tolerant indifference or unrealistic moralistic claims. We do not have to be embarrassed that our understanding of morality is still so contradictory and incomplete. Like science and religion, our understanding of morality too is a progressive revelation, but that is no reason not to make our moral learning central to our public discourse.

We cannot raise critically conscious young people by modeling a public discourse dominated by oppositional, self-centered debate which does not emphasize learning as a collective consultative process. Even our best news shows, such as the "MacNeil-Lehrer NewsHour," which try to give a more in-depth coverage and discussion, fall into the pattern of short snippets of thought exchanged like swords crossed by opposing camps, rather than a more thoughtfully and serenely unfolding conversation. These public models reveal our assumptions about the way to arrive at truth, as well as our failure to recognize and respect the wisdom of others.

Children have to grow up in a climate of authentic moral discourse central to society, a discourse which models tolerance of ambiguity, respectful and truly open and thoughtful *consultation* across different worldviews, and a fundamental recognition of our collective journey as a human family. Anything less than that is not about peace in the world, authentic moral values, and education for CC, but is rather about our continuing adolescent love affair with war and power.

In summary, consistent education for critical consciousness would have to be based on an integrative large-scale view of the global historical processes in which we are engaged and an equally integrative understanding of the relationship between the spiritual and material aspects of human life. Such an education would have to transcend the political swings between conservatism and liberalism, between nationalism and globalism, in order to equip people to negotiate a balanced, permeable approach to past, present, and future, guided by moral agency.

There are some heartening examples of such a vision emerging. Among them is the issuing, in March 2000, of the final version of the Earth Charter, after eight years of deliberations, involving more than 100,000 people in at least fifty countries. The charter, which is now recognized as "the definitive earth ethics declaration" (Pokorny, 2000, p. 14), not only identifies this as a critical moment in Earth's history, but also points to the need to integrate the understanding of interdependence and responsibility as an educational tool in formal and nonformal education for global citizenship and sustainable development.

Thus, education for CC is no less than all-encompassing spiritual education, and the construct of CC offers many insights as to how to orient education toward cultivating a pervasively moral, spiritually awakened, and intellectually integrated global consciousness.

DIMENSIONS OF SPIRITUAL EDUCATION

The principles discussed above as central to cultivating critical consciousness (recognizing, and orienting education toward the human spiritual potential; serious integration of science and religion; and recognizing the centrality of moral values) can be implemented along the four dimensions of moral motivation, using these four dimensions as overarching interdisciplinary objectives. The degree to which specific educational interventions are consistent with principles of CC can be continuously assessed using the expanded motivational template offered in chapter 3 as a qualitative tool for focused critical reflection and examination.

It is impossible in this chapter on education to discuss all the educational implications of the profiles examined in earlier chapters or to do justice to the educational insights contained in the original study (Mustakova-Possardt, 1996). Suffice it to say that until education focuses on the cultivation of character and the development of a moral sense of identity and moral imperative; until it begins to purposefully emphasize models of authentic moral authority and to foster moral responsibility and agency; until it makes central the cultivation of expanding levels of empathy, progressively embracing the human race; and until it is willing to entertain an explicit spiritual conversation about truth and meaning in life, it cannot really fulfill its responsibility to the human potential.

The challenge education is facing is to transcend the collective paralysis of relativistic, stage 4/5 (Lahey et al., 1988) thinking and to integrate the best understanding gained through postmodern thought into a spiritual vision of human potential and a commitment to that vision. Without that vision, even our greatest achievements and most honest efforts are tinged with bitterness, if not cynicism, and we are left estranged from our own powers. This can be clearly seen in studies of the lives of moral leaders, such as human rights activist Virginia Durr, as described by Colby and Damon (1992).

The study of CC offers many possibilities for an in-depth interdisciplinary revisioning of holistic education across the curriculum. A detailed examination of these possibilities would have to be a separate enterprise. The next section offers some initial suggestions on how public education can foster moral motivation in concordance with developing more sophisticated structures of reasoning.

Moral Identity

Parenting and education need to cultivate in a child a sense of his or her inner nobility. Why do people love children? Because in their presence, through their innocence and purity of heart, we get in touch with our own. Children are naturally spiritual, but they do not know it, and they also have other inclinations as the ego develops. They need to learn from us that they are primarily spiritual beings, and they need to learn to identify themselves as such. Their inherent moral sense needs to be continuously drawn forth through discussion and living examples of virtues such as patience, trustworthiness, kindness, justice, mercy, generosity, courtesy, respect, purity, and love. Discovering these capacities, and learning to develop these potentialities in themselves, is tremendously empowering to children. So is observing and reading about these capacities in others, for example, through collections of folk stories and world spiritual teachings (Taafaki, 1986).

As the study of lives in Mustakova-Possardt (1996) showed, spiritual self-understanding naturally leads to a striving to develop spiritual qualities of character. Virtues become increasingly internalized as personal values, and a conscious striving develops to live as a moral being. This is the root of habitual morality.

Recognizing the spiritual nature of a human being, and helping every person develop rootedness in a sense of his or her inherent nobility, underlies any effort to release the human potential. People can be freed from the inner oppression of having to identify primarily with transient and questionable social configurations and to struggle to build a sense of identity in fear, anxiety, and social competition. As we saw in some of the case studies, a person's socialization can be mediated by a recognition of his or her own spiritual nature, its potential for love, mercy, kindness, service, generosity, and justice, and the power of moral behavior to express that spiritual nature (Noguchi, Hanson and Lample, 1992). Embracing these values as ideals is fundamental to positive development in adolescence. They provide a buffer of critical discernment, high personal standard, and resilience, which will mediate socialization. Such a process would be the source of moral character, normative ends, moral imperative, and habitual morality.

With the emergence of a child's sense of spiritual identity, educators need to foster the recognition of the oneness of the human family and the affective capacity of children to embrace the human race (Rutstein, 1999).

Authority, Responsibility, Agency

The development of discernment of and respect for authentic moral authority in others, and the gradual evolving of personal moral authority and responsibility depends on the presence of figures of authentic moral authority in one's life. Most of the people whom this author spoke to had few such figures in their immediate environments. As social critics point out, the disintegration of the fabric of family and community life is a reality in relatively alienated Western societies. The lack of models of authentic moral authority has become particularly prominent in academe, where "the disparity between intellect and character" was recently captured in Coles' (1995) account of his encounter with an earnest and disillusioned Harvard student quitting her college education and "fancy, phony Cambridge" because she found no answer there to her burning question: "What's the point of knowing good, if you don't keep trying to become a good person?" There is a general outcry for authentic moral authority, different from hypocritical, self-righteous, and moralistic pseudo-religious authorities, and from equally hypocritical, alienated, and ideological secular intellectual authorities (Abdullah, 1995; Bellah et al., 1985; Rutstein, 1994; Wilshire, 1990).

Research (Mustakova-Possardt, 1996) has shown that authentic moral authority is the meeting ground of the best of traditional character-building values, with the best democratic ideas of the progressive movement, without the stereotypes of the first and the disorientedness of the second. It is not a battleground between liberals and conservatives or between religious and secular approaches to contemporary social reconstruction. Its spiritual essence unites these opposites and integrates dualistic polarities.

No person, regardless of economic or family background, need be deprived from an education that develops intimate understanding of the lives and teachings of human models of transcendence throughout civilization. Education cannot fulfill its purpose of *educare* (in Latin, to draw out the human potential) if the living examples of the most transformative figures in human history, humanity's spiritual and moral leaders, are not integral to the content that is taught. While such content needs to be central to the study of literature, religion, and history, the focus on outstanding examples of the human spirit from all cultures and historic periods can enrich the current approach in all the sciences and social sciences. Engaging young people in an ongoing dialogue with authentic exemplars of the human spirit is a powerful way to help them recognize and develop their own moral authority, responsibility, and agency.

Relationships

Developing an understanding of what it means to be in a relationship with the world is the focal point of any authentic spiritual education. In the examination of educational opportunities along this dimension, Noguchi, Hanson, and Lample's (1992) approach is particularly helpful. As they point out,

The development of the moral structures of a new age implies a profound change in the conception of essential relationships: between man and nature, among individuals and groups, within the family, and between the individual and social institutions. . . . Beset by turbulence, some of the relationships have been corrupted, some shattered, and others rendered meaningless. Fundamental to the reconceptualization of these relationships is awareness of the spiritual aspects of social structures and relationships. (p. 8)

As we saw in the stories in earlier chapters, relatedness can and needs to be taught and is best learned in an authentic spiritual environment which practices it on every level.

Relationship with Nature. The fact that environmentally sustainable education is practically nonexistent in the public school system and is still viewed as peripheral to the central concerns of society is testimony of our short-sighted, adolescent view of life on this planet. Much has been written on this topic, but in essence, the emerging field of ecopsychology has shown that children's growing alienation from the natural world and primary attraction to technological artifacts as well as adults' greedy and exploitative attitudes have become the source of much psychological disorder.

Spiritual education needs to cultivate, on all educational levels, a new sense of "the responsibility to conserve and use rationally the earth's resources" (Noguchi, Hanson, and Lample, 1992, p. 9). Such education needs to examine "the very goals and structures according to which society has been organized. Endless acquisition of material goods impelled by individual and collective greed can only aggravate the destruction of the environment" (Noguchi, Hanson, and Lample, 1992, p. 9).

Finally, spiritual education needs to cultivate a consciousness of the interconnectedness of the universe and of the beauty and necessity of diversity.

Relationships among Individuals and Groups. The current reality of these relationships is succinctly captured by Noguchi, Hanson, and Lample (1992):

Just as establishing a healthy relationship between humanity and the environment requires a cultivation of attitudes of humility rather than pride, serenity rather than greed and interconnectedness rather than exploitation, the relationships among individuals and groups can also be set on a more mature footing through attention to the spiritual characteristics of the social order. At present, most societies are pervaded by relations of dominance and most of the world's people find themselves enmeshed in such relations, as victims, as perpetrators, or both. (p. 10)

In reaction to this reality, we see two types of phenomena—rigid and closed group identifications that Daloz et al. (1996) call tribalism and individualistic distrust toward society, which we saw in many of the stories.

Hence, education at all levels needs to foster in young people an understanding of and an ability and commitment to develop further democratic grassroots processes to redress social injustice. Such education needs to include the full range from Socratic dialogues on contemporary moral dilemmas, to Kohlbergian just community approaches developing students' moral responsibility and capacity for self-governance, to cultivating participatory community development efforts.

Service has to become a central component of education, and it has to open up for young people realistic opportunities to find "where the heart's deep gladness meets the world's deep hunger" (Daloz et al., 1996, pp. 196–97). For service to become a genuinely meaningful component of education, rather than a formal requirement, education needs to overcome the current fractured view of the structure of humanity (Rutstein, 1999) and its expression in various forms of tribalism and to cultivate true understanding of the oneness of the human race.

At the dawn of our transition to a global civilization, relatedness between races is amid the ultimate tests of true relatedness and needs to be consistently taught through the spiritual principle of the oneness of humanity (Rutstein, 1999). This is the only way to overcome racism, sexism, and class and ethnic prejudice in the world of the future.

When we internalize the reality of the oneness of humankind, we become able to see possibilities we would never have seen in our previous state of mind. . . . The idea of the

Earth's being one country no longer seems like a pipedream. In fact, we begin to view the internationalization of our planet as a necessary step toward establishing world peace, and we find we want to dedicate ourselves to sharing with others what we now feel is so obvious. When a great number of people attain such an outlook, individuals and institutions will undergo metamorphosis. As a result, the collective spirit in the world will be more caring and optimistic than it is today. Changes that once seemed impossible before we embraced the concept of oneness will begin to seem realistic, workable, and manageable. (Rutstein, 1999, p. 165)

As experience has shown (Rutstein, 1997), it is not enough to teach young people the intellectual concept of human rights, especially in view of the painful reality that the United States, the greatest proponent of human rights in the world, has failed to ratify for years a number of the most important Human Rights Conventions of the United Nations. Such an intellectual approach can easily be perceived by young people as hypocritical and can breed more disillusionment. In addition to discussing in realistic terms the uneasy movement of world history in the direction of human rights, young people need to experience the oneness of the human family. Their faith and hope need to strengthen amid communities that truly embrace the diverse members of humanity and that have the force of love and the will to carry through their intellectual commitments. Participation in such experiences can help young people grow up with the conviction that every human being counts. Such an approach

enables each individual to feel as one part in an organic whole and to realize that injury to any part results in injury to all, that one's accomplishments are built on the sacrifices and achievements of others, and that one's own fulfillment lies in the welfare and happiness of one's fellow human beings. Awareness of these truths helps delineate the beginning of a path that will lead humanity out of the conflicts that have characterized relations between individuals and groups in every society throughout the world. . . . Moral action is infused with the feelings of love, harmony and kindness that can only be engendered by an unshakable belief in the unity of humankind. (Noguchi, Hanson and Lample, 1992, p. 7)

Relationships within Families. The social breakdown syndrome, which involves the disintegration of the traditional family as well as other social institutions, has become an increasingly pervasive reality throughout the twentieth century. Most of the U.S. interviewees for this study came from one-parent homes. They related lifelong struggles with insecurity related to instability in the early family environment, as well as excessively casual, laissez-faire, or authoritarian single-parent styles. Relatively few had had an experience with authoritative parenting and parents as models of authentic moral authority.

In this context, Western education has made significant progress in helping young people to develop a new conception of family relationships based no longer on domination but on mutual respect. With the overall spiritualizing of education, this area of human relationships too needs to be infused with a much deeper appreciation of the sanctity of family relationships.

Relationships between the Individual and Social Institutions. Education can help bridge the gap between individualistic distrust of social institutions that curtail individual freedom and excessively collectivist tendencies. Since there are sociocultural examples of the limitations of both, education needs to take a dialectical historical view and help individuals become more aware of their particular cultural conditioning and of the possibility of a balanced middle ground. Here again, the concepts of human freedom, human nature, and the nature and purpose of institutions need to be profoundly reexamined.

Meaning of Life

The essence of spiritual education is to teach a greater, self-transcending purpose in life, which helps the growth, transformation, and well-being of the individual and society (Noguchi, Hanson and Lample, 1992). Authentic spiritual education does that by fostering the independent and interdependent investigation of truth and reality. What does that mean?

As Wilfred Cantwell Smith ([1979] 1998) points out in his distinction between faith and belief,

Faith . . . [is] that human quality that has been expressed in, has been elicited, nurtured, and shaped by, the religious traditions of the world. . . . Faith . . . precedes and transcends the tradition, and in turn sustains it. (pp. 5–6)

Faith is a quality of human living. At its best it has taken the form of serenity and courage and loyalty and service: quiet confidence and joy which enable one to feel at home in the universe, and to find meaning in the world and in one's own life, a meaning that is profound and ultimate, and is stable no matter what may happen to oneself at the level of immediate events. Men and women of this kind of faith face catastrophe and confusion, affluence and sorrow, unperturbed; face opportunity with conviction and drive; and face others with a cheerful charity. . . . Faith . . . is an orientation of the personality, to oneself, to one's neighbour, to the universe; a total response; . . . a capacity to live at a more than mundane level; to see, to feel, to act in terms of, a transcendent dimension. (p. 12)

Education can and needs to cultivate faith in the ultimate meaningfulness of life and in our capacity to respond to life fully and completely, with both hearts and minds. What education cannot do is to teach religious beliefs, except as comparative religion, which should be part of the basic curriculum. It is for families to teach beliefs, but education can foster faith. In a nurturing and strengthening educational environment, in which young people learn that humanity has forever been sustained by its capacity for faith in life and are exposed to rich examples of that from the history of world religions, young people can do their own independent and interdependent investigation of truth. They will find beliefs and traditions they can relate to and which can sustain them in their life journey. A content area that has the potential to support in significant and unexplored ways the cultivation of faith across the curriculum is the emerging global ethic discourse (Swindler, 1999).

If education is to recognize the human spiritual potential and consistently amplify it along the four motivational dimensions discussed earlier, thus strengthening the attraction of the heart to truth, beauty, and goodness while engaging the mind in an ongoing examination and reconstruction of truth, beauty, and goodness, then education needs a historical perspective. Education needs to view the cultivation of the powers of the individual against the background of evolving collective human consciousness in the context of grand historical shifts. An education that truly empowers individuals to not simply adjust to existing social conditions, but to overcome what critical psychologists call false consciousness (Martin-Baro, 1994; Sloan, 1996), to achieve a critical understanding of themselves, their world and where they stand in it, needs to help people understand the historical context in which their lives are unfolding. Only then can education truly do justice to its task.

EDUCATIONAL VISION: A DYNAMIC HISTORICAL PERSPECTIVE

For education to stand on the grounds of authentic authority, rather than be perceived by young people as an arbitrary conglomeration of socialization strategies, it has to be based on an ethical orientation to history (Saiedi, 2000). It has to help young people view themselves as part of a large collective process, in which humanity's spiritual potential is progressively "unveiled" and manifested "through successive stages of humanity's cultural and spiritual development" (Saiedi, 2000, p. 166).

Young people need to understand that in the current stage of this historical unfolding of collective human consciousness the greatest battle is for global justice and peace. As part of their educational development, they need to ask themselves what will be their individual roles in this grand historical process of learning to establish justice and peace on the planet. They need to be assisted in articulating not just a career but a personal calling in service to the sustainable development of the human family. The ultimate testimony of their successful education would be the evolving of a world-embracing vision, an understanding of the historical processes convulsing different parts of the world, and a choice to commit to a specific field of human endeavor as a conscious localized contribution to the peaceful and sustainable globalization of the planet. Such an understanding of one's place in history is what Freire (1973) considered true empowerment. As he succinctly captured it, people's ability "to perceive the epochal themes of their times," and to enter into conscious relationships with them largely determines the degree to which they can become "Subjects" or "are carried along in the wake of change" (Freire, 1973, p. 7).

In this most education-oriented and information-filled century, relatively few people understand history in context, and even fewer are able to see their lives as part of larger historical processes at work. Education, in the age of globalization, is challenged to shift to a whole new level of dynamic historical perspective, to a genuinely spiritual understanding of history, as suggested by Saiedi (2000) in his *Logos and Civilization*: "Human history in its totality can be seen as the progressive realization and unfoldment of this primordial unity and dignity in the form of social relations, cultural transitions, and spiritual orientations which, in ever more complex and complete ways, express and reflect that characteristic of unity and integration" (p. 166).

Such an approach to historical reason goes beyond the familiar critique of historical reason in Western philosophy, which

applied the concept of historicity and historical progression to the realm of economics, society and culture. These theories rejected the eighteenth century Enlightenment view that held human nature to be static and unchanging; reduced society and culture to expressions of individual natural characteristics; identified nature as a mechanistic and dead object; saw humans as self-interested and utilitarian entities; and took capitalism and liberalist institutions to be eternally rational, moral and natural social forms. The advocates of historical reason, in contrast, saw society as a dynamic and organic reality, stressed the historical specificity of cultural practices and institutions, and rejected the utilitarian definition of human beings. Many major schools of nineteenth-century social theory advocated a critique of historical reason which emphasized that dynamic view and insisted on the dependence of human reason and social ideologies on the stage of social and historical development. Human knowledge was defined as a historically specific and socially conditioned phenomenon. (Saiedi, 2000, p. 167)

From the perspective of the twenty-first century, however, the nineteenth-century critique of historical reason does not recognize human spiritual potential or the larger spiritual potentiality of life. Historically changing human constructions are understood relativistically, where all historical constructions of truth and value are equally arbitrary (Saiedi, 2000). Such a historical understanding legitimized a thesis/antithesis, action/reaction type of education, where each new educational paradigm is a reaction to some past trends, and in that sense adopts an opposite extreme.

Perhaps the most significant example of this action/reaction type of educational decision making is the place of religion in education. After having dominated education for centuries, often stunting scientific investigation and critical reflection and repressing minority religious views, religious dogma has now been thrown out of public education, and along with it, the recognition of spiritual reality, as well as of the role of faith in the formation of character. Contrary to what most of the great scientists in human history have believed (Wilber, 1984), science and religion in the twentieth century have been viewed as two irreconcilable opposites, creating a gaping chasm in the human experience, compartmentalizing it beyond the possibility of any meaningful integration.

From a developmental perspective, ideological reactions like the ones our world appears to be caught in characterize the adolescent worldview, which faces the challenge of evolving a meaningful synthesis of old and new, past, present, and future. An example of such reactive education is the understanding of the role of communism in the twentieth century. Depending on the ideology, it is seen either as a disaster or as a just idea. Yet the whole modern and postmodern era has been a time of massive movements toward democratization, debunking of centuries-old ways and beliefs, and strikingly large-scale experiments around the theme of equality and social justice. Communism was one such experiment with an adolescently one-sided abstract idea: that if religion has been used to numb people's minds, we should do away with it; if classes have been the source of exploitation, we should do away with them; if workers have been exploited, they should now rule in order to bring justice; if social tools of production mediate human development and socialization, then consciousness can be fully explained by historical materialism; if material means so obviously determine the quality of life, then that's all there is to life.

Absurd as these propositions sound, many other twentieth-century ideas reveal the same thesis/antithesis quality of thinking, and they have all been sources of learning for humanity. In the case of communism, one of the big lessons has been that crude materialism can never bring true and lasting social justice, because it cuts off the very branch on which social justice sits—the attraction of the human spirit toward achieving harmony of the true, the good, and the beautiful.

The mature synthesis that our public understanding needs can occur only from the point of view of a large-scale metasystematic understanding of the historic advancement of human civilization. Such an understanding would be reflected in the educational curriculum by requiring high school history courses such as "The Evolution of the Idea of Social Justice in Human Civilization"; or "The Role of Religion, and Its Rises and Declines, in the History of Human Civilization." This understanding would also be reflected in considering it an integral part of education to train young people in all fields to think of their specific work in the context of global issues of justice and sustainability. It would require involving young people in first-hand experience with displaced populations, victims of war, repression and poverty, so that their explicit formalized knowledge can be stretched further, challenged, and ultimately supported by the deeper knowledge of praxis (Martic-Baro, 1994).

People entering the new millennium need to be educated to see the history of human civilization as a grand process of gradual emancipation of the majority of people by choice of free will, an emancipation both material and spiritual, and at great historical costs. Such understanding of history, however, implies a paradigmatic shift in the social sciences from a positivistic piecemeal approach to larger, more encompassing paradigms of knowledge. This large-scale integrative approach to teaching history and to preparing young minds to participate in history is yet to emerge. It has the potential to release young minds from the crushing burden of anomie and to strengthen them to explore how they can contribute to an ever-advancing diverse and interdependent human civilization.

Chapter 7

Spiritual Psychology: The Emerging Psychology of Integration

Only when the lamp of search, of earnest striving, of longing desire . . . is kindled within the seeker's heart . . . will the darkness of error be dispelled, the mists of doubts and misgivings be dissipated, and the lights of knowledge and certitude envelop his being.

Baha'i Faith, Baha'u'llah, [1952] 1983, p. 267

Beware! Your clinging-to-ego is greater than yourself; Pay heed! Your emotions are stronger than yourself. . . . Your habitual thought is more characteristic than yourself; Your ceaseless mental activity is more frantic than yourself.

Buddhism, Milarepa, in Wilson, 1995

Knowledge is a single point, but the ignorant have multiplied it.

Islamic Hadith, qtd. in Baha'u'llah, 1988

How can social science to transcend its piecemeal approach and develop more encompassing paradigms of knowledge, characterized by dynamic historical vision, on the basis of which a new level of collective social praxis can emerge? Such a shift implies a movement beyond the radical doubt of Cartesian rationalism, considered for centuries the highest standard of critical scientific thought (Wilson, 1995). It implies bridging the current gap between theory and praxis, and recognizing that "[N]o knowledge can be true if it has not attached itself to the task of transforming reality" (Martin-Baro, 1994, p. 41). We have to recognize the fallacy of scientism in separating knowledge from love and will. We have to develop scientific approaches which work rigorously with the dialectical interdependence of the three faculties in understanding any aspect of reality. As perennial philosophy (Huxley, 1974) sums it, "We can only love what we know, and we can never know completely what we do not love. Love is a mode of knowledge, and when love is sufficiently disinterested and sufficiently intense, the knowledge becomes unitive knowledge" (p. 95).

As part of this shift, the last decades of the twentieth century have seen the emergence of a fast-growing body of proposals regarding the paradigmatic challenges facing contemporary psychology (Claxton, 1994; Donaldson, 1992; Griffin, 1988a, 1988b; Grof, 2000; Jacoby, 1975; Lewis, 1998, 2000; Martin-Baro, 1994; Prilleltensky, 1997; Sloan, 1996; Sternberg, 1992; Wade, 1996; Wilber, 1998, 2000). While this chapter can hardly do justice to the full complexity of the question, this study would not be complete if it did not address the need for psychology to expand beyond the study of conditioning, personal constructs, and emotions and to speak to questions of motivation and volition, collective and individual, in a historic context.

THE MYSTERY OF HUMAN MOTIVATION

Psychology reveals useful insights about human motives and buried feelings, the content and structure of our thinking, and the dimensions of personality. We have developed a wide range of conceptualizations of existing personal form/content and corresponding interventions. Unfortunately, current theories of human motivation are fragmentary and often mutually exclusive. In seeking to understand human functioning, one can be either a behaviorist or a Jungian analyst, a constructive developmentalist or a Freudian psychoanalyst. Because these different theoretical frameworks are so mutually contradictory, one cannot move in any coherent way among them. Yet all supposedly seek to describe aspects of the one and single human experience. While the elements of any system by definition are interrelated and subject to the same all-embracing governing principles, psychology has not yet been able to identify and articulate the underlying principles of human potentiality.

Until the humanistic/transpersonal movement, it was not even scientifically acceptable to talk about potentiality behind form. With the breakthrough of transpersonal studies in the last decades, it has become increasingly clear that we cannot really understand mind while we focus solely on personal mind. To see mind, we have to look beyond mind.

Perhaps the most compelling proposal in terms of moving psychology to a new level of analysis and synthesis which has the capacity to answer these unanswered questions is offered by Wilber's (2000) landmark study in human development, *Integral Psychology*, which charts the possibility for psychology to become a truly integrative human science:

Psychology is the study of human consciousness and its manifestations in behavior. . . . The great problem with psychology as it has historically unfolded is that, for the most part, different schools of psychology have often taken one of those aspects of the extraordinarily rich and multifaceted phenomenon of consciousness and announced that it is the only aspect worth studying (or even that it is the only aspect that really exists). Behaviorism notoriously reduced consciousness to its observable, behavioral manifestations. Psychoanalysis reduced consciousness to structures of the ego and their impact on the id. Existentialism reduced consciousness to its personal structures and modes of intentionality. Many schools of transpersonal psychology focus merely on altered states of consciousness, with no coherent theory of the development of structures of consciousness . . . Cognitive science admirably brings a scientific empiricism to bear on the problem, but often ends up simply reducing consciousness to its objective dimensions, neuronal mechanisms, and bio-computer-like functions, thus devastating the lifeworld of consciousness itself.

What if . . . all of the above accounts were an important part of the story?

Under Wilber's influence, transpersonal psychology has identified consciousness as the central unit of study, aligning itself with the emerging post-Newtonian view of reality in the physical sciences (quantum physics, field and chaos theory, holography), which suggests that consciousness pervades all realities and is the creative principle of all existence; that "consciousness is not personal but transpersonal, not mental but transmental" (Walsh and Vaughan, 1993, p. 14). Wilber (2000) suggests that we cannot really begin to understand human consciousness until we recognize its spiritual nature. He reminds us that the earliest thinkers, on the shoulders of whom the science of psychology emerged, recognized

that the whole universe is spiritual in character, the phenomenal world of physics being merely the external manifestation of this spiritual reality. Atoms are only the simplest elements in a spiritual hierarchy leading up to God. Each level of this hierarchy includes all those levels beneath it, so that God contains the totality of spirits. Consciousness is an essential feature of all that exists. (Fechner, qtd. in Wilber, 2000, p. x)

Opening up psychology to Eastern wisdom traditions and modern holographic theory, both of which describe an implicit essential reality which is unknowable, nondualistic, and self-organizing and from which reality as we know it in space and time arises, Wilber proposes a way of looking at the levels of being (matter, body, mind, soul, spirit) as different levels of manifestation of the potentiality of Spirit in the "Great Nest of Being." Such an understanding indeed begins to provide a macro-map for integrating science and religion (Wilber, 1998) and for opening dialogue across scientific methodologies and paradigmatic assumptions. For psychology, it has tremendous implications in understanding motivation as the human yearning to realize itself as spirit, part of Spirit as the essence of life. In that sense, Jung saw as the major force in human behavior "an innate purposeful drive to attain wholeness and completeness of self" (Nugent, 2000, p. 115) through "a process of integration of world consciousness with the inner world of unconsciousness" (Bennet, 1983, p. 172).

Without such an understanding, motivation remains one of the most ambiguous areas of human development. Neither the Piagetian organism-environment conflict-based approach (Rosen, 1985) nor the Vygotskian shared-goals-and-mental-tools approach (Cole and Scribner, 1974; Rogoff, 1990; Tudge and Winterhoff, 1993; Valsiner, 1989; Wertsch, 1985) account fully for the energy behind development and its significant individual variations. Recent studies in personality theory have begun to link motivation with spirituality and have proposed an important connection between religion and personality integration and a new organizing concept of "spiritual intelligence" (Emmons, 1999). Such work has validated the place of spiritual striving in the psychological literature.

The profiles of Jim, Danton, Ramina, Ivan, Tom, Finnigan, William, Eliot, Ada, Emily, and Gandhi show they shared similar life conditions. However, some of them chose to listen to the yearning of their hearts after truth, beauty, and goodness; others became too frightened and took a different path. How can psychology help us understand this phenomenon, and what can it tell us about motivation and volition in specific historical contexts without merely reducing them to conditioning?

Studies of moral leaders (Bembow, 1994; Colby and Damon, 1992; Daloz et al., 1996) show that the choice to follow the yearning after truth, beauty, and goodness often happens early in life (although it can happen at any time) and often it is not experienced as a choice. Bembow's (1994) interviewees recounted again and again a childhood awareness of there not really being another option but the choice on the side of love and truth. Describing his childhood, Paul, one of her interviewees, says:

I was very consciously using Jesus as a model; and I had this image that Jesus sometimes had a lot of people saying "right on, right on," and other times he'd look around and no one would be there. . . . [M]y understanding of Jesus at that time was that going Jesus' way was different than going the way of the crowd or "the world." . . . Later I rejected most of those ideas, but what I retained . . . was this sense of there being a transcendent dimension to our lives and that it's not enough to live our lives by public opinion polls. By the age of 19 I knew my vocation was with social change, and with struggling for justice and peace. I knew that's why I was on the planet. . . . I don't know how I came to know that. I remember environments in which I became aware of it. (Bembow, 1994, pp. 75, 86, 90)

Colby and Damon's (1992) exemplars even "disclaim entirely the experience of moral courage" (p. 71): "Why does one need courage when one has no morally acceptable choice in the matter?. . . It would be more difficult for me not to do it. . . . How could I live with myself afterwards? . . . It was a normal act" (pp. 71, 75).

We heard the same in Emily's account, as well as in Jim's, Eliot's, William's, and Tom's. Colby and Damon (1992) describe it as a "belief in the moral necessity of their position" and the "willing suspension of fear and doubt." (p. 79) In Danton, we saw much more of a struggle with fear and an overall choice on the side of love coming much later in life. In Ramina, we saw a person paralyzed in the limbo between love and fear.

Colby and Damon (1992) explain this phenomenon with the very nature of moral goals, which, by definition, transcend the self. They draw on Heckhausen's "Rubicon effect" to describe the single-mindedness of moral commitment (p. 86). As they point out, "Heckhausen distinguishes between *motivation*, the state in which one makes a choice, and *volition*, the state in which the choice has already been made and all energies are directed toward the question of how to implement it" (p. 86).

If adult moral commitment is an act of volition, an act of free will, somewhere along the way, to bring closer and closer together the separate meaning systems of self and morality (Damon and Hart, 1988), then what is that motivation in children, as well as adults, which has the potential to lead to such volitional acts? An emerging area of serious study within the discipline of psychology is the identification and elucidation of the linkages among spirituality, morality, and motivation (Emmons, 1999; Lewis, 2000; Mustakova-Possardt, 1996).

One aspect of this motivation is clearly and expanded sense of identity, which encompasses increasingly wider aspects of humankind, life, the cosmos. Transpersonal psychology has begun a groundbreaking process of describing both the horizontal and vertical expansion of the Eastern and Western sense of identity. The transpersonal psychologists are studying the spectrum of individual manifest consciousness from instinctual to egoic to spiritual modes, from prepersonal to personal to transpersonal experiences, from subconscious to self-conscious to superconscious structures, from prerational to rational to transrational states (Wilber, Engler, and Brown, 1986). The intellectual intricacy of the transpersonal ontology of levels of being and epistemology of levels of knowing, as well as applied studies of the effect of spiritual practices of prayer and meditation on the level of healthy psychological functioning have attracted significant attention. (Dalai Lama and Cutler, 1998; Epstein, 1995; Goldstein, 1976; Kabat-Zin, 1995; Shapiro, 1995; Tan, 1996; Thich Nhat Hahn, 1991) However, these studies of the expansion of consciousness do not view consciousness as a psychosocial reality, related to collective consciousness in a concrete historical context (Martin-Baro, 1994). In these studies, history is present as little more than an abstract quadrant of human activity. The interdependent dialectic between individual and collective historical development is yet to be understood.

Offsetting the dominant Eastern emphasis of transpersonal psychology on detached individual reflection, studies in the Judeo-Christian tradition have attempted to speak more to the heart of human motivation—love, or what Danesh (1994) calls the power of attraction to beauty, truth, and goodness. Christian scholars describe spirituality as the very creative and relational essence of a human being that bears upon every aspect of a person's being in the world. Matthew Fox (2000), Scott Peck (1978), Fowler (1980, 1981)

In the tradition of Lonergan, Helminiak (1987, 1996) defines *spirit* as intentional consciousness and proposes, in keeping with other earlier thinkers (Robert MacLeod, 1944, 1970; Sigmund Koch, 1971, 1981), the existence of an intrinsic human principle of self-transcendence as a broader heuristic principle. Helminiak (1987) defines *spiritual development* as "the ongoing integration that results in the self-responsible subject from openness to an intrinsic principle of authentic self-transcendence" (p. 41).

Significantly, Christian studies of spiritual development contribute decisively to transpersonal understanding of the fundamental aspect of action. Helminiak's perspective on spiritual development as a development toward personal wholeness or integrity, which implies self-consistency and self-constitution, is very helpful in the study of empowered ways of being in the world. "They become as they do. They constitute themselves in an ongoing dialectic between themselves as agents in an outer world and their own dynamism toward authenticity in the realm of interiority" (Helminiak, 1987, p. 36).

Helminiak's intrinsic principle of self-transcendence is in harmony with the way the field of advanced adult development defines transcendence, as "the conscious apperception of an underlying unity of life" (Miller and Cook-Greuter, 1994, p. xvii). While many studies see the motive for transcendence as pertaining to the far reaches of adult development, Helminiak's model opens the door to encompassing the core of human motivation, which is naturally expressed even in early childhood as the power of love, the inherent attraction to the true, the good, and the beautiful (Coles, 1990; Erricker et al., 1997; Robinson, 1977). Helminiak differentiates spiritual from theistic connotations, and links theistic to the philosophical question whether there is "an ultimate truth and goodness toward which this human dynamism points" (Helminiak, 1987, p. 102).

This recognition of the subject's openness to the spiritual principle of self-transcendence opens up psychology to the long-avoided question of free will. The closest psychology has previously come to the question of will has been in incorporating existentialist insights into the psychotherapeutic context (Young-Eisendrath and Miller, 2000). Existential understanding of free will, however, is partial and pessimistic. It is colored by a distinctly individualistic understanding of social context as a static inimical force, "a kind of natural phenomenon . . . before whose 'objective' demands the individual must seek, individually and even 'subjectively,' the solutions to his or her problems" (Martin-Baro, 1994, pp. 37–38). Existential psychotherapy identifies itself as "skeptical spirituality" (Young-Eisendrath and Miller, 2000, p. 4) and recognizes as the sole symbol of spiritual maturity the individual's increased sensitivity to the urge for authentic self-transcendence in a therapeutic context.

The fact that psychology predominantly understands free will in an individual, often therapeutic, context speaks to the current limitations of the field. In line with the positivistic boundaries between disciplines, free will has been considered a theological category. As Martin-Baro (1994) points out,

[T]he most serious problem of positivism is rooted precisely in its essence; that is, in its blindness toward the negative. Recognizing nothing beyond the given, it necessarily ignores everything prohibited by the existing reality; that is, everything that does not exist but would, under other conditions, be historically possible. . . . To consider reality as no more than the given . . . constitutes an ideologization of reality that winds up consecrating the existing order as natural. (p. 21)

The model of the development of critical consciousness offered by this author builds on the contributions of both transpersonal research and Christian studies of spiritual development, as well as moral psychology and critical psychology. It takes the study of potentiality to its next step—understanding the human exercise of free will in its defining historical context. This model offers a conceptual framework for exploring motivation and volition, the exercise of free will under the constraints of specific historical contexts.

This approach draws on the Baha'i spiritual paradigm, which, in the last century and a half, has developed a heuristic that overcomes the split between transcendental and mystical approaches to understanding the spiritual nature of the human experience, and restores to the psycho-spiritual examination of human consciousness its fundamental historical context. The Baha'i concept of divine manifestation as an ethical orientation to history integrates asceticism and mysticism into "the perspective of harmonious transcendence" (Saiedi, 2000, p. 165). The Baha'i concept suggests that "the essence of human nature is . . . the hidden sign of the unity of God"; that this nature is only gradually revealed in the history of collective humanity through the guidance of successive divine manifestations, around which the world religions emerged; that "all divine revelation is historically progressive and in accordance with the level of spiritual and social development of humanity"; and that "it is only through these successive, historically specific, and progressive revelations that the divine Reality makes itself known" (Saiedi, 2000, pp. 166–67). Hence, behind the sociocultural evolution of collective human consciousness (see Wilber, 2000, pp. 149–57), historically centered around the figures of the manifestations of each religious tradition (Sorokin, 1959), is an ongoing relationship of individual and collective consciousness to universal consciousness, of individual and collective humanity to its spiritual essence. This spiritual essence is only progressively revealed through the unfolding of increasingly complex social relations and cultural institutions, reflecting "stages of the realization of unity in diversity" (Saiedi, 2000, p. 166).

Thus, the focal point of the most recent historically specific revelation, the Baha'i Faith, is the achievement of individual and collective maturity through recognizing the fundamental oneness of the diverse human family and through global social praxis toward the establishment of the foundation for social justice and peaceful global integration as the next stage in collective social evolution. The Baha'i spiritual paradigm suggests that the fulfillment of human spiritual potentiality in this age can only occur through the praxis of liberation of all members of the human family from all forms of oppression, inner and outer.

Viewed from this perspective, the cases of Jim, Emily, Eliot, William, and Tom, as well as Gandhi, illustrate how an activated depth dimension of existence allows people to transcend the specific limitations of their historical contexts, to liberate themselves from both inner and outer historical oppression, and to critically redefine these contexts, becoming effective, contextually specific agents for change. The actualization of their spiritual potential does not suggest a decontextualized, universal, ahistorical consciousness (Martin-Baro, 1994), as is often the case with transpersonal studies. Theirs is an empowered historical consciousness firmly grounded in concrete historical praxis oriented toward social justice.

What unites Jim, Emily, Eliot, William, and Tom with Freire's illiterate, oppressed Brazilian peasants? Different as their historical experience is, they are all writing their own history, as Martin-Baro (1994) puts it. We saw how the inherent love of truth, beauty, and goodness became amplified in varying degrees in the lives of Jim, Emily, Eliot, William, and Tom, and began to interact synergistically with their capacity to know, producing degrees of an empowered consciousness. Comparably, Freire's orientation toward the virtues and potentialities of simple illiterate people amplified their love for truth and justice, and allowed them to become the subjects of their own conscienticizing, liberating literacy (Martin-Baro, 1994). He engaged them in defining their own critical participation in life. In essence, he engaged in action research, "theorizing with them and from them"; trying to find out what "mental health would look like from the place of a tenant farmer on a hacienda, or personal maturity from someone who lives in the town dump, or motivation from a woman who sells goods in the market" (Martin-Baro, 1994, p. 28). He did not think for them; he approached them from a place of unity of knowledge, love, and will, with faith in their own potentiality, and through his participation in life awakened their own capacity to engage life consciously. His approach was fundamentally spiritual. It raises many profoundly generative questions regarding the potential power of psychology to not just describe but transform if it were to be redefined from a spiritual perspective.

Hence, the construct of critical consciousness and the understanding of its ontogenesis in the lifespan (Mustakova-Possardt, 1995a, 1996, 1998, 2000) allow a rethinking of psychology in the direction of moving it away from inadvertently naturalizing global conditions of social injustice, as has been compellingly pointed out by critical psychologists (Fox and Prilleltensky, 1997; Martin-Baro, 1994); toward making psychology more directly relevant to the current turbulent processes of globalization. As Martin-Baro (1994) wrote,

[t]he fundamental horizon for psychology as a field of knowledge is
conscientization. . . . (p. 39)
[t]he awakening of critical consciousness (*conscientization*) joins the psychological dimension of personal consciousness with its social and political dimension, and makes manifest the historical dialectic between knowing and doing, between individual growth and community organization, between personal liberation and social transformation. . . . Given what psychology deals with, we must ask ourselves whether, with the tools at our disposal today, we can say, or more important, do something that will make a significant contribution to solving the crucial problems of our communities. (p. 18)
{c}onscientizacion requires the psychologist . . . to produce an answer to the great problems of structural injustice, of war and national alienation, that overwhelm our peoples. (p. 41)

This study of critical consciousness conceptualizes the fundamental rethinking of psychology as beginning with a reorientation of psychology from a primary emphasis on already existent historical forms as 'natural' realities to a focus on the study of potentiality and its historically specific unfolding. A fundamental step in that direction is recognizing human spiritual motivation, human striving toward truth, beauty, and goodness, which takes historically specific individual and collective forms in various contexts and under different political, socio-economic, and spiritual conditions. Such a rethinking, as Martin-Baro (1994) also points out, involves a new horizon, a new epistemology, and a new praxis in the discipline; he calls this needed shift a movement toward liberation psychology.

The relationship of human beings to unknowable Spirit is essentially a love relationship, an attraction toward the unity of truth, beauty, and goodness, and an urge to fulfill that potentiality in life. It is what Wilber (2000) vaguely refers to as "Eros," "the same Spirit-in-action that originally threw itself outward to create a vast morphogenetic field of wondrous possibilities (known as the Great Nest) . . . This Eros moves through you and me, urging us to include, to diversify, to honor, to enfold" (p. 194).

Such an understanding begins to account for the stirrings we witnessed in the profiles in earlier chapters. It also explains the choices that we saw on the side of fear. To understand those choices, it helps to turn for a moment to the profound analysis of the twentieth century offered by the Baha'i international community's governing body, the Universal House of Justice, in its millennial publication, *The Century of Light*.

This analysis discusses the aggressive ideologies of nationalism, in its twin manifestations as fascism and nazism, as well as racism and communism, which came to dominate the twentieth century, leaving on the most educated century in human history the stamp of bestial atrocities and a violent "conspiracy against human nature" that sought to "systematically extinguish faith in God" and thus committed "deliberate violence to the roots of human motivation" (Universal House of Justice, 2001, p. 62). This analysis of the twentieth century poses a painful question:

Looking back on the twilight world in which such diabolical forces loomed over humanity's future, one must ask what was the weakness in human nature that rendered it vulnerable to such influences . . . [s]o willful an abandonment of reason on the part of considerable segment of the intellectual leadership of society demands an accounting to posterity. If undertaken dispassionately, such an evaluation must, sooner or later, focus attention on a truth that runs like a central strand through the Scriptures of all of humanity's religions. In the words of Baha'u'llah: "Upon the reality of man . . . He hath focused the radiance of all His names and attributes, and made it a mirror of His own Self. . . . These energies . . . lie, however, latent within him, even as the flame is hidden within the candle and the rays of light are potentially present in the lamp. . . . Neither the candle nor the lamp can be lighted through their own unaided efforts, nor can it ever be possible for the mirror to free itself from its dross." (pp. 62–63)

This quote suggests that the development of the human faculty of discernment is subject to how we choose to exercise our free will, what we choose to love. It is only to the degree that we acknowledge our attraction to the spiritual essence of life that we begin to develop and manifest this potentiality. Attraction to human ideologies and rationalizations cannot fully light the lamp of potentiality.

If we return to the stories of Ivan, Ramina, Ada, Finnigan, we see that, in varying degrees, these people chose not to follow the yearnings of their hearts after truth, beauty, and goodness and instead rationalized them into what *Century of Light* calls "humanity's worship of idols of its own invention" (p. 62). Their choices against the core of their own motivation snowballed into lifelong battles with fear and inner paralysis. St. Augustine describes this internal fragmentation as "a house divided" (qtd. in Emmons, 1999, p. 119).

Hence, while understanding human motivation does not change the fact of ultimate individual free will, it can provide a context for the cultivation of an enlightened use of volition, which ultimately forms moral character and habits, and builds health and resilience. A psychology that can speak in depth to these processes, by virtue of its understanding of human potentiality and its historical unfolding, is in essence spiritual psychology. The gradual shift in the discipline toward spiritual psychology is most evident in recent intensified efforts to define a holistic approach to mental health. Therefore, the section below reviews briefly the most significant developments in this area.

A HOLISTIC PSYCHOLOGY OPEN TO THE WISDOM WITHIN

In the last few decades of psychological research, there has been a growing recognition of the interrelatedness among morality, wisdom, and psychological health (Maslow, 1999; Mills and Spittle, 2001). Amid the proliferation of publications, there seem to be two groups of studies, both coming out of psychological praxis. The first group comes from the practice of psychotherapy. The second comes from psychoeducational interventions in education, counseling, prevention and community development.

Studies of the Relationship between Spirituality
and Healing within Counseling Psychology

With the immense multiplication of therapeutic approaches, psychological practitioners have increasingly recognized that, while case formulation is heavily influenced by the clinician's theoretical perspective, diagnosis itself points to depth processes underlying cognitive, somatic, emotional, and behavioral functioning. In search for a deeper unitive dimension of health, in the last decade or so counseling psychologists have become increasingly aware of the link between spirituality and successful healing (Adams, 1996; Fukuyama and Sevig, 1997; Hurding, 1996; Ingersoll, 1997; Ivey, 1993; Jimenez, 1994; Kelly, 1995; Larson, 1994; Levin, 1994; Miller, 1999; Richards and Bergin, 1997; Westgate, 1996; Worthington, 1989). A range of applied studies is increasingly pointing to two dimensions of spirituality that need to be explored in terms of their relationship to healing: the search for a deeper purpose and meaning in life and the search for deeper relatedness to life in all its forms (Batson et al., 1992; Burke, 1996; Kennedy, 1996; Leifer, 1996).

For example, in the treatment of trauma, there has been an increasing interest over the last several decades in the intensified searching for purpose and meaning in life that trauma seems to induce. Therapists have observed that even though this intensified search for meaning may not bring about immediate improvement of psychological functioning, it causes a spurt in spiritual development, in the course of which healing happens (Decker, 1994). As a result, clients frequently show an increased internal locus of control and an overall empowerment as a result of the belief that the reinforcements they seek are brought about by their own change of attitude and behavior (Jimenez, 1994). Hence, the spiritual search for meaning is being increasingly proposed as an organizing construct in psychotherapy (Elkins, 1995).

In its pure form, known as logotherapy (Frankl, 1962), this approach to healing was developed in the most dramatic of life circumstances, Nazi concentration camps. Not only was it remarkably effective, but also its organizing principles have become embedded in many more contemporary approaches, such as twelve-step programs and existential approaches (Brown, 1994). Clearly, the spiritual dimension of the need for deeper meaning and purpose in life can no longer be disregarded.

Another spiritual dimension increasingly gaining recognition is the effect of deeper relatedness in nourishing the soul and reenergizing its capacity for healing through effective engagement. A whole area of ecopsychology has emerged which, along with feminist psychology, recognizes in human beings natural inborn feelings of love and understanding which need expression not only in human relationships but also in a living relationship with nature. Estrangement from these feelings is seen as bringing about personal, social, and environmental stress, the emotional void of which is filled by destructive habits, dependencies, abandonment feelings, and other negative effects. On the other hand, nature-connecting ecopsychological practices seem to rejuvenate biological and spiritual integrity (Cohen, 1994; Conn, 1998; Feral, 1998; Roberts, 1998).

These two central dimensions, which have been increasingly associated with living a healthy, wholesome, and spiritually integrated life, the search for ultimate meaning in life, and the search for wholesome connections, have been described by Thomas Moore (1994) as spirit and soul. In Moore's terminology, the spirit is that aspect of the human being that seems to be eternally striving to transcend itself and bring greater meaning and coherence to life. The soul is that aspect which seeks groundedness in depth relatedness with all life beyond immediate pragmatic needs and interests. Trauma and crisis may be the result of a breakdown in either spiritual striving or soulful relatedness. Even if trauma is the result of physical suffering, it still prompts seeking healing through soul and/or spirit. Overall, counseling practice now recognizes that being able to bring about a particular personal and immediate experience of the human soul and spirit is the foundation of effective healing. Counseling and psychotherapeutic practice have begun to discover the connection between spirituality and well-being, to which the best of the Judeo-Christian tradition points (Lewis, 1970; Miller, 1999; Ryff and Singer, 1998; Tillich, 1957).

Advances in psychoneuroimmunology (PNI) have required researchers to recognize the influence of mind on the body (Bryson, 1999). Quantum physics is bringing to the fore the possibility of understanding material life as forms of expression of energy, where biology, as well as psychosocial behavior, can be understood as expressions of a deeper spiritual reality. We are increasingly discovering that working from that level brings about substantially different results on the manifest levels of biology as well as psychosocial behavior. Even hard-core "scientific" medicine is slowly but surely learning the painful lesson that no real healing can occur without drawing first and foremost on the mysterious resources of the spirit and the powers of the mind (Bryson, 1999; Leifer, 1996; Ross, 1995).

Holistic Health Psychology

Out of the above understanding and practice has emerged a whole new field—health psychology. Its focus has been on the phenomenon of human resilience—the mysterious capacity of the human spirit to rebound from all kinds of circumstances in life and to transform them into learning, strength, and growth, as opposed to what Seligman and Csikszentmihalyi (2000) have summarized as the past focus of psychology on "victimology." We are beginning to realize that the social sciences may have gone a little too far in the direction of a deterministic biological understanding of human development. As Danesh (1994) points out,

Together with the psychoanalytic schools, the behavioral, cognitive, existential, developmental, humanistic, and other major schools of psychology have all made great contributions to our understanding of the instinctual, biological, and psychosocial forces that affect the formation of our personalities and life styles. We have also begun, with some success, to apply our psychological insights into socio-economic and political aspects of human life. However, along with these major achievements, modern psychology has become increasingly mechanistic and lifeless in its orientation and approaches. An ever-greater and all-inclusive emphasis is placed on the development of chemical agents that will calm our anxieties, counter our depression, and decrease our confusion. . . . We are told we are victims . . . of our parents, family members, friends, or strangers. In their attempts to analyze and explain away the root causes of such disturbing behavior as violence, cruelty, inequality, prejudice, greed, selfishness, war, and so on, psychologists and psychiatrists have resorted to instinctual, hereditary, biophysiological, and ethological . . . explanations. (pp. 16–17)

Yet, there are great differences in how individuals deal with similar circumstances (Bowman, 1997). In order to understand people's deeper resources, two things need to find an appropriate place in overall psychological understanding—the innate human urge for transcendence, or what Tillich (1957) has called ultimate concerns, and the ultimate free will of every individual, regardless of circumstances, to make moment-to-moment choices in keeping with the inner voice of conscience. Neither can be easily proven, but an abundance of work has pointed to them. Hence, rather than denying them, it appears more constructive to accept them as hypothetical heuristic concepts and find out what tangible, assessable possibilities they open up.

We have tended to see conscience as a late development, associated in Kohlbergian thought with postconventional stages of moral reasoning. However, Helminiak (1987), in his review of psychological accounts of spiritual development, writes:

Philibert argues for a broader notion of conscience: conscience is operative in all the stages of moral development—in different ways in different stages, to be sure. Expressing itself through an urge toward self-congruence, it moves one not only to know the good but also to do it. It is thus a factor in one's being and becoming and leads one in growth towards transcendent value. (p. 20)

Philibert (1979) points out that Rogers recognized "an energizer in the subject—the need to achieve congruence between ideas and experience," the tendency to seek affective consonance (see Helminiak, 1987, p. 20). Philibert describes this urge toward affective consonance as "something akin to the dynamic present in Augustine's 'Our hearts are made for Thee, and they shall not rest until they rest in Thee' " (qtd. in Helminiak, 1987, p. 21). Such an understanding points to the depth motivation of a human being to not just know, but also love, and act in accordance with truth, beauty, and goodness—a depth motivation we saw clearly amplified in the lives of the CC individuals in earlier chapters. Philibert (1979) recognizes "the energy in the agent's pursuit of the good, the impulse to pursue the object of duty," and explains it as "an intrinsic orientation of the moral agent to the good" (qtd. in Helminiak, 1996, p. 20).

A branch of resilience studies, recently known as health realization, has found out that conscience, understood in this way, is a fundamental characteristic of healthy psychological functioning at *all* levels of development (Mills, 1995; Pransky, G. 1998). Conscience will reappear even in the most troubled people in moments when their habitual frenetic thinking slows down and their minds clear. The presence or absence of conscience in a person's moment-to-moment functioning seems to be a good indicator of the level of mental health from which they are operating in that moment.

As people drop below the mental health line into states of greater stress and distress, these messages of conscience are drowned out by process thinking. . . . The lower a person drops below the mental health line, the less guidance the person has from the innate intelligence of their conscience and as a result the more maladaptive and self- and socially-destructive their behavior. (Pransky, G. 1998, p. 95)

Recent studies identify an in-built self-correcting mechanism in people, innate mental health, which surfaces at any moment that excessive and obsessive analytical thinking is suspended (Bailey, 1990; Banks, 1998; Mills and Spittle, 2001; Pransky, G., 1998; Pransky, J., 1998, 2000). This phenomenon is familiar in psychiatry as lucid moments in even the most dysfunctional people.

The understanding of innate mental health points to the inherent capacity of individual mind to function in a balanced and responsive way, to the extent that the mirror of consciousness is directed toward the spiritual essence of life and away from narrow constructions of personal reality. Such functioning is highly intelligent, regardless of the level of intellectual development, and allows the individual to both be aware of and respond to the inner yearning toward truth, beauty, and goodness. This default capacity helps explain the natural spiritual inclinations of children, which can be thwarted by fearful conditioning. It also helps explain the dramatic positive transformations that adults sometimes undergo in extreme circumstances.

Regardless of how heavily overlaid by fearful conditioning this capacity for balanced, responsive, and moral functioning has been, it never disappears. As soon as the intensely personal thinking quiets down, this self-correcting mechanism takes over and allows the individual to experience moments of clear understanding and goodness; that is, to return to his or her inherently moral way of being. This way of being may be experienced for only a moment before it becomes overlaid again, or it may become the dominant modus operandi. That is the infinite continuum between CC and non-CC ways of being.

Moments of clear moral understanding are accompanied by remarkable common sense and creativity. Their affective experience is often one of love, gratitude, and awe, a sense that all is right with the world (Mills and Spittle, 2001). Such moments can always bring about a more lasting permanent transformation. Hence, it is impossible to know at what point people will experience a critical mass of innate mental health that will tip their overall motivation toward the moral end of the continuum and allow them to begin to function as CC people.

To the extent that this understanding of innate mental health and resilience in moment-to-moment functioning has been applied to work with crime-ridden projects (Pransky, J., 1998), to individual and family therapy and counseling Pransky, G. 1992), to organizational development (Sedgeman, 2001), to prevention and education (Pransky, J., 2001), it assists people in reorienting themselves toward the processes that precede the psychological content in which they were living, and profoundly and lastingly transforms their experience of life. Remarkable successes have been recorded in the relatively short-term treatment, without later remission, of depression, schizophrenia, panic attacks, addictions, PTSD, sexual offences, migraine headaches, allergies, and other afflictions (Bailey, 1990; Pransky, G., 1998). A recent one-year follow-up study of the effect of Health Realization training on helping professionals reported that people experienced

more calm and comfort in life; more lightheartedness; fewer and less intense emotional reactions; less stress; higher quality relationships. They attributed changes to realizing 1) their own power of creation of their life experience through Thought; 2) a source of "health" within; 3) a clear, calm mind as the pathway to their health; 4) using feelings as guides to monitor their health; 5) their choice to see an inside, nonpersonal vs. outside, personal world; 6) their ability to transcend their habitual patterns via higher levels of understanding. (Pransky, 1999, p. 4)

The same study reported a 57 percent reported decrease in arguments with children, a 49 percent decrease in fights with spouse or partner, a 40 percent stress-level reduction, and an 18 percent improvement of quality of life or perceived well-being.

Much of the work in health psychology, which grew out of the humanistic psychology movement of the 1960s, as well as the work in health realization, has remained largely outside the narrow scientific model of mainstream psychology. Yet, a recent awakening in mainstream academic psychology to the need for a deeper understanding of health and optimal psychological functioning has led to the official launching of a new movement sanctioned by the American Psychological Association (APA) under the name positive psychology, committed to studying issues of happiness, excellence, and optimal human functioning (American Psychologist, January 2000, volume 55, #1). Even though this movement has paid no tribute to the contributions of humanistic psychology or the very existence of health realization studies and applied work for a few decades now and has not even begun to acknowledge the spiritual nature of human resilience and its connection to morality, positive psychology is an important indicator of the growing realization within the field of the need to move to a new level of integration in psychology.

In an integrated psychology, mental health and optimal functioning need to be studied not just in terms of relatively permanent personality and behavior characteristics but also in terms of the moment-to-moment alignment and realignment of individual thinking with larger spiritual reality. As Ryff and Singer (1998) also suggest (see Emmons, 1999), studies of health and well-being should not be separated from studies in moral psychology.

EMERGING PRINCIPLES OF SPIRITUAL PSYCHOLOGY

In view of everything said in the previous sections of this chapter, there are reasons to believe that we are, in fact, seeing the emergence of spiritual psychology as a discipline. Both the growing understanding of the lifespan development and macrodynamics of optimal moral consciousness, and the growing understanding of the microdynamics of resilience as connected to the moment-to-moment capacity for realignment of the individual mind, redirect primary focus from individual and collective formations viewed as relatively permanent and an overall emphasis on memory to the study of our moment-to-moment relationship to potentiality. It appears that the quality and content of moment-to-moment individual and collective formations depends on their relationship to the spiritual forces of life. Hence, there is a need for a larger perspective for psychology, an "out-of-the-box" view on psychological content and its inherent dilemmas.

Does assuming spiritual reality as preceding form seriously conflict with our findings in the last 150 years of rapid scientific development? The answer, at least from leading scientists such as Heisenberg, Schroedinger, Einstein, Planck, and Eddington (Wilber, 1984), seems to be no. Just the opposite, such an understanding not only brings together previously disparate findings but also provides the missing links and accounts for otherwise unanswerable questions.

The main premise of this book is the need to focus our efforts on an individual and collective integration of minds and hearts as the essence of optimal human development and to evolve a psychology that understands and speaks to that integration. Recently, at least two other works have attempted to speak directly to the same challenge. One is Vokey's (1997) dissertation entitled *Reasons of the Heart: Education for Critical Dialogue in a Pluralistic World*. Another is

Lewis' (2000) article *Spiritual Education as the Cultivation of Qualities of Heart and Mind*.

Vokey's work constitutes an impressive effort, stemming from moral psychology, to establish a nonfoundational justification for a wide reflective equilibrium beyond intellectual bias in psychology. Vokey (1997) points out that this intellectual bias, "firmly rooted in Hellenic dualism" and "a persistent feature of mainstream Western culture" (p. 159), leaves out several important questions. The first question is "What is perception," and "how do we come to see things as they are, the varieties of ways in which we may fail, the varieties of causes of failure, and the kind of discipline that can overcome these obstacles." The second question is "how does habit educate the passions." The third question is "how can we know which actions to perform in order to educate the passions" (pp. 159–61). Drawing on Buddhist psychology, Vokey describes our capacity for "unconditioned awareness or wakefulness" as our basic nature (p. 196) and a potential foundation for holistic psychology.

J. Lewis' (2000) discussion of the possibilities for synthesis between psychological and spiritual understanding builds further on these ideas, drawing on significant work in cognitive psychology (Bohm, 1994; Claxton, 1994, 1997; Donaldson, 1992; Sternberg, 1992; Sternberg and Davidson, 1995; Sternberg and Wagner, 1986). Lewis' (2000) main premise is the need for a holistic approach to the human being which cultivates qualities of both mind and heart. Lewis (2000) points to the culture-specific Western separation between mind and heart, in contrast to the ancient Pali term *cita*, translated as "heart-mind," or the seat of ultimate understanding (Lewis, 2000, p. 273). Lewis draws on several significant bodies of cognitive research, namely, Claxton's (1994, 1997) work on slow ways of knowing, Bohm's (1994) work on proprioception of thought, Donaldson's (1992) work on modes of thought, and Sternberg's (1992) work on wisdom and intuition, to show that "an increase of the prevalence of qualities of the heart leads naturally into the development of a wider range of qualities of the mind" (p. 273).

As some of the mind's most important and systematically ignored potentials, Claxton (1994, 1997) identifies slow ways of knowing, which he calls "Tortoise Mind," contrasting them to "Hare Brain," and terming them the *undermind*. These capacities—insight, intuition, wisdom—are central to many of life's ill-defined problems (Mills, 1995; Carlson and Bailey, 1997) and are cultivated through spiritual practice. In contrast, education and psychology generally emphasize the "Hare Brain," or what Claxton calls "d-mode" activity— conscious, deliberate, purposeful thinking.

Health realization has independently identified these two modes of using mind as flow mode and process mode and has developed further the understanding of the dynamic of what Claxton calls "tortoise mind." It describes this slowed down way of using mind as moving away from the intensely personal nature of ordinary, memory-based thinking and accessing an innate intelligence, characterized by insight and highly responsive thinking in the moment. This intelligence is experienced as "no thought" or "clear mind," and is at the heart of peak performance (Bailey, 1990; Carlson and Bailey, 1997; Maslow, 1970). It has been found to be fairly universal across personality types, as the following account shows:

A young psychiatrist, who went as a medical observer on five combat missions of the Eighth Air Force in England, says that in times of great stress and danger men are likely to react quite uniformly, even though under normal circumstances they differ widely in personality. He went on a mission, during which the B-17 plane and crew were so severely damaged that survival seemed impossible. He had already studied the "on the ground" personalities of the crew and had found that they represented a great diversity of human types. Of their behavior in crisis he reported: "During the violent combat and during the acute emergencies that arose during it, they were all quietly precise on the interphone and decisive in action . . . unobtrusively cheerful and ready for anything." . . . [W]hen the crisis came, each of these young men forgot the particular personality which he had built up out of the elements provided by his heredity and the environment in which he had grown up. (Huxley, 1974, pp. 51–52)

Health realization practitioners have found that as people learn to quiet their minds and become aware of the powerful capacities of "tortoise mind," the overall balance in their daily functioning changes, exhibiting an epistemological shift to a deeper knowing of the heart and a correspondingly broader use of mind. In moments of mental health, people's thinking is characterized by a balanced movement back and forth between a spontaneous epistemological reliance on intuition and insight, and a periodical resorting to analysis wherever necessary, without getting stuck in the analytical mode. Hence, in moments of mental health, people exhibit a different epistemology, which has recently begun to attract attention as "the knowing of the heart" manifested in various healing practices (Katz, Biesele, and Denise, 1997). Characteristic of this epistemology is that the heart leads the way, while the mind is a faithful and well-disciplined servant; in contrast to the typical Western mindframe in which we associate intelligence with effortful linear analytical thinking noticeably dissociated from intuition, and in service to ego, personal views and opinions.

In view of these discoveries regarding "tortoise mind" and the experience of "no thought", cognitive psychologists have begun to recognize that the term "thought" may refer to two qualitatively different processes: thoughts as content and neurophysiological reflexes, and thought as an "unbroken field" of thinking in the here and now (Bohm, 1994). As Lewis (2000) puts it,

thought often interferes in the ability to think fully . . . because for reasons of evolutionary significance, thought has evolved in such a way that it . . . forms neurophysiological reflexes. . . . Through repetition, emotional intensity, and defensiveness, these reflexes have become hard-wired in consciousness to such an extent that they respond independently of our conscious choice . . . so that much of our thought is no more than reflex, though it appears to be volitional. (pp. 274–5)

While the power of representational thought to induce feelings of necessity to act was evolutionarily significant in life-threatening situations, it no longer is at this stage in our social evolution. The "reflexive, habituated nature of thought" creates the illusion of a thinker who is "steadfastly committed to preserving some variation of its own reflexive structure." (Lewis, 2000, p. 275) Psychologists are increasingly recognizing the importance of cultivating the ability to be present to our thoughts without being impelled by them. In this way, the momentum of our reflexes is dissipated and our awareness broadens.

In order to both integrate and further differentiate these various uses of the terms mind, consciousness, and thought in the psychological literature, and in the effort to begin to consistently describe the moment-to-moment relationship of psychological phenomena to potentiality, there has emerged a recent proposal to redefine mind, consciousness, and thought on two levels: the pre-form or formless level of spiritual principles, and the level of form (Banks, 1998; Mustakova-Possardt, under review).

Mind, Consciousness, and Thought can be understood as immanent spiritual principles that operate in unity to create the individual human mind. They can be conceptualized as both a pure potentiality, and as an expression of that potentiality in the world of form. Such an approach brings forth the controversial debate between mind and matter. However, it transcends materialistic monism, dualism, or parallelism (DeQuincey, 2000), and proposes a spiritual monism that embraces mind, consciousness, and thought as a unity, expressed and evidenced in dimensions of being, personal realities, and moment-to-moment awareness. This view of life as a dynamic, on-going relationship between the formless life force and form is consistent with current understanding in quantum physics and neurophysiology (Talbot, 1991).

From this perspective, Mind, at the formless level, can be considered the universal life force - the source of life - referred to in history by many different names including Self, divine ground, spirit, absolute, universal intelligence, and so forth. On the level of form, this life force is continuously manifested in, and flows through, "personal mind," the individual minds of living things. This on-going formation of personal minds can be conceptualized as occurring through the interplay of the twin processes of Thought and Consciousness, understood as higher order constructs.

Thought can be understood as the creative agent, the capacity to give form to formless life energy; it is the link between the source and the form our experience is taking in the moment. On the level of form, thought manifests itself as our personal moment-to-moment thinking. Consciousness can be conceptualized as the neutral energy of Mind that allows us to be aware—to be cognizant of the moment in both a sensate and a knowing way; the pure light of awareness referred to in every mystical tradition. In the new physics (Wilber, 1984), light occupies a special place. While its inner nature has proven impossible to know directly, it is clear that it stands outside of, and in that sense is more fundamental than, time, space, and matter. In the same way, a number of mystical traditions consider the light of consciousness to be what has always been there, and what underlies every process in the present moment (Russell, 1999). On the level of form, consciousness manifests itself as levels and degrees of awareness, including intuitive, direct ways of knowing (Hart, Nelson, & Puhakka, 2000). Seen in this way, thought and consciousness are the two sides of the same process of experiencing life: "*Consciousness* allows the recognition of form, form being the expression of *Thought*" (Banks, 1998, p. 39). Such differentiation of the role of thought and the role of consciousness breaks down and operationalizes what is otherwise rather globally referred to as consciousness in the transpersonal literature. It also suggests a dialectic between thought and consciousness.

This treatment of consciousness and thought is clearly very different from the prevailing understanding. While transpersonal psychology has moved away from the purely constructivist focus on consciousness as content (Friedman, 1996), and has defined consciousness as a structural universal (Wade, 1996), the understanding of thought proposed here is more generic than is typically associated with the concept in conventional cognitive psychology.

Generally, thought has been used to refer to cognitive processes such as perceiving, thinking, remembering, evaluating, planning, and organizing, as well as to the contents of thought (Frager & Fadiman, 1998). However, some interesting possibilities emerge when thought is considered to be a neutral psychological force or power that gives form to life. To understand thought as a generic creative agent does not suggest that matter does not exist separately from thought, as is a standard accusation against idealism (DeQuincey, 2000). Rather, it suggests that our only way to know matter, or anything at all, is via thought; that human reality is essentially psychological. An understanding of thought as a generic creative power, which is at work throughout life, including under coma, embraces different ways of giving form (e.g., perception, apperception, insight, and so forth), and compels psychology to focus on the essential creative nature of the human experience, and on the fact that different forms of thought create a qualitatively different moment-to-moment experience of life.

Understood as higher order constructs, mind, thought, and consciousness allow us to conceptualize the infinite macro and micro-fluctuations in the quality of our experience as fluctuations in the quality of the relationship between form and formless energy. Such an understanding embraces what psychology has so far seen as its domain—the study of relatively permanent individual configurations of personal mind, and their potential for adjustment or maladjustment. In addition, however, it opens the door to a study of the moment-to-moment fluidity and flexibility of any human configurations, which is at the heart of human resilience and potential. For example, there is empirical evidence throughout the history of human civilization that the more the individual mirror of consciousness turns toward the source of all form, Mind, the purer that consciousness is, the less contaminated by conditioned personal form (Huxley, 1974).

Such a redefining of mind as the focus of psychology makes it easier to see that whether we are studying the individual or collective unconscious, social conditioning and socialization, individual thinking and beliefs, perception and apperception, behavior, or the phenomenology of human experience in the here-and-now, we are studying various levels and sub-levels of manifest form, none of which are as permanent as we experience them to be. Until now, competing schools of psychological thought have proposed different levels of form as defining of the human experience. However, understanding *the fact of* thought and consciousness as the basic principles through which the human experience is generated in the moment gives psychology an important over-arching view of the role of form and content, and opens the door to a more foundational Aristotelian causal analysis (Aristotle, 1991; Diessner, 2002). It also bridges in a coherent theoretical way the long-perceived gap between the psychology of wisdom traditions and Western psychology. It provides a structural understanding of the microdynamics of mental health and spirituality.

This structural understanding has guided this author's action research in the empowerment and community development of marginalized Latino immigrants in rural West Georgia. As people focus on the fact of thought, rather than the thought content that shapes their experience at any moment, they experience a surfacing of their innate mental health and resilience regardless of circumstances. They regain their creative, responsive, and insightful thinking, accompanied by deeply satisfying noncontingent affective states, and are ready to take charge of their lives, engage issues of social justice constructively, and begin to change their living environments. It appears that Freire's approach to the conscientization of illiterate Brazilian peasants started in precisely that place: he approached and drew out the healthy potentiality in otherwise disempowered ordinary people. As they experienced more confidence and security, they engaged with him in a dialog about reality.

Sternberg's (Sternberg, 1992; Sternberg and Davidson, 1995; Sternberg and Wagner, 1986) work on intuition and wisdom shows remarkable convergence with the above basic premises. The contributors to both volumes recognize the power of the still quiet moments as the source of a fresh way of seeing and thinking. In addition, much in concert with health realization's emphasis on the impersonal nature of wisdom in the moment, Csikszentmihalyi and Rathunde suggest "That wisdom has a cognitive component, which attempts to understand the world in a disinterested way, seeking the ultimate consequences of events as well as ultimate causes. . . . [T]hey see wisdom as . . . 'an intrinsically rewarding experience that provides some of the highest enjoyment and happiness available' " (Lewis, 2000, p. 278).

Mills and Spittle (2001) suggest that wisdom is a natural innate capacity to use the full range of the mind's capacities responsively in the moment and that people delve into this capacity to the extent to which they become aware of the impersonal, universal spiritual nature of reality and distance themselves from their intensely personal constructions. Much like Krishnamurti (1969), Mills and Spittle (2001) also suggest that although wisdom has a cognitive component, it cannot be accessed purely analytically in the way that we have learned to predominantly use our minds; that wisdom springs out of the capacity to trust the unknown.

This general convergence, spanning the range from theoretical physics and cognitive psychology to moral psychology and holistic health psychology, points to what may prove to be the beginning of a long-sought generic understanding of principles of psycho-spiritual functioning. This understanding embraces biological and psychosocial factors, but leaves room for free will and sees the link between individual mind and Universal Mind as that intrinsic motivating force, discussed as the urge for self-transcendence. From such a perspective, the individual mind has the sense of being part of something larger and can exercise its free will to strive to align itself with that larger reality. To the extent that that happens the individual exhibits optimal functioning. Where such tendency to seek alignment with larger life becomes a dominant characteristic, we see moral motivation and critical consciousness.

Within a macrodynamic view of human life which understands individual mind not only as a relatively permanent, biologically based, and separate configuration, but also as a dynamic and continuously transforming manifestation of Mind, with unlimited moment-to-moment potentialities, it becomes more possible to speak in scientifically grounded terms about human interconnectedness as part of the interconnectedness of all life; of human resilience, and of human spiritual potential, and its relative historical actualization. From this perspective, it is also possible to begin to ask and answer questions regarding how psychology can become more directly relevant in addressing the most pressing challenges of the current age of globalization. We can begin to address the crisis of large displaced and terrorized populations, victims of war, gaping disparities between extreme wealth and poverty, and the ecological crisis on the planet. We can articulate a transformative educational psychology and a clinical and preventive practice that transcends social class and embraces the masses of humanity.

A METAPSYCHOLOGY ENCOMPASSING UNITY IN DIVERSITY

What kind of metapsychology can truly speak to the global human condition in the twenty-first century? How can we integrate clinical, experimental, moral, critical, personality, community, cross-cultural, and holistic health psychology? How can we synthesize an integrated understanding of optimal human development? What kind of psychology can transmute or transcend the entrenched ideological oppositions of the past? How can we study the dynamic interaction of individual and collective becoming, encompassing the full range of human motivation and free will? How can we, in the psychology community, become a progressive force in the global efforts to create a civil society based on unity and justice? Who among us can speak with compelling understanding and integrative vision of the eternal human choice between love and fear at this portentous crossroad in human history?

In order to understand the emerging global-community psychology, let us pause and reflect on the nature of the century which has just come to a close.

Century of Light (Universal House of Justice, 2001) provides a poignant large-scale historical analysis of the age. The fundamental premise is that the twentieth century, despite all of its unprecedented atrocities and large-scale betrayals of humanity, will be regarded by future historians as "the century of light," because in it emerged "the universal recognition of the oneness of humankind" (p. 127).

As Anthony Marsella (1998) writes:

Human survival and well-being is now embedded in an entangled web of global economic, political, social, and environmental events and forces. Global events and forces are now local events and forces! Willingly or unwillingly, the world has become the fabled "global village" ... and the global village is multicultural, multinational, and multiethnic. The scale, complexity and impact of these forces constitute a formidable challenge for psychology as a science and profession. (p. 1282)

At the beginning of the twentieth century, at the threshold of two world wars, when none could yet foresee what we know today, one of the central figures of the Baha'i Faith, Abdu'l-Baha, wrote:

Behold how its light is now dawning upon the world's darkened horizon. The first candle is unity in the political realm, the early glimmerings of which can now be discerned. The second candle is unity of thought in world undertakings, the consummation of which will erelong be witnessed. The third candle is unity in freedom which will surely come to pass. The fourth candle is unity in religion which is the cornerstone of the foundation itself. . . . The fifth candle is the unity of nations—a unity which in this century will be securely established, causing all the peoples of the world to regard themselves as citizens of one common fatherland. The sixth candle is unity of races, making of all that dwell on earth peoples and kindreds of one race. The seventh candle is unity of language, i.e. the choice of a universal tongue in which all the people will be instructed and converse. Each and every one of these will inevitably come to pass. (Abdu'l-Baha, qtd. in Universal House of Justice, 2001, pp. 127–28)

Century of Light further points out that these essential features are now recognized processes throughout the world, and although imperfect, are well under way. The movement beyond national sovereignty and the establishment of the United Nations, which embodies the recognition of the nations of the world that "however great the differences among them may be, they are the inhabitants of a single global homeland," illustrates the emerging unity in the political realm (p. 129). This unity was marked by the Millennium Summit at the United Nations in New York in September 2000. The Summit Resolution was signed by 149 heads of state and government, which illustrates dramatically "the difference between the world of 1900 and of 2000":

We solemnly reaffirm, on this historic occasion, that the United Nations is the indispensable common house of the entire human family, through which we will seek to realize our universal aspirations for peace, cooperation and development. (United Nations General Assembly, qtd. in Universal House of Justice, 2001, p. 130)

The emerging unity of thought in world undertakings, a concept for which the most idealistic aspirations at the opening of the twentieth century lacked even reference points, is also in large measure everywhere apparent in vast programmes of social and economic development, humanitarian aid and concern for protection of the environment of the planet and its oceans. (Universal House of Justice, 2001, p. 128)

The movement toward "official languages" in the United Nations, universal education, and universal aspirations for unity in freedom have all become aspects of our collective consciousness. They have been embodied in the Human Rights movement and the efforts of over one thousand nongovernmental organizations, which gathered in New York on May 22–26, 2000, at the invitation of United Nations Secretary General Kofi Annan, as spokespersons of the emerging global civil society.

These historic processes, the legacy of the twentieth century, have, however, been relatively poorly understood and appreciated by both the media and the public mind. The general lack of enthusiasm or even interest in these significant and complex global transformations "exposes the depth of the crisis the world is experiencing at the century's end" (Universal House of Justice, 2001, p. 131). Behind this distrust are "two phenomena which undermine such confidence. The first . . . the collapse of society's moral foundations has left the greater part of humankind floundering without reference points in a world that grows daily more threatening and unpredictable" (Universal House of Justice, 2001, p. 131).

The second is the shadow side of the process of globalization, which has mistakenly been attributed to globalization itself rather than to the prevailing philosophy of materialism that is driving it. "Globalization itself is an intrinsic feature of human society." (Universal House of Justice, 2001, p. 134) However, it has brought to a crisis the gross disparities in the distribution of wealth in the world, with the gulf between wealth and poverty widening dramatically each year, according to the United Nations Development Program.

What kind of psychology can adequately address the needs of humanity in the twenty-first century against the backdrop of these twin processes of the collapse of old institutions and social decay and the blossoming of a new way of thinking?

First, it has to be a psychology that understands the historical process in its complexity and is bigger than the liberal relativism that has been the philosophical and political ideology behind capitalism. The challenge we are facing is, above all, a spiritual challenge. We need a fundamental change in consciousness, a movement away from reductionistic materialism as a dominant philosophy, as well as from its forms of social and political expression. If social science is to plumb the depths of our current reality, we have to recognize collective and individual spiritual potential as the motivating force behind the evolution of human civilization (Sorokin, 1959; Universal House of Justice, 2001).

The social science and psychology communities can then begin to incorporate the specific proposals for a global-community psychology offered by Marsella (1998). We can resist "the hegemonic imposition or privileged positioning of any national or cultural psychology," avoid a dominant voice with excessive "emphasis on individualism, mechanism and objectivity" (Marsella, 1998, pp. 1284–85). It can subject to a penetrating analysis the moral implications of each alternative psychological approach, in a way compellingly modeled by Prilleltensky (1997). Such a psychology can be the meeting ground of East and West, North and South. It can create a broader forum for both appreciating and learning from the wealth of indigenous psychologies, and discovering the common ground among them. It can begin to cultivate an emerging understanding of unity in diversity and a psychospiritual understanding of collective human history. Since concepts are historically constructed categories that gain meaning in relation to what they enable us to do, a social science which truly grasps the human condition in the twenty-first century needs to understand and foster those capacities of individual and collective consciousness that are propelling the current painstaking movement to a new level of sociohistorical organization.

Appendix: Descriptive Statistics of Interviewees

Pseudonym	Unique Characteristic	Age	Gender	Education [1]	Occupation	Evaluation
U.S. Sample						
Lin	Chinese American (Taiwan)	50+	F	16 (English/ Spanish.lit.)	University research assistant	Pre-CC
Tom	Town activist Former policeman	50	M	11 quit high school	Florist	Pre-CC
Sim	Former drug addict	39	M	11	Truck driver	Preconventional non-CC/ early conformist
William	Lodge member	60+	M	12+2 college	Retired computer technician	Transitional CC/ achievement
Finnigan		48	M	12+2 college	After-school counselor	Conventional non-CC/ achievement
Agnes	Cancer patient	64	F	16	Retired teacher	Conventional non-CC/ achievement

Ann	Jewish German immigrant	60	F	16	Teacher, buyer	Transitional CC (close to call)
Ken	Former drug addict	48	M	16 (sociology)	Airline caterer	Conventional non-CC/conformist
Loyd	Gay	36	M	16+2 MA	Town commissioner	CC (close to call)
Jim	Black activist Vietnam veteran	49	M	12+3 (biology/ chemistry)	Train conductor	CC
Manny	Rape victim	50+	F	12	Retired computer trainer and insurance agent	Preconventional non-CC/early conformist
Ben	Alcohol problem	62	M	12	Carpet installer/cleaner	Transitional CC/ conformist
Mac	Alcoholic	52	M	13	Unemployed	Preconventional non-CC thoroughly amoral
Ron	Vietnam veteran	48	M	16 (psychology)	Tax examiner	Conventional non-CC

Mansueto	Italian	60	M	12+ college courses	Glass blower	Conventional non-CC/ conformist
Cathy	Rehabilitated suicidal alcoholic	44	F	12+ 3 Bible school	Clerk	Postconventional/ non-CC (close to call)
Margo	"All American Businesswoman"	30+	F	16 (psychology/ sociology)	Clothing buyer	Conventional non-CC/ achievement
Landorf		59	M	16+ continued education	Pharmacist	Conventional non-CC
Don	"Mother Teresa of cats"	48	M	16+1 job training	Components tester	Preconventional non-CC/early conformist
Cynthia	Upper class	50+	F	16	Nursing	Conventional non-CC/ conformist

Bulgarian Sample

Ivan	Communist	52	M	18 (criminal law)	Internal Affairs Police	Preconventional non-CC/early conformist
Eliot	Political activist (Democrat)	37	M	18 (medical)	Dentist	Transitional CC/ achievement
Ada	Communist allegiances	55	F	18 (medical)/ PhD	Pediatrician/ professor	Conventional non-CC/ achievement (close to call)
Danton	Bulgarian Jew	49	M	18 (medical)? PhD	Psychiatrist	CC
Emily	Single mother/ Retarded child	38	F	12 +1	Chemical lab technician	CC
Ramina	Conservative democrat	40	F	16+ 2 special.	Res. chemist/ business	Postconventional non-CC (close to call)

| Katja | Democrat/communist | 37 | F | 19 teacher+
School director | Day care | CC/
(borderline post-
conventional)/
achievement
(close to call) |
| Nat | Democrat | 45 | M | 16+ special. | High school
music teacher | CC |

[1] 12 years considered high school graduate; 13–16 years college; 16+ postgraduate.

References

Abdu'l-Baha. [1917] 1969. *An early pilgrimage*. Oxford, UK: George Ronald.

————. [1930] 1999. *Some answered questions*. Wilmette, IL: Baha'i Publishing Trust.

————. 1978. *Selections from the writings of Abdu'l-Baha*. Chatham, UK: W&J Mackay.

————. 1982. *The promulgation of universal peace*. (Howard MacNutt, comp.). 2 Edition, Wilmette, IL: Baha'i Publishing Trust.

Abdullah, S. 1995. Feeding our hunger for the sacred. *Noetic Sciences Review* (winter: 18–23.

Adams, N. 1996. Spirituality, science and therapy. *Australian and New Zealand Journal of Family Therapy*, 16 (4): 201–208.

Adorno, T. 1989. The culture industry reconsidered. In S. Bronner and D. Kellner (Eds.) *Critical theory and society: A reader*. New York: Routledge, Chapman and Hall.

Allport, G. 1959. Normative compatibility in the light of social science. In A. Maslow (Ed.), *New knowledge in human values*. New York: Harper & Brothers.

American Psychologist. 2000. *Special issue on happiness, excellence, and optimal functioning*, 55, 1.

Arendt, H. [1958] 1998. *The human condition*. Chicago, IL: University of Chicago Press.

Argyris, C., and Schon, D. A. 1978. *Organisational learning: A theory of action perspective*. Reading, MA: Addison-Wesley.

Aristotle. 1991. *The Metaphysics* (J. H. McMahon, trans.). Amherst, NY: Prometheus.

Aull, B. 1988. The faith of science and the method of religion. *Journal of Baha'i Studies* 1 (2): 11–23.

Baha'u'llah. [1931] 1983. *Kitab'i'Iqan: The book of certitude*. Wilmette, IL: Baha'i' Publishing Trust.

————. [1941] 1988. *Epistle to the son of the wolf*. Wilmette, IL: Baha'i Publishing Trust.

————. [1952] 1983. *Gleanings*. Wilmette, IL: Baha'i Publishing Trust.

————. 1988. *Tablets of Baha'u'llah*. Wilmette, IL: Baha'i Publishing Trust.

————. 1991. *The hidden words*. Kuala Lumpur, Malaysia: Baha'i Publishing Trust.

Bailey, J. 1990. *The Serenity principle: Finding inner peace in recovery.* New York: Harper San Francisco.

Banks, S. 1998. *The missing link.* Edmonton, Canada: Lone Pine Publishing.

Basseches, M. 1984. *Dialectical thinking and adult development.* Norwood, NJ: Ablex Publishing.

————. 1986. Dialectical thinking and young adult cognitive development. In R. A. Mines and K. S. Kitchener (Eds.), *Adult cognitive development: Methods and models,* pp. 76–91. New York: Praeger.

Batson, C. D., Schoenrade, P., and Ventis, W. L. 1992. *Religion and the individual: A social-psychological perspective.* New York: Oxford University Press.

Belenky et al. 1986. *Women's ways of knowing: The development of self, voice, and mind.* New York: Basic Books

Bellah, R. et al. 1985. *Habits of the heart: Individualism and commitment in American life.* California: University of California Press.

Bembow, J. 1994. *Coming to know: A phenomenological study of individuals actively committed to radical social change.* Doctoral dissertation, University of Massachusetts at Amherst.

Bennet, E. A. 1983. *What Jung really said.* New York: Schocken Books.

Best, R. (Ed.). 1996. *Education, spirituality and the whole child.* London: Cassell.

Blake, N. 1996. Against spiritual education. *Oxford Review of Education* 22 (4): 443–56.

————. 1997. Spirituality, anti-intellectualism, and the end of civilization as we know it. In R. Smith and P. Standish (Eds.), *Teaching right and wrong.* Stoke on Trent, UK: Trentham Books.

Blasi, A. 1995. Moral understanding and the moral personality: The process of moral integration. In Kurtinez and Gewirtz (Eds.), *Moral Development.* Needham Heights, MA: Allyn & Bacon.

Bohm, D. 1993. Science, spirituality and the present world crisis. *ReVision* 15 (4): 147–153.

————. 1994. *Thought as a system.* New York: Routledge.

Boud, D., Keogh, R., and Walker, D. 1985. *Reflection turning experience into learning.* London: Kogan Page.

Boud, D., Cohen, R., and Walker, D. (Eds.). 1993. *Using experience for learning.* Bristol, PA: Open University Press.

Bowers, C. A. 1974. *Cultural literacy for freedom: An existential perspective on teaching, curriculum, and school policy.* Eugene, OR: Elan Publishers.

————. 1984. *The promise of theory: Education and the policies of cultural change.* New York: Longman.

Bowman, M. 1997. *Individual differences in posttraumatic response: Problems with the adversity-distress connection.* Mahwah, NJ: Lawrence Elbaum.

Boyd, E. M. and Fales, A. W. 1983. Reflective learning: Key to learning from experience. *Journal of Humanistic Psychology* 23: 99–117.

Bronner, E. and Kellner, D. M. 1989. *Critical theory and society: A reader.* New York: Routledge.

Brookfield, S. 1998. Understanding and facilitating moral learning in adults. *Journal of Moral Education* 27 (3): 283–300.

Brown, H. P. 1994. Tools for the logotherapist: A twelve-step spiritual inventory. In *International Forum for Logotherapy* 16 (2): 77–88.

Bryson, A. 1999. *Healing mind, body and soul.* New Delhi, India: Dawn Publisher.

Burke, M. T. 1996. Using the spiritual perspective in counseling persons with HIV/AIDS: An integrative approach. *Counseling and Values* 40 (3): 185–95.

Burnett, J. 1916. The Socratic doctrine of the soul. *Proceedings of the British Academy* 7: 3–27.

Carlson, R. and Bailey, J. 1997. *Slowing down to the speed of life: How to create a more peaceful, simpler life from the inside out.* New York: Harper San Francisco.

Carr, D. 1995. Towards a distinctive conception of spiritual education. *Oxford Review of Education* 21 (1): 83–98.

————. 1996a. Rival conceptions of spiritual education. *Journal of Philosophy of Education* 30 (2): 159–78.

————. 1996b. Songs of immanence and transcendence: a rejoinder to Blake. *Oxford Review of Education* 22 (4): 457–63.

Cavanaugh, J. C. 1991. On building bridges, developing positively, and postformal thinking coming of age: Confessions of a nonconformist. In J. D. Sinnott and J. C. Cavanaugh (Eds.) *Bridging Paradigms: Positive development in adulthood and cognitive aging.* New York: Praeger.

Cell, E. 1984. *Learning to learn from experience.* Albany: State University of New York Press.

Chopra, D. 1993. *Creating affluence: Wealth consciousness in the field of all possibilities.* San Rafael, CA: Amber-Allen/New World Library.

Christians, C. 2000. Ethics and politics in qualitative research. In K. Denzin and Y. Lincoln (Eds.), *Handbook of qualitative research* (pp. 133–55). Thousand Oaks, CA: Sage.

Claxton, G. 1994. *Noises from the dark room: The science and mystery of the mind.* London: Fourth Estate.

————. 1997. *Hare brain, tortoise mind: Why intelligence increases when you think less.* London: Fourth Estate.

Cohen, M. J. 1994 Integrated ecology: The process of counseling with nature. *The Humanistic Psychologist* 21 (3): 277–95.

Colby, A. and Damon, W. 1992. *Some do care.* New York: Macmillan.

————. 1994. *Social responsibility at midlife: Research plan for 1994–95.* Unpublished manuscript.

Cole, M. and Scribner, S. 1974. *Culture and thought.* New York: Wiley & Sons.

Coles, R. 1990. *The spiritual life of children.* Boston, MA: Houghton Mifflin.

————. 1995. The disparity between intellect and character. *The Chronicle of higher education* September 22: A68.

Commons, M. and Rodriguez, J. A. 1990. "Equal access" without "establishing" religion: The necessity for assessing social perspective-taking skills and institutional atmosphere. *Developmental Review* 10: 323–40.

Commons, M., Straughn, J., Meaney, M., Johnstone, J., Weaver, J. H., and Lichtenbaum, E. 1990. *Measuring stage development across domains: A universal scoring system.* Paper presented at the fifth symposium of the Society for Research in Adult Development.

Conn, S. A. 1998. Living in the Earth: Echopsychology, health and psychotherapy. *The Humanistic Psychologist* 26 (1/2/3): 179–98.

Cook-Greuter, S. 1990. Maps for living: Ego-development stages from symbiosis to conscious universal embeddedness. In Commons et al., *Adult development: Models and methods in the study of adolescent and adult thought,* 2. New York: Praeger.

Cranton, P. 1994. *Understanding and promoting transformative learning.* San Francisco, CA: Jossey-Bass.

Csikszentmihalyi, M. 1993. *The evolving self: A psychology for the third millennium.* New York: HarperCollins.

Dalai Lama and Cutler, C. 1998. *The art of happiness: A handbook for living*. New York: Riverhead.

Daloz, L., Keen, C., Keen, J., and Parks, S. 1996. *Common fire: Lives of commitment in a complex world*. Boston, MA: Beacon Press.

Damon, W. and Hart, D. 1988. *Self-understanding in childhood and adolescence*. New York: Cambridge University Press.

Danesh, H. 1994. *The psychology of spirituality*. Ontario, Canada: Nine Pines Publishing.

Decker, L. R. 1994. The role of trauma in spiritual development. *Journal of Humanistic Psychology* 33 (4): 33–46.

DeQuincey, C. (2000). Consciousness: Truth or wisdom. *IONS: Noetic Studies Review*, 51: 8-46.

Diessner, R. 2002. *The Psyche: A descriptive and interpretive investigation based on Bahá'í Holy Text*. Unpublished manuscript, Landegg International University.

Dillon, J. 2000. The spiritual child: Appreciating children's transformative effect on adults. In *Encounter: Education for meaning and social justice* 13 (4): 4–18.

Donaldson, M. 1992. *Human minds: An exploration*. London: Penguin.

Elkins, D. 1995. Psychotherapy and spirituality: Toward a theory of the soul. *Journal of Humanistic Psychology* 35 (2): 78–98.

Emmons, R. 1999. *The psychology of ultimate concerns: Motivation and spirituality in personality*. New York: Guilford.

Epstein, M. 1995. *Thoughts without a thinker: Psychotherapy from a Buddhist perspective*. New York: Basic Books.

Erikson, E. H. 1969. *Gandhi's truth: On the origins of militant nonviolence*. New York: W.W. Norton.

————. 1980. *Identity and the life cycle*. New York: W.W. Norton.

Erricker, C., Erricker, J., Ota, C., Sullivan, D. and Fletcher, M. 1997. *The education of the whole child*. London: Cassell.

Feral, C. H. 1998. The connectedness model and optimal development: Is ecopsychology the answer to emotional well-being? *The Humanistic Psychologist* 26 (1/2/3): 243–74.

Fifth Annual State of the World Forum. (1999). *To envision and create a sustainable and compassionate civilization*.

Foucault, M. 1980. *Power/knowledge: Selected interview and other writings, 1972–1977*. (C. Gordon, Ed.). New York: Pantheon.

Fowler, J. 1980. Stages and the development of faith. In B. Munsey (Ed.), *Moral development, moral education and Kohlberg: Basic issues in philosophy, psychology, religion, and education*. Birmingham, AL: Religious Education Press.

————. 1981. *Stages of faith: The psychology of human development and the quest for meaning*. New York: HarperCollins.

Fox, D. and Prilleltensky, I. 1997. (Eds.). *Critical psychology*. Thousand Oaks, CA: Sage.

Fox, M. 2000. *One river, many wells: Wisdom springing from global faiths*. New York: Putnam Publishing Group.

Frankl, V. E. 1962. *Man's search for meaning*. Boston, MA: Beacon Press.

Freire, P. 1973. *Education for critical consciousness*. New York: The Continuum Publishing Company.

Friedman, M. (1996). Becoming aware: A dialogical approach to consciousness. *The Humanistic Psychologist*, 24 (2): 203–220.

Fromm, E. 1989. Politics and psychoanalysis. In S. Bronner and D. Kellner (Eds.), *Critical theory and society: A reader*. New York: Routledge, Chapman and Hall.

Fukuyama, M. A. and Sevig, T. D. 1997. Spiritual issues in counseling. A new course. *Counselor education and supervision* 36: 233–44.

Gandhi, M. K. 1927. *An autobiography or the story of my experiments with truth.* Ahmedabad, India: Navajivan Publishing House.

Gardner, H. 1983. *Multiple intelligences.*

————. 1993. *Creating minds.* New York: BasicBooks.

Gibbs, J. C. 1991. Toward an integration of Kohlberg's and Hoffman's moral development theories. *Journal of Human Development* 34: 88–104.

Goldstein, J. 1976. *The experience of insight.* Boston, MA: Shambhala.

Griffin, D. (Ed.). 1988a. *Spirituality and society. Postmodern visions.* Albany: SUNY.

————. 1988b. *The re-enchantment of science: Postmodern proposals.* Albany: SUNY.

Grof, S. 2000. *Psychology of the future.* Albany: SUNY.

Hart, M. 1985. Thematization of power, the search for common interests, and self-reflection: Towards a comprehensive concept of emancipatory education. *Adult Education Quarterly* 40: 125–38.

Hart, T. 2000. From information to transformation: What the mystics and sages tell us education can be. *Encounter: Education for Meaning and Social Justice* 13 (3): 14–29.

Hart, T., Nelson, P., and Puhakka, K. 2000. *Transpersonal knowing: Exploring the horizon of consciousness.* New York: SUNY.

Havel, V. 1994. "The new measure of man." *The New York Times*, July 8.

Helminiak, D. 1987. *Spiritual development.* Chicago, IL: Loyola University Press.

————. 1996. *The human core of spirituality: Mind as psyche and spirit.* Albany: State University of New York Press.

Higgins, A. 1995. Educating for justice and community: Lawrence Kohlberg's vision of moral education. In Kurtinez & Gewirtz (Eds.), *Moral development.* Needham Heights, MA: Allyn & Bacon.

Hoffman, M. L. 1983. Affective and cognitive processes in moral internalization. In E. T. Higgins, D. N. Ruble, and W. W. Hartup (Eds.), *Social cognition and social development: A sociocultural perspective.* Cambridge, MA: Cambridge University Press.

————. 1989. Empathy and prosocial activism. In N. Eisenberg, J. Reykowski, and E. Staub (Eds.), *Social and moral values.* New Jersey: Hillsdale.

————. 1991. Commentary. *Journal of Human Development* 34: 105–10.

Hornby, H. 1997. *Lights of guidance.* New Delhi, India: Baha'i Publishing Trust.

Huddleston, J. 1999. *Standing up for humanity: Thoughts on the world economy, the politics of world peace, and the role of religion.* New Delhi, India: Baha'i Publishing Trust.

Hurding, R. F. 1996. Pathways to wholeness: Christian journeying in a postmodern age. *Journal of Psychology and Christianity* 14 (4): 293–305.

Huxley, A. 1974. *The perennial philosophy.* London: Chatto & Windus.

Ingersoll, R. E. 1997. Teaching a course on counseling and spirituality. In *Counselor Education and Supervision* 36: 224–32.

Irwin, R. R. 1991. Reconceptualizing the nature of dialectical postformal operational thinking: The effects of effectively mediated social experiences. In J. D. Sinnott and J. C. Cavanaugh (Eds.), *Bridging paradigms: Positive development in adulthood and cognitive aging.* New York: Praeger.

Ivey, A. E. 1993. Counselling and psychotherapy as moral and spiritual practice: Facing a major paradigm shift. *Counseling and Values* 37 (1): 39–46.

Jacoby, R. 1975. *Social amnesia: A critique of conformist psychology from Adler to Laing.* Boston, MA: Beacon Press.

Jimenez, M. J. 1994. The spiritual healing of post-traumatic stress disorder at the Menlo Park Veteran's Hospital. *Studies in formative spirituality* 14 (3): 175–87.

Kabat-Zin, J. 1995. *Wherever you go, there you are.* New York: Hyperion.

Katz, R., Biesele, M., and Denis, V. 1997. *Healing makes our hearts happy.* Rochester, VT: Inner Traditions International.

Kegan, R. 1982. *The evolving self.* Cambridge, MA: Harvard University Press.

————. 1994. *In over our heads: The mental demands of modern life.* Cambridge, MA: Harvard University.

Kelly, E. W., Jr. 1995. *Spirituality and religion in counseling and psychotherapy: Diversity in theory and practice.* Alexandria, VA: American Counseling Association.

Kennedy, J. E. 1996. Psychic and spiritual experiences, health, well-being, and meaning in life. *Journal of Parapsychology* 58 (4): 353–83.

Kitchener, K. S. and King, P. 1990. The reflective judgment model: Ten years of research. In Commons et al. (Eds.), *Adult development: Models and methods in the study of adolescent and adult thought.* New York: Praeger.

Koch, S. 1971. Reflections on the state of psychology. *Social Research* 38: 669–709.

————. 1981. The nature and limits of psychological knowledge: Lessons of a century qua "Science." *American Psychologist* 36: 257–69.

Kohlberg, L. 1974. Education, moral development and faith. *Journal of Moral Education* 4 (1): 5–16.

————. 1984. *The psychology of moral development: Essays on moral development.* (Vol. 2). San Francisco, CA: Harper & Row.

Kretovics, J. R. 1985. Critical literacy: Challanging the assumptions of the mainstream. *Journal of Education* 167: 50–62.

Krishnamurti, J. 1969. *Freedom from the known.* New York: HarperCollins.

Kuhn, T. 1970. *The structure of scientific revolutions* (2nd ed.). Chicago, IL: University of Chicago Press.

Labouvie-Vief, G. 1980. Beyond formal operations: Uses and limits of pure logic in life span development. *Human Development* 23: 141–61.

Lahey, L., Souvaine, E., Kegan, R., Goodman, R., and Felix, S. 1988. *A guide to the subject— object interview: Its administration and interpretation.* Cambridge, MA: The Subject-Object Workshop.

Lambo, A. 2000. Constraints on world medical and health progress. In Lanza (Ed.) *One World: The health and survival of the human species in the 21st century.* Santa Fe, NM: Health Press.

Lambourn, D. 1996. "Spiritual" minus "Personal-Social"=?: A critical note on an empty category. In R. Best (Ed.), *Education, spirituality, and the whole child.* London: Cassell.

Lankshear, C. and McLaren, P. (Eds.) 1993. *Critical literacy: Politics, praxis ,and the postmodern.* Albany: SUNY Press.

Lanza, R. 2000. (Ed.). *One world: The health and survival of the human species in the 21st Century.* Santa Fe, NM: Health Press.

Larson, D. B. 1994. A paradigm shift in medicine toward spirituality. *Advances* 9 (4): 39–49.

Laszlo, E. 1989. Science and prophecy: Humankind's path to peace in global society. *The Journal of Baha'i Studies* 2 (2): 19–37.

Lee, D. M. 1994. Becoming an expert: Reconsidering the place of wisdom in teaching adults. In J. D. Sinnott (Ed.) *Interdiscipinary handbook of adult lifespan learning.* Westport, CT: Greenwood Press.

Leifer, R. 1996. Psychological and spiritual factors in chronic illness. *American Behavioral Scientist* 39 (6): 752–66.

Levin, J. S. 1994. Esoteric vs. exoteric explanations for findings linking spirituality and health. *Advances* 9 (4): 54–6.

Levinson, D. 1978. *The seasons of a man's life.* New York: Alfred A. Knopf.

Lewis, C. S. 1970. *The grand miracle.* New York: Ballantine.

Lewis, J. 1998. Embracing the holistic/constructivist paradigm and side-stepping the post-modern challenge. In C. Clarke, A. Dyson, and A. Millward (Eds.), *Theorising special education.* London: Routledge.

————. 2000. Spiritual education as the cultivation of qualities of heart and mind: A reply to Blake and Carr. *Oxford Review of Education* (June), 26 (2): 263–284.

Lohman, D. F., and Scheurman, G. 1992. Fluid abilities and epistemic thinking: Some prescriptions for adult education. In A. Tuijnman and M. Van Der Kamp (Eds.), *Learning across the lifespan: Theories, research, policies.* New York: Pergamon.

MacLeod, R. B. 1944. The phenomenological approach to social psychology. *Psychological Review* 54: 193–210.

————. 1970. Newtonian and Darwinian conceptions of man; and some alternatives. *Journal of the History of the Behavioral Sciences* 6: 207–18.

Malaska, P. 1993. Threefold harmony and societal transformation. In Bushrui, Ayman and Laszlo (Eds.), *Transition to a global society.* Oxford, UK: Oneworld Publications.

Marcuse, H. 1989a. From ontology to technology: Fundamental tendencies of industrial society. In S. Bronner and D. Kellner (Eds.), *Critical theory and society: A reader.* New York: Routledge, Chapman and Hall.

————. 1989b. Liberation from the affluent society. In S. Bronner and D. Kellner (Eds.), *Critical theory and society: A reader.* New York: Routledge, Chapman and Hall.

————. 1989c. The obsolescence of the Freudian concept of man. In S. Bronner and D. Kellner (Eds.), *Critical theory and society: A reader.* New York: Routledge, Chapman and Hall.

Marsella, A. 1998. Toward a "global-community psychology". *American Psychologist,* (December), 53 (12): 1282-1291.

Martin-Baro, I. 1994. *Writings for a liberation psychology.* Cambridge, MA: Harvard University Press.

Maslow, A. 1959. (Ed.). *New knowledge in human values.* New York: Harper & Brothers.

————. 1999. (reprint). *Towards a psychology of being.* New York: Harper & Brothers.

————. 1970. Religions, values, and peak experiences. New York: Penguin.

Matousek, M. 2001. Life force. In *Modern maturity,* May/June, pp.25-29.

Mezirow, J. 1991. *Transformative dimensions of adult learning.* San Francisco, CA: Jossey-Bass.

Miller, M. and Cook-Greuter, S. (Eds.). 1994. *Transcendence and mature thought in adulthood: the further reaches of adult development.* Lanham, MD: Rowman & Littlefield.

Miller, W. 1999. *Integrating spirituality into treatment.* Washington, DC: APA.

Mills, R. 1995. *Realizing mental health.* New York: Sulzburger & Graham.

Mills, R. and Spittle, E. 2001. *The wisdom within.* Renton, WA: Lone Pine Publishing.

Moore, T. 1994. *Soul mates: Honoring the mysteries of love and relationships.* New York: HarperCollins.

Moravcsik, J.M.E. 1974. "Aristotle on adequate explanations." *Synthese* 28: 3–17.

Mustakova-Possardt, E. 1995a. Building critical consciousness in the context of an ever-advancing human civilization. *Dialectics, Cosmos and Society* 8: 9–19.

———. 1995b. *Critical consciousness and social responsibility among Bulgarian midlifers: research proposal for the Henry A. Murray Dissertation Award.* Unpublished manuscript.

———. 1996. Ontogeny of critical consciousness. Doctoral dissertation, University of Massachusetts at Amherst.

———. 1998. Critical consciousness: An alternative pathway for positive personal and social development. *Journal of Adult Development* 5(1). New York: Plenum.

———. 2000. The construct of critical consciousness and its ontogeny in the life-span. In M. Miller and A. West (Eds.), *Spirituality, ethics, and relationships: The emotional and philosophical challenges of the adulthood years.* Madison, CT: Psychosocial Press/International Universities Press.

———. Under review. *Discovering our health: Rethinking mind, consciousness, and thought.*

Nicolov, N. 1988. *World conspiracy.* Newport Beach, CA: Noontide Press.

Noguchi, L., Hanson, H., and Lample, P. 1992. *Exploring a framework for moral education* Riviera Beach, FL: Palabra.

Novak, M. 1998. *New York Times*, May 24, Sec. 4, p. 11, col. 2.

Nugent, F. 2000. *Introduction to the profession of counseling.* Upper Saddle River, NJ: Merrill/Prentice Hall.

Peck, S. 1978. *The road less traveled.* New York: Touchstone.

Perry, W. G., Jr. 1968. *Forms of intellectual and ethical development in the college years.* New York: Holt, Rinehart & Winston.

———. 1970. *Forms of Intellectual and ethical development in the college years: A scheme.* New York: Holt, Rinehart & Winston.

Philibert, P. J. 1979. Conscience: Developmental perspectives from Rogers and Kohlberg. *Horizons* 6: 1–25.

Piaget, J. [1932] 1965. *Moral judgement of the child* (M. Gabain, Trans.). New York: Free Press.

Pirsig, R. 1974. *Zen and the art of motorcycle maintenance: An enquiry into values.* New York: Bantam Books.

———. 1991. *Lila: An enquiry into morals.* New York: Bantam Doubleday Dell.

Plato. 1937. *The dialogues of Plato* (B. Jowett, Trans.). New York: Random House.

Pokorny, Brad. (Ed.). 2000. Earth charter final draft issued. *One Country* 11 (4): 14.

Pransky, G. 1992. *The relationship handbook.* New York: McGraw-Hill.

———. 1998. *The renaissance of psychology.* New York: Sulzburger & Graham.

Pransky, J. 1998. *Modello: A story of hope for the inner-city and beyond.* Cabot, VT: NEHRI.

———. 1999. *The experience of participants after health Realization training: A one-year follow-up phenomenological study.* (Dissertation).

———. 2000. What is innate mental health, and what does it mean to live it? *POM/HR Communique*, Feb. 2000, Vol. 6, No. 1.

———. 2001. *Prevention: The critical need.* Bloomington, IN: 1st Books Library.

Prilleltensky, Issac. (1997). Values, assumptions, and practices: Assessing the moral implications of psychological discourse and action. *American Psychologist*, 52, 5, pp. 517–535.

Rabbani, R. 1969. *The priceless pearl*. London: Baha'i Publishing Trust.

Richards, P. S. and Bergin, A. 1997. *A spiritual strategy for counseling and psychotherapy*. Washington, DC: APA.

Roberts, E. 1998. Place and the human spirit. *The Humanistic Psychologist* 26 (1/2/3): 5–34.

Robinson, E. 1977. *The original vision*. Oxford, UK: Alister Hardy Research Centre.

Rogoff, B. 1990. *Apprenticeship in thinking*. New York: Oxford University Press.

Rogoff, B. and Lave, J. 1984. *Everyday cognition: Its development in social context*. Cambridge, MA: Harvard University Press.

Rosen, H. 1985. *Piagetian dimensions of clinical relevance*. New York: Columbia University Press.

Ross, L. 1995. The spiritual dimension: Its importance to patients' health, well-being and quality of life and its implications for nursing practice. *International Journal of Nursing Studies*, 32 (5): 457-468.

Ruhe, D. S. 1994. *The Grand transition*. Paper presented at the 1994 North American Baha'i Conference on Social and Economic Development.

Russell, P. (1999). Sierious. *IONS Noetic Studies Review*, Dec. 1999-March 2000.

Rutstein, N. 1994. *There is a way out of the trap*. Springfield, MA: Whitcomb.

————. 1997. *Racism: Unraveling the fear*. Washington DC: The Global Classroom.

————. 1999. *Coming of age at the millennium: Embracing the oneness of humankind*. Albion, MI: Starr Commonwealth.

Ryff, C. D. and Singer, B. 1998. The contours of positive human health. *Psychological Inquiry* 9: 1–28.

Saiedi, N. 2000. *Logos and civilization: Spirit, history and order in the writings of Baha'u'llah*. Bethesda: University Press of Maryland.

Schaefer, U. 1994. *Beyond the clash of religions*. Prague, Czech Republic: Zero Palm Press.

School Curriculum and Assessment Authority (SCAA). 1995. *Spiritual and moral development*. London: SCAA.

————. 1996. *Education for adult life: The spiritual and moral development of young people: A summary report*. London: SCAA.

Sedgeman, J. (2001). *Monthly reflections*. Retrieved September, 2001, from the Sydney Banks Institute for Innate Health Website: http://www.hsc.wvu.edu/sbi/

Seligman M. and Csikszentmihalyi, M. (2000). Positive psychology. *American psychologist*, 55, 1, pp. 5-14.

Shapiro, D. 1995. Examining the content and context of meditation: A challenge for psychology in the areas of stress management, psychotherapy, and religion/values. *Journal of Humanistic Psychology* 34 (4): 101–35.

Shapiro, E. and Shapiro, D. 1992. *Voices from the heart: Inspirations for a compassionate future*. New York: Putnam.

Shoghi Effendi. [1939] 1990. *The advent of divine justice*. Wilmette, IL: Baha'i Publishing Trust.

Shor, I. and Freire, P. 1987. *A pedagogy for liberation: Dialogues on transforming education*. South Hadley, MA: Bergin & Garvey.

Sifton, K. and Hornsby, R. 1998. *Energy: A practical guide to personal achievement, health, and transformation*. Bowdon, GA: InnerChi.

Sloan, T. 1992. *Understanding major life decisions: A life history approach. New Ideas in Psychology* 10 (1): 63–77.

————. 1996. *Life choices: Understanding dilemmas and decisions*. Boulder, CO: Westview.

Smith, R. M. (Ed.). 1990. *Learning how to learn across the lifespan.* San Francisco, CA: Jossey-Bass.

Smith, W. C. [1979] 1998. *Faith and belief: The difference between them.* Princeton, NJ: Princeton University Press.

Sober, E. and Wilson, D. S. (1998). *Unto others: The evolution and psychology of unselfish behavior.* Cambridge, MA: Harvard University Press.

Sorokin, P. 1959. The powers of creative unselfish Love. In A. Maslow (Ed.), *New knowledge in human values.* New York: Harper & Brothers.

Stanage, S. 1987. *Adult education and phenomenological research: New direction for theory, practice, and research.* Malabar, FL: Krieger.

Sternberg, R. and Davidson, J. (Eds.). 1995. *The nature of insight.* Cambridge, MA: MIT.

Sternberg, R. J. and Wagner, R. K. 1986. *Practical intelligence: Nature and origins of competence in the everyday world.* New York: Cambridge University Press.

Sternberg, R. (Ed.). 1992. *Wisdom, its nature, origins, and development.* Cambridge, MA: Cambridge University Press.

Swindler, L. (Ed.). 1999. *For all life: Toward a universal declaration of a global ethic.* Ashland, OR: White Cloud Press.

Taafaki, I. 1986. *Thoughts, education for peace and one world: a studybook for moral education.* Oxford, UK: George Ronald.

Talbot, M. 1991. *The holographic universe.* New York: HarperPerennial.

Tan, S. Y. 1996. Practicing the presence of God: The work of Richard J. Foster and its applications to psychotherapeutic practice. *Journal of Psychology and Christianity* 15 (1): 17–28.

Taylor, C. 1982. The diversity of goods. In A. Sen and B. Williams (Eds.), *Utilitarianism and beyond* (pp. 129–44). Cambridge, MA: Cambridge University Press.

Thich Nhat Hanh. 1991. *Peace is every step.* New York: Bantam.

Tillich, P. 1957. *Dynamics of faith.* New York: Harper & Row.

Tudge, J. and Winterhoff, P. 1993. Vygotsky, Piaget, and Bandura: Perspectives on the relations between the social world and cognitive development. *Human Development* 36 (2): 1–81.

Tuijnman, A. and Van Der Kamp, M. (Eds.). 1992. *Learning across the lifespan: Theories, research, policies.* New York: Pergamon.

Universal House of Justice. 1985. *The promise of world peace.* Thornhill, Canada: Baha'i Peace Council of Canada.

————. 2001. *Century of light.* Wilmette, IL: Baha'i Publishing Trust.

Valsiner, J. 1989. *Human development and culture: The social nature of personality and its study.* Boston, MA: Lexington Books.

Vokey, D. J. 1997. *Reasons of the heart: Moral objectivity, MacIntyre, and education for critical dialogue in a pluralistic world.* Doctoral dissertation, University of Toronto.

Wade, J. 1996. *Changes of mind: A holonomic theory of the evolution of consciousness.* Albany: State University of New York Press.

Wagner, R. K. 1994. Practical intelligence. In A. Tuijman and M. Van Der Kamp (Eds.) 1992, *Learning across the lifespan: Theories, research, polices.* New York: Pergamon.

Walker, S. J. 1995. *College students, alcohol and drugs, and culture: An application of the theories and practices of Robert Kegan and Paolo Freire.* Doctoral dissertation, Harvard University.

Walsh, R. and Vaughan, F. 1993. *Paths beyond ego: A transpersonal vision.* New York: Putnam.

Weinstein, G. and Alschuler, A. 1985. Educating and counseling for self-knowledge development. *Journal of Counseling and Development* 64: 19–25.

Wertsch, J. V. 1985. *Vygotsky and the social formation of the mind.* Cambridge, MA: Harvard University Press.

Westgate, C. E. 1996. Spiritual wellness and depression. *Journal of Counseling and Development* 75 (1): 26–35.

White, R. A.1989. Spiritual foundations for an ecologically sustainable society. *Journal of Baha'i Studies* 2 (1): 33–57.

Wilber, K. (Ed.). 1984. *Quantum Questions: Mystical writings of the world's great physicists.* Boston, MA: Shambhala.

————. 1998. *The marriage of sense and soul: Integrating science and religion.* New York: Random House.

————. 2000. *Integral psychology: Consciousness, spirit, psychology, therapy.* Boston, MA: Shambhala.

Wilber, K., Engler, J., and Brown, D. 1986. *Transformations of consciousness: Conventional and contemplative perspectives on development.* Boston, MA: Shambhala.

Wilshire, B. 1990. *The moral collapse of the university: Professionalism, purity, and alienation.* Albany: State University of New York.

Wilson, A. (Ed.). 1995. *World Scripture:A comparative anthology of sacred texts.* St. Paul, MN: Paragon House.

Wilson, E. O. 1975. *Sociobiology.* (Abr. ed.) Cambridge, MA: Harvard University Press.

Woodall, J. 1996. Racism as a disease. In Rutstein and Morgan (Eds.), *Healing racism: Education's role.* Springfield, MA: Whitcomb.

World Hunger Statistics. Retrieved February 12, 2002 from http://www.unicef.org

Worthington, E. L., Jr. 1989. Religious faith across the lifespan: Implications for counseling and research. *Counseling Psychologist* 17: 555–612.

Wuthnow, R. 1991. *Acts of compassion.* Princeton, NJ: Princeton University Press.

Young-Eisendrath, P. and Miller, M. (2000). *The psychology of mature spirituality.* Philadelphia, PA: Taylor & Francis.

Index

About the Author

ELENA MUSTAKOVA-POSSARDT is Assistant Professor of Psychology at the
State University of West Georgia.

CPSIA information can be obtained
at www.ICGtesting.com
Printed in the USA
LVOW10*2259130318

569736LV00002B/62/P